ALSO BY CHRISTINA ASQUITH

The Emergency Teacher:
The Inspirational Story of a New Teacher
in an Inner-City School

SISTERS
IN WAR

SISTERS
IN WAR

A STORY OF LOVE,
FAMILY, AND SURVIVAL
IN THE NEW IRAQ

CHRISTINA
ASQUITH

RANDOM HOUSE · NEW YORK

Published in the United States by Random House, an imprint of
The Random House Publishing Group, a division
of Random House, Inc., New York.

RANDOM HOUSE and colophon are registered trademarks
of Random House, Inc.

Asquith, Christina.
Sisters in war: a story of love, family, and survival in the new Iraq / Christina Asquith.
p. cm.
ISBN 978-1-4000-6704-6
eBook ISBN 978-1-58836-761-7
1. Women—Iraq—Social conditions.   2. Women, Arab—Iraq—Social conditions.
3. Women's rights—Iraq.   4. Iraq War, 2003—Women.   5. Iraq—Social conditions.   I. Title.
HQ1735.A627 2009
305.48'89275670090511—dc22   2009006692

Printed in the United States of America on acid-free paper

www.atrandom.com

2 4 6 8 9 7 5 3 1

First Edition

Book design by Victoria Wong

To my sister, Nikki

SISTERS
IN WAR

CHAPTER ONE

WHEN THE SISTERS heard the roar of U.S. military planes overhead, they clambered up the wooden steps onto the roof of their uncle's mud-brick farmhouse. "Maybe they can see us!" cried Nunu happily. She shouted to the sky, for once not caring who heard: "*Go!* Good luck! But don't kill any innocent people."

Zia laughed with her, glad to have something, at last, to celebrate. The Americans were here to free them from Saddam. She watched her little sister waving at the distant black specks, skipping over the mud and straw in her fancy shoes. A few days ago, Nunu had overheard on her shortwave radio that American troops were marching through Iraqi villages, going door-to-door, and ever since then she had been getting up an extra hour early in the morning just to do her hair and makeup. So far, no war heroes had shown up, but it was so good to see Nunu happy that Zia hadn't even teased her for it. They could feel the electricity in the air: after years of oppression, the government was about to be overthrown, and Iraq would be free—a "freedom" they had only ever known through their mother's stories of Iraq's glorious past. After weeks and months of waiting, these military planes were their first, welcome sign of that immense promise.

As the sound of the planes died away and Nunu scanned the horizon for more, Zia's own thoughts grew darker. In her mind she followed the bomber planes to Baghdad, 115 miles to the east, where her father, stubborn as ever, had insisted on waiting out the invasion to protect their house from looters. As a child she had heard bombs falling around their neighborhood during the Iran-Iraq war, and she remembered the terror, as she moved through adolescence, of the American bombing raids on Baghdad in 1991 and 1998. She couldn't bear to imagine anything happening to Baba, or to her beloved city—though she tried to tell herself that some destruction was necessary and understandable. Her throat tightened as she remembered Baba's admiration of the "incredible precision" of American bombs, and his insistence that the Americans weren't interested in targeting civilians. That had been three weeks ago, though, and they'd had no news from him since. Though she knew it was forbidden to doubt her own father, she still whispered a silent prayer, under her breath, that he'd be safe.

Nunu skipped toward her across the roof. "Zia, let's go tell Mamina! Now that the Americans are here, soon we'll be able to go home!"

As they climbed down the ladder into their uncle's home, Zia wished, again, that women's lives would change with the Americans' arrival. She was tired of being an outcast. As the eldest daughter, Zia had unconsciously stepped into the patriarchal role usually assumed by the eldest son, earning income in her job, driving the car, tutoring Nunu, and even handling financial matters with her uncles. She liked being in charge, even though she knew her outspokenness had earned her a reputation as "unmarriageable" around the neighborhood.

"The Americans are advancing toward Baghdad!" Nunu cheered when they found Mamina, folding her prayer mat in the bedroom the women shared downstairs. Their mother's darkly lined eyes lit up, and she gave them a tight, perfume-scented hug. Even with her hair hidden under a veil, Mamina radiated the warmth and beauty of a woman twenty years younger, Zia thought. This time, they all felt sure, the Americans would get the job done.

Mamina sighed contentedly. "Like he parted the sea for Moses, we pray God makes a smooth path for the Americans. Then, my dears, you will know how it feels to be proud of your homeland—you'll see the progressive, cultured Iraq your father and I loved so much when we were young. Iraq was once a paradise for women, and the Americans will help us restore that. I dream that you will be able to live as you wish from now on."

Zia caught Nunu's eye and they both collapsed into excited giggles like children, unable to believe this fantasy would soon be real. Clapping her hands, Nunu cried, "Mamina, when the American soldiers see us, maybe they will fall in love and want to marry us!"

"Shhhh!" Mamina scolded, though her eyes belied her joy. "Keep your voice down. Remember we are in Hit."

INDEED, LIVING WITH Uncle Jalal, the women were all too aware that not every Iraqi was celebrating the end of Saddam's twenty-five-year rule. Although their uncle's family had agreed to shelter Zia, Nunu, and Mamina because Mamina's sister, Sahra, was married to Jalal, the imminent invasion had awoken dormant religious tensions across the country. They, like most of the other townspeople of Hit, were conservative Sunni Muslims, while Sahra and the rest of Zia's family were Shia. It was a divide that had arisen in the seventh century, over which group held true claim as descendants of the Prophet's rightful successor. Saddam and his government were mostly Sunni, and during the quarter century he'd been in power Saddam had deepened the distrust between the two groups by overtly favoring Sunni villages, granting them more reliable electricity and public funding. Although in recent years most residents in the educated areas of Baghdad dismissed infighting between religious sects as backward, and intermarriages like Sahra and Jalal's had become common, there was still strong religious feeling in conservative tribal centers. As the American invasion neared, politics had begun to increasingly break down along these religious lines, with provincial areas like Hit remaining deeply loyal to Saddam while the more urban Shia were suspected, often rightly, of supporting and even helping the USA with the imminent invasion.

THESE TENSIONS WERE certainly making the evening meals increasingly awkward. That night, as Mamina, Zia, and Nunu sat cross-legged on the floor around the embroidered tablecloth, they tried not to betray too much of their excitement. Inevitably, though, as the family began to eat, roughly tearing off pieces of flat bread and using it to spoon the stuffed onions, rice, cucumbers, and kebabs, the discussion turned to the war. Everyone had heard the planes overhead that afternoon, and knew that the long weeks and months of suspense would soon be over, for better or worse.

Jalal's mother, eyeing her guests, openly praised Saddam. "He is a strong man who will stand up to the infidel Americans." She looked around the room bitterly, her fierce face swathed in a black abaya. The tribal tattoos on her wrists were visible as she waved her arms in defiance. Mamina glanced in alarm over at Zia, knowing how hard it was for her daughter to keep her opinions to herself when she was angry, but Zia just shot their hostess a hostile look and swallowed hard. Nunu, who never said anything in public anyway, kept her eyes downcast, refusing to risk anyone's disapproval. Mamina hurriedly tried to move the conversation to safer ground. Saddam's secret police could be anywhere, and no one had dared criticize the dictator for more than two decades. It wasn't yet safe to start.

Luckily, Jalal's sister, who was far less interested in politics, soon dominated the conversation. She wanted to gossip about the woman next door, whom she considered "barren" because she had only two children: "I have sixteen children, mostly sons," she haughtily reminded her city cousins, and the dinner discussion soon settled into a polite appraisal of these young men's virtues.

After dinner, Nunu and Zia retreated to the bedroom to listen to the news on Nunu's little shortwave Sony radio. Although most channels were government-controlled and spewed pure propaganda, the girls had found an international station, Radio Monte Carlo, where they could get reliable outside information. They listened anxiously for news about their Baghdad neighborhood, praying nothing would happen to Baba and their neighbors, but there wasn't much information available. "Do you think our relatives are listening to these same stations, too, from London?" Nunu asked.

"Maybe," Zia mused. The family had little contact with their family members who lived in exile. They suspected their phone calls were monitored by Saddam's Ba'ath Party, so they didn't dare speak openly with exiled family members on the rare occasion when they called them. Letters addressed to foreign countries were also opened and screened, and Iraqis had no access to the Internet or email. "I hope our uncles are not too worried. I wonder if they'll want to come visit, now that Iraq is going to be safe again."

As snatches of broadcasts interrupted the static, the sisters talked about how different life would be once Saddam was defeated: Zia would finally get her medical degree, and Nunu would "marry Redha al-Abdullah"—a famous Iraqi singer—and "have *seventeen* children!"

"And they'll *all* be boys!" Zia added. They laughed. These impoverished, aggressively conservative villagers were looked down upon by the well-educated city girls, who had grown up among much more liberal attitudes, even under Saddam's brutality. Baba generally let them wear pants and makeup, if they wanted to, but here the old women's abayas covered their faces, hands, and feet. Barefoot young women and their dirt-smudged children carried urns of water alongside the roads. Few of the women in the village had gone to school beyond elementary, while Zia had graduated from university and Nunu would too, in a few years. These villagers' lives were not governed by the modern strictures of Parliament, police, and the court of law, but instead by a small band of tribal elders and Islamic clerics whose families had ruled the region for generations.

Still, Hit and Baghdad did have one thing in common: the center of town had a monument to Saddam. Every town and city in Iraq was peppered with government-ordered murals and statues of the dictator. There was "Uncle Saddam," the loving patriarch; "Muslim Saddam," shown in religious attire to underscore his devotion to Islam; and, most frequently, the armed "Warrior Saddam," perpetually victorious against the modern-day evils of America and Israel. Everyone knew these symbols, but it had been a long time since any of the government's rhetoric held even an echo of truth; Saddam had stopped caring for or protecting his countrymen long ago. Nunu and Zia found the statues both ridiculous and terrifying—even the smallest act of vandalism to one of these images could mean a painful death.

Mamina came into the bedroom and found her girls gossiping about Saddam, Jalal's family, and the backwardness of Hit. Nunu looked up at her mother. "Saddam has done nothing but steal from Iraqis for two decades, and yet they are still loyal to him over the Americans. How can they defend him?"

Mamina settled on the bed between them, curling her fingers absentmindedly through Nunu's glossy hair. "Did you know Aunt Sahra and I grew up in a world very much like Hit? There were twelve of us children, and your grandparents were very poor. When we were young, Iraq had few roads, and no cars or airports. Most people in these rural areas traveled by donkey or walked, married their cousins to preserve family unity, and never ventured beyond their villages. The old ways are deeply ingrained, and there was never a lot of reason to change. You can't call them backward just for carrying on the ancient traditions— after all, Iraq is famously known as the cradle of civilization. All great history and culture began here. The epic of *Gilgamesh* was first told by Mesopotamians more than five thousand years ago; the ancient tales of Kalila and Dimna inspired Aesop's fables, and, as you know, the story of the *Arabian Nights* is set in a Baghdad neighborhood right near our apartment. We have much to be proud of."

"But Mamina," Zia pointed out, "you left your village, and you're *not* like Uncle Jalal's sister. And you're always telling us that women can be as good as men at some things. These people certainly don't believe that."

Mamina sighed. "One of the things I loved best about Iraq, in the years before you girls were born, was how we led the Arab world in culture, education, and women's rights. Iraq had the best of both worlds— the ancient heritage and modern, secular policies. When I was in elementary school, General Kassim overthrew King Faisal the Second. He was just a puppet for the British government, which had been running Iraq for almost forty years. We adored General Kassim. For him, Iraq's women and children *were* just as important as the men. When an interviewer asked him why he wasn't married, he said, 'Iraq's old women are my mothers, the young women are my sisters, and the baby girls are my daughters.' " Mamina laughed. "That made us *all* want to marry him! Under his rule, the public schools gave out milk, yogurt, and vitamins, the government tested children's health annually, and medicine was free. In the winters our headmaster gave the poorer students pieces of thick material and dinars to take to the tailor for jackets."

"That's what Saddam *should* be doing if he wants to have those statues of him as our 'uncle,' " Nunu interjected. "Instead we have nothing to be proud of—no nice shampoos, no fancy cheeses, no fruits, bread, or milk half the time, and the markets have nothing to sell."

Mamina reminisced about the period of great freedom, creativity, and intellectual activity in the 1950s and early '60s, which flourished after the country began to grow rich from its oil reserves, and as the strict ways of conservative Islam started to fade into the background. Much the same had happened in the neighboring countries of Saudi Arabia, Egypt, and Iran, as young Arabs embraced Western styles and attitudes. Then, in 1963, to everyone's shock and horror, General Kassim was assassinated by a little-known group with Syrian ties called the Ba'ath Party. Women cried in the streets, and the whole country was plunged into mourning.

For a long time, though, even after the new Ba'ath leadership came to power, Iraq continued to prosper on its exploding oil wealth. The political ideology of Ba'athism was a secular, pan-Arab socialism that was generally well received. In those years there was talk of returning Baghdad to the capital of a cosmopolitan Middle East, as it had not been since the thirteenth century. The phrase "Cairo writes, Beirut prints, and Baghdad reads" was popularized, as Islamic traditions took a backseat. When eighteen-year-old Mamina met Baba, he was one of thousands of forty-something Iraqi men who had returned from Europe with PhDs, bearing tantalizing stories and impressions of the modern West.

But there was a darker side to the Ba'ath Party. Not long after Kassim's death, a rising soldier in the party named Saddam Hussein began bragging that he had personally assassinated Kassim. Although no one believed him, he nonetheless rose through the ranks in the late 1960s and '70s, eventually taking complete control as president in 1979. Terrifyingly, in one of his first acts, Saddam executed all the top party members whom he suspected of betraying him, including the minister of education. Appalled, Mamina and Baba watched the executions broadcast on state television, and worried that "He who begins in blood, ends in blood."

At first, however, Saddam's social programs proved to be popular. Furthering the initiatives of General Kassim, he used the country's oil wealth to eradicate illiteracy, improve health care, and provide free higher education. He even encouraged women's rights, and soon women were allowed to own property, join the police force, drive cars, and have bank accounts. He mandated that all children enroll in school, especially girls, and he won a UNESCO prize in 1982, the year Zia was born, for improving girls' education.

He even selected a remarkably strong representative for women's rights, Manal Yunis, to head the General Federation of Iraqi Women, which was the only women's group allowed in Iraq. Iraq's women were surprised and delighted by her policies, joking that "All men hate Manal Yunis!" She helped strengthen women's rights after divorce, fighting for a law that granted women custody of the children, mandated alimony payments, and eliminated a rule that, under certain conditions, prevented a divorcée from remarrying for seven years. Yunis instituted day care at many of the government ministries and introduced partially paid one-year sabbaticals for new mothers. She wasn't completely progressive, however, and one of her policies banned birth control pills, which had become popular among married women who already had several children.

Yet Iraqi women felt they were moving forward under Saddam, particularly given the way conditions for Muslim women elsewhere were deteriorating. In the late 1970s and '80s, many neighboring Muslim countries had begun to reject Western ideas, worrying that the abandonment of Islam was causing only economic and cultural decay. The Arab world had been agitated by the Israeli army's victories against Egypt in the 1967 and 1973 wars, and fundamentalist fervor for the destruction of Israel and the overthrow of pro-Western Arab governments was on the rise. In 1979, when neighboring Iran underwent an Islamic revolution, clerics and angry citizens toppled the U.S.-backed shah, seized the U.S. embassy in Tehran, and established a strictly religious, Islamic government. (Mamina had been surprised at the vehemence of their anti-Americanism, since at that time Saddam had good relations with the United States.) When the Iranian revolution degenerated into mayhem, stories emerged about the brutal treatment of women, in Iran and other countries that gravitated to Islamic rule. Women were being beaten or stoned to death for wearing nail polish or showing a little of their hair. In such an environment, Mamina and Baba were proud that their country had chosen Western traditions over religious fanaticism.

But the good times wouldn't last. When similar stirrings of religious fervor appeared in Iraq in the 1980s, Saddam's efforts to brutally crush them would drag the entire nation into the gutter. He began by banning all religious groupings, including Friday-night mosque sermons, and discouraging believers from wearing the Islamic headscarf. Soon, senior Shia clerics were being assassinated, and their young followers were disappearing. Criticizing Saddam's regime was equated with treason and punishable by torture and death. Worrying that the Shia in Iran would encourage the Iraqi Shia to rise up, Saddam launched a war with Iran in the early 1980s, and the population suffered through years of terror as low-flying Iranian fighter planes regularly dropped bombs across the neighborhoods of Baghdad. By the time the war exhausted itself in 1988, it was estimated that hundreds of thousands of Iraqi men—many of whom had been kidnapped and forced into battle—had lost their lives; but Saddam spoke only of "victory."

Disillusion set in, and in an effort to contain rising dissent, Saddam banned free media and foreign travel and began a propaganda campaign that included erecting billboards and the monstrous statues of himself across the country. His government-controlled television channels began showing only positive images of Saddam and Iraq and demonized Israel. Just three years later, in 1991, Saddam made the disastrous decision to invade oil-rich Kuwait, provoking the ire of the Americans who had been his longtime allies. The Iraqi army was driven back by U.S. forces. Saddam's government was weak, but rather than overthrow Saddam itself, the United States encouraged hundreds of thousands of Shia in southern Iraq to rise up against him. But the American support never arrived. Although their friendship with Saddam was over, the Americans decided at the last minute that toppling him would empower neighboring Iran. Saddam brutally crushed the southern Iraqis, bulldozing tens of thousands of the dead into mass graves. To deter Saddam's further aggression, the United Nations imposed sanctions on Iraq in 1993, forbidding all imports and exports, locking the country in isolation and driving almost all Iraqis into poverty as salaries plummeted and inflation ran wild. The supermarket shelves became bare. Fathers began to marry off their daughters younger and younger.

For a long time, as things got worse, Mamina had comforted herself that, at the very least, her daughters would grow up among strong female role models, friends and family members who were lawyers, doctors, and engineers and who enjoyed many more liberties compared to women in other Arab countries. Given the short workday, nationalized health care, and close family circles, Iraqi women had for several years been able to maintain both a family life and a full-time career—a balance, Saddam's government pointed out, that had not been attained even by women in many Western countries. By the 1990s, though, the happy times had definitely ended, and women's rights became a forgotten luxury as mothers struggled to fill hungry mouths.

After Saddam's own sons-in-law tried to defect and tell the world of his chemical-weapons programs in 1996, Saddam unleashed a brutal police state that tortured people just for criticizing the regime. His secret police, the Mukhabarat, would imprison anyone whose loyalty was in question, and it paid tens of thousands of dinars to spies in neighborhoods, offices, and university classrooms. The social fabric of society was shredded as friends betrayed friends and family members turned on one another.

Baba, too, was suffering. Saddam had nationalized the German company where Baba had worked and filled the management ranks with Ba'ath Party loyalists. Eventually, Baba was pushed out for his refusal to join the party, and he started his own lucrative construction company, but its building sites were looted during the Kuwait war, and by the time the UN sanctions started, he could no longer import materials. Eventually, he lost his business, as did so many other Iraqis. Many of Baba's friends joined the Ba'ath Party, either for the money and power or merely to protect themselves. Some became rich, driving Mercedes and flaunting their wealth, but on principle, Baba still refused. Within just a few years, corruption and poverty destroyed a country that had once been at the forefront of the Arab world. Mohammed joined tens of thousands of other young professionals who began secretly fleeing the country, but not everyone could leave. Zia and Nunu's generation came of age in a time that knew only dictatorship, repression, hunger, and barbarism. No one in Iraq talked about women's rights anymore. They had no human rights.

As Mamina lay on the bed in the farmhouse in Hit, gently stroking the hair of her sleeping daughters and thinking about the arrival of the

Americans, for the first time in more than fifteen years she felt hope. She wanted so badly for her girls to understand that women's equality was not just a Western concept that the Americans would introduce. It was a proud Iraqi tradition that they must all work to restore.

A FEW NIGHTS later, during dinner, when they heard a bomb land and felt the ground vibrate, Zia grinned boldly at Uncle Jalal's mother, thinking how her parents' dreams were finally coming true, how Iraq would soon be restored to its glory days, the way it was in Mamina's stories. The next day, they heard that Hit's communication tower had been bombed. Nunu's shortwave radio still worked, and it assured them that U.S. troops were advancing toward Baghdad, though they had been slowed by the dust storm. Everyone started talking at once. Would the Americans get rid of Saddam, or back out at the last minute? Would the Iraqi army defend the government or defect? How fiercely would Saddam fight back? The next few days passed slowly until the radio announced, to the Shia women's surprise and delight, that the Americans had taken Baghdad International Airport.

After that, the news moved quickly. American tanks had knocked through the gates of Saddam's Republican Palace and rolled down Abu Nawass, a major street in their family's Baghdad neighborhood. Zia and Nunu danced around the room.

"Saddam is falling, Saddam is falling," they sang, no longer caring who in Hit overheard them. Saddam's information minister, Saeed al-Sahaf, came on to the state-run station to deny the presence of American troops on Iraqi soil, but the women just laughed at the ludicrous propaganda.

"The Iraqi army is controlling the situation," he announced.

"Oh yeah?" joked Zia to the radio. "Which situation are you controlling?" The Americans were clearly winning. Saddam's huge statue in Baghdad's Firdos Square had been torn down, the news reports were saying, and Iraqis were beating his face with their shoes.

Nunu couldn't believe that. "How dare they do this? They will be killed!"

Zia hugged her little sister. "Not with the Americans here. Saddam's army is afraid of them!"

Suddenly, after all these weeks of tension—all these years of fear—it was over. Saddam's army had barely put up a fight.

Within hours, Mamina, Zia, and Nunu piled into a car full of other refugees staying at the house next door and headed home to Baghdad and Baba. Aunt Sahra and Uncle Jalal would return separately to Baghdad later. The women squeezed in together and put a stick with a white cloth out the window, to indicate they were civilians.

As the car pulled away, Mamina thanked Jalal's family for housing them, but goodbyes were forced, as the family's opinions had turned ugly. "Those who welcome foreigners onto Iraqi soil are dirty, shameless *kafirs,*" Jalal's mother spit out, using a derogatory term for non-Muslims. Never would they support the occupation of their country by a Western, Christian army—to them this was clearly forbidden in the Quran.

"Saddam will be back," Jalal's sister muttered.

"We pray to God that never happens," Mamina replied loudly, surprising even herself with her directness and marveling at her defiant tone, which she had not heard in twenty years.

A FEW HOURS later, the scene in Baghdad was beyond anything the sisters could have imagined. Cars jammed the roads back into the capital, despite the plumes of ink-black smoke dissolving above it into the cloudless horizon. Shell casings and shattered glass littered the streets. Though they had seen war before, this was much bigger. An entire nation was in revolt, a government in shambles and its dictator overthrown. A state of silent shock settled over the car, punctured by gasps, as the enormity of events sunk in. Suddenly Zia didn't know if she felt more happy, nervous, or terrified. Although smoldering, Baghdad was still standing, and while physical devastation was widespread, there was little sign of bloodshed. Zia, Nunu, and Mamina squeezed one another's hands quietly in the car, each hoping nothing had happened to their home.

Far more shocking still than the destruction, however, was the joyous mob scene in downtown Baghdad, so different from the somber faces they had left behind in Hit. Just as the radio had said, Iraqis were banging murals of Saddam with their shoes and climbing atop his statues to beat them. Nunu marveled again at the scene, unable to believe her eyes. Only two weeks earlier, those men would have been tortured by electrical shocks or had members of their family killed for such behavior. Yet now people were cursing Saddam openly, and it was the Ba'athists who hid in their houses. The streets teetered with wild, carefree energy. Men with AK-47s leaned out car windows, shooting celebratory gunfire into the air. Drivers blew their horns musically and groups of men jumped up and down, playing instruments and cheering. Iraqis shouted to the American soldiers parked in their Humvees: "Yes, yes, Bush! Down, down, Saddam!" Zia knew exactly what they were all thinking: *The nightmare is over.*

Their car was caught in a long line of slow-moving traffic, which they soon realized was caused by a military checkpoint. Seeing U.S. soldiers standing on the familiar streets where she and her siblings had learned to ride bicycles made Nunu feel like she had stepped onto a movie set. The Americans were tall and rich-looking, with well-made uniforms and expensive gear attached to their broad chests. To the sisters, they looked like celebrities in their black sunglasses and helmets.

One approached their car with his finger on his rifle's trigger, and Zia's heart pounded. She and Nunu were the only passengers who spoke English.

"Do you have any weapons in the car?" the soldier asked gruffly. His helmet said HARRIS.

"We are civilians," Zia said. "We have no arms," she added nervously.

They held each other's gaze for what felt like forever. At last, he smiled at Zia and stretched out his hand, but Mamina interrupted in her limited English. "Thank you, thank you," she said, holding back her daughter's hand. "God bless you. Bush good." As the car moved on, the soldier's gaze followed the sisters, and Nunu waved prettily. "They are so flirtatious!" Zia gasped, not unhappily.

WHEN THEY FINALLY arrived at their street, Baba was standing outside with their neighbor Abu Hassan, his wife and son, and many others. They looked exhausted, their cheeks unshaven and their clothes wrinkled, but they were all, thankfully, alive. Baba threw up his hands in celebration when he saw them come around the corner. Everyone was laughing, full of giddy joy as they kissed in greeting. All the neighbors were pointing to a nearby residence, where a high-ranking member of Saddam's government had lived. Someone had scrawled graffiti on his front wall: *Let the Ba'ath Party Fall.*

Despite the wear of the last several weeks, Baba's face looked flushed and youthful, as though the twenty-five years of Saddam had been suddenly erased. "The Americans have done it," he said, clapping his hands and grinning at his daughters. "They stood up to Saddam. They were the only ones willing to do that." Zia couldn't remember the last time her family had been so happy.

CHAPTER TWO

WHEN THE NEWS came that Baghdad International Airport
had fallen, the soldiers of the U.S. Army's 354th Civil Affairs
Brigade cheered wildly. Shortly thereafter, the unit packed
their duffel bags and began traveling in convoy up the supply route that
snaked from Umm Qasr, near Kuwait, toward Baghdad. On the stifling,
slow drive through southern Iraq, Lieutenant A. Heather Coyne
couldn't resist taking a few photos of herself to email back to her friends
in Washington, D.C., who knew her as Heather, an examiner in the
White House's Office of Management and Budget; a wonky bureaucrat
with a desk covered in policy papers, who wore a sensible gray suit and
had a degree in Arabic from the Defense Language Institute. Her decision, at almost thirty years old, to quit her job and join the army had
thrown her off her career path—and her coworkers, all vying up the
White House ladder, were shocked she'd give it all up. But this is what
it's all about, she told them. While she was scared and nervous about
poison gas attacks, her fear faded as the WMD attacks never material-
ized. She felt alive and excited to be liberating the Iraqis, and to be center stage in this world event. Her D.C. friends would certainly never
recognize her now, sweating under forty pounds of gear and a bulletproof vest, and with the chin strap of the Kevlar helmet digging into her
smiling cheeks. The gear was cumbersome, but she didn't mind; it gave
her a certain authority, which she knew she needed as a relatively recent
recruit and as one of the few women in her unit.

When, after two weeks of travel, they finally arrived in Baghdad, the
mood coming down the chain of command was victorious. There had
been no WMD attacks, and practically no resistance at all from the Iraqi
army; the only disturbing news was about rampant looting of national in-

stitutions such as universities, the library, and the museum. When she had asked her commanding officers why the U.S. soldiers weren't doing more to halt the looting, they pointed out that the troops were still taking fire, and that they didn't have the personnel to guard the museum, which housed artifacts that dated back ten thousand years, through the Sumerian, Babylonian, and Assyrian periods. She argued with commanders about it, but they seemed nonchalant. Their fears had been of a chemical weapons attack, fierce fighting, and millions of Iraqi refugees—none of which was happening. Back in Washington, Secretary of Defense Donald Rumsfeld was dismissing the looting as "cathartic" for Iraqis who had suffered under Saddam's repression. If the worst thing to happen was looting of toasters and sneakers—or even pre-Islamic artifacts—well, they reasoned, this was war and bad stuff happened. She felt uncomfortable about this answer, but was in no position as a lowly lieutenant to challenge it.

Her commander's sense of victory was confirmed when, on Heather's first tour of Baghdad, the locals kissed the soldiers' cheeks and played trumpet and drums in the dirt roads. Heather felt vindicated, given that so many of her friends and family back home had believed that the Iraqis didn't want war. She recalled their stunned reaction upon learning that she, an avid Democrat who was vehemently anti-Bush, would participate in what many saw as a Republican war for oil. But she never thought of it as "joining Bush's war." Iraqis suffered horribly under Saddam's police state, and she saw this war as the chance to release an oppressed people and free subjugated women, just as in Afghanistan. Looking triumphantly around her now, she was confident that events had proven her right.

IN ONE WAY or another, Heather had been thinking about the plight of Iraq for much of her adult life. The country had first come across her radar in high school, when Saddam Hussein was accused of gassing to death thousands and thousands of Kurds, including women and children, in the Iraqi town of Halabja. The eldest daughter of two science professors, young Heather Coyne was raised in the San Francisco Bay area, which proudly considered itself the most liberal city in America.

Outraged, she and her teacher had talked about how the world had, essentially, stood by and done nothing. She came to believe that the United States had a moral obligation to intervene in the world to stop injustice. Heather's rebel streak drew back to her mother, Lelia, who had fought her way into the PhD program at Cal Tech in the 1960s and had been one of the first women to graduate, and to her grandmother, a civil-rights activist in Kansas who had marched for African American rights; and her great-grandmother had been a suffragette. Heather adopted that passion, as well as their belief that the system could be changed—although they never imagined Heather would try to make a difference by becoming a soldier.

The road that brought Heather to Iraq began after she had attended Bryn Mawr College, when she went on to get her MA at Johns Hopkins University's School of Advanced International Studies (SAIS) in Washington, D.C., in international relations and international economics. The then-dean of SAIS was Paul Wolfowitz, who would later become President Bush's deputy undersecretary for defense and so-called architect of the Iraq invasion. As a student, Heather interacted with Wolfowitz only a few times, but she came of age, intellectually, as Wolfowitz and others were first making their case to get rid of Saddam. Wolfowitz, along with the future defense secretary Donald Rumsfeld, was actively campaigning for a coup d'état—in 1998 they penned an open letter to President Clinton calling for Saddam's removal. Heather was still in her mid-twenties and working her way up the career ladder. At the White House, her office at the OMB oversaw $350 billion in federal spending on national security programs, and she focused on counterterrorism when few others did. In the late 1990s, Al Qaeda was a familiar term around the OMB, but little known among those who worked outside of Middle Eastern issues. Much to her and her colleagues' frustration, they couldn't get people in power to pay attention to terrorism. Heather became known around the office as intense, whip-smart, ambitious, and yet also very idealistic. Anti-American sentiment couldn't be overcome from a desk in Washington, D.C., she realized. We need Arabic speakers, living in Arab countries, promoting aid programs and education. And yet few in the Pentagon or the State Department even spoke Arabic. "I want to get my hands dirty and make a difference," she told her boss. Shortly thereafter, she stunned her office by announcing she was quitting her well-paid, well-connected job as a bureaucrat and signing up for the U.S. Army Reserve. She underwent training and then enrolled in the Defense Language Institute in Monterey, California, to learn Arabic. It was early 2001, and she had no idea what the future held in store for her. Some days, she feared she had thrown away her career.

Then, one morning, she was driving to language class when she heard that four commercial airliners had been crashed into New York City, the Pentagon, and Pennsylvania. Tears flowed as she listened to the mounting death toll. *We saw that coming,* she immediately thought, her anger and sadness mixed powerfully with guilt. *We should have fought harder, worked longer, raised more hell to get terrorism on the agendas of people who mattered.* She didn't believe Saddam Hussein had anything to do with 9/11, but hadn't America just learned a lesson about ignoring rogue international actors such as Bin Laden? Tyranny breeds terrorism, and democracy is the antidote. If Saddam wasn't a threat right then, he would become one soon enough and he had to be taken down. If the rest of the world wouldn't help, America should do it anyway, she had felt. The Bush administration, obviously, agreed.

Heather didn't get called up for the 2001 Afghanistan mission. Finish language school, her commanding officers told her. We're going to need Arabic-speakers.

AFTER THEIR TOUR of the streets, and the gratifying sight of jubilant, grateful Iraqis celebrating the toppled statue of Saddam, Heather and the other soldiers returned to their new base in Saddam's palace and relaxed. The worst was over. They spent the next several days sweeping out the ballrooms, reattaching doors blown off by the bombs, writing emails home, and setting up their cots. On her walls, Heather hung up postcards of Saddam, to remind her why she was there. One morning at four a.m., on early guard duty, she walked out onto Saddam's veranda in night-vision goggles. Early-morning hues of pink and orange silhouetted the date palms, and the warm desert air felt like silk on her face. She was intoxicated by such exotic surroundings and filled with a sense of adventure and optimism. She knew there was hard work ahead—the details of which she hadn't even begun to consider—and she was ready to work harder than ever to make it succeed. Yet as she stood there, surveying Saddam's former world through the goggles' grainy green, she was suddenly hit by the scope of what she was part of: a vicious dictator had been toppled, a country had been liberated, and the course of history had been forever changed. And she had been a part of it.

CHAPTER THREE

WHEN TALK OF a war in Iraq began, Manal Omar was on the front row at the antiwar rallies.

"Iraqis have been through enough! We should help them, not bomb them," she shouted from the Washington stages, to cheering crowds of thousands.

Amid a sea of Caucasian college students, many of whom had only just found Iraq on the map, Manal stood out: a veiled woman in her late twenties, who laced her powerful speeches with Muslim slang, like political hip-hop. Manal was an outspoken and active member of the international aid world who had lived in Baghdad and still had family in the Palestinian territories. As an aid worker and an observant Muslim herself, she cared deeply about the plight of Iraqis under Saddam's reign, particularly Iraqi women, but she felt strongly that an invasion was unequivocally the wrong answer. She and other U.S. women's rights activists opposed the war on the grounds that war was, quite simply, *always* bad for women. The violence and insecurity of an invasion and military occupation would devastate the lives of the average citizens the Bush administration purportedly wanted to save. On the heels of a supposed victory in Afghanistan, the administration had pointed to the liberation of women there from the Taliban. But Manal suspected the situation on the ground in Iraq would be more complicated. With a decade of experience in aid work in the Arab world, she knew the first casualties of war were the most essential ingredients to women's freedom—security and stability. Without these things, women couldn't even leave the house. There was no way it could ever turn out well, and no way the Iraqis were going to welcome an American army, she felt sure.

Almost all women's aid groups agreed. In recent years, women's rights had risen in precedence inside the U.S. administration, with Colin Powell declaring in 2002, "It is the firm policy of the Bush administration that the worldwide advancement of women's issues is not only in keeping with the deeply held values of the American people, it is strongly in our national interest as well." Encouraged by this policy but worried by the impending invasion, on March 7, 2003, eight prominent U.S. women's organizations signed a letter to the White House requesting a meeting to discuss their concerns that "Violence often simply begets violence. . . . For Iraqi women, the war carries the danger that their nation will degenerate into an even more militarized or extremist Iraq that dramatically could restrict women's rights." The letter was signed by the National Council for Women, the National Organization for Women, the Feminist Majority, and the Ms. Foundation for Women. Their request for a meeting was denied and their concerns were dismissed as politically motivated, anti-Bush rhetoric.

As it turned out, this was because the Bush administration was hearing much more welcome news from another quarter: specifically, from a group called Women for a Free Iraq, which included a number of professional Iraqi expat women whose families had been living in exile in the United States and Europe in fear of Saddam. Most hailed from prominent Shia families who had been pushed out of power by the Ba'athists, and recently groups of these expats had been receiving tens of millions of dollars from the U.S. Congress in support of their efforts, including a publicity campaign that fed anti-Saddam stories into U.S. magazines and newspapers. Women for a Free Iraq had also teamed up with a Republican women's organization, the Independent Women's Forum (IWF), which had been started in the 1990s by Lynne Cheney as an alternative to other women's groups, which Cheney saw as deeply left-wing and highly critical of the United States.

The groups' position was welcomed inside a presidential administration making a case for war, particularly as images of Afghan women lining up to vote and rushing back into schools helped shore up support for the invasion of Afghanistan on the basis of strengthening women's rights. Some of the pro-war activists from Women for a Free Iraq were invited to meet with President Bush, and one would be given a seat near the first lady at the State of the Union address as a way of reminding

Americans that this war was not only about WMDs. These conservative women argued that Iraqi women had suffered horribly under Saddam, at least in recent years, and they promised that the war would start a feminist wave that would ripple across the Middle East. In Kuwait, women still couldn't vote. In Saudi Arabia, they couldn't drive or travel without a male companion. In Jordan, women could be murdered for having premarital contact with a man. All this needed to change, and liberating Iraq, they argued, was the first step.

Manal, for her part, didn't buy it. She had fought for Muslim women's rights, and she knew firsthand how unbearable life was in Iraq. She had been there in 1997 and '98 while working for the United Nations, and seen the poverty, corruption, and fear. But did people really imagine that women's rights and democracy would simply flourish in the wake of Saddam's removal? No one had a crystal ball, but Manal knew that distrust of the United States was strong across the Arab world, even after 9/11. Iraq sat between Iran, Saudi Arabia, Syria, and Jordan, and these countries would not simply throw open their doors for the pro-Israel Bush administration's military bases. The destruction caused by the bombings could leave hundreds of thousands dead. Worse still, she could tell from the speeches by top White House officials that they understood little about Middle Easterners. The American troops would not be greeted as liberators, Manal thought. This was going to be a mess.

AS SOON AS the invasion began, however, it seemed as though Manal and the other activists had been wrong. CNN beamed images of Iraqis celebrating and greeting the troops with flowers. Excitement overflowed as many realized that Saddam was on the run, and the Americans were establishing a clean slate: a new government, a new economic model, and a new constitution. Suddenly the invasion looked, indeed, more like a liberation. Women for a Free Iraq brimmed with confidence that they stood on the threshold of the greatest opportunity for women ever. With the Americans' help, Iraqi women's rights could be enshrined into the new constitution, and a quota of women in government could be mandatory by law. Parallels were drawn with revolutionary America: had American women had a role in the formation of the first government, in the writing of the U.S. Constitution, perhaps it wouldn't have taken them 150 years to earn the right just to vote—and 200 years to start getting elected in earnest to Congress. (Even in 2003, fewer than 15 percent of members of Congress were women.) Iraq could do better.

Manal cared deeply about the fate of Iraqi and Muslim women, and, watching the unexpected success of the invasion, she suddenly realized that, in a time of promise, she had been cynically sitting on the sidelines. At the moment, Manal was working as an analyst for the World Bank in Washington, D.C., focusing on the Middle East, but that wasn't her calling. High-energy, daring, and unafraid of being pushy, Manal thrived on the front lines of the action. In April, Manal was contacted about applying for a job in Iraq with a small D.C.-based women's rights organization called Women for Women International. The director was Iraqi, a woman named Zainab Salbi, who had fled Saddam's regime in her early twenties. She hated Saddam, but, like Manal and others, she had been against war because she knew the dangers an invasion could create for women. Now that it had happened, she was eager to have a staff on the ground to help those women who needed them most. Manal knew the Afghanistan director for Women for Women from high school and had volunteered for Women for Women in Kabul for several weeks. She had been impressed by the organization's ear-to-the-ground style of aid work. The group's method was to train women to be self-sufficient, mostly by starting their own businesses: beauty parlors in Afghanistan, fruit-pulp production in Colombia, and peanut-oil marketing in Nigeria. But despite Women for Women's good reputation, many of Manal's aid-worker friends tried to shame her into not accepting the job. They were feeling embarrassed by the reports of happy, grateful Iraqis who were greeting the soldiers with open arms. "You'll just be helping Bush's war," they said, arguing for her political loyalty. *Hell no,* she thought. *This is about women's lives, not political football, and someone has to help them.* So she quit her job with the World Bank, accepting the 50 percent cut in salary, and headed to Jordan to meet Zainab.

DURING THE FOURTEEN-HOUR drive into Iraq from Amman, her iPod at hand, Manal tried not to be freaked out. What if there was a chemical weapons attack, she wondered, or the U.S. soldiers shot at her SUV? Her loving parents would never forgive her for volunteering for such a dangerous assignment. Saddam's Iraq had been one of the safest countries in the world, as long as you kept your mouth shut about the regime. The rules for survival were unknown now. Who knew what to expect? Zainab, sitting up front, was as perky as a firecracker, chatting the entire time about all the ways Iraq had changed since she had last lived there ten years earlier. Zainab had already made a trip into Baghdad in May 2003, shortly after the invasion, rented an office in the Hay al-Jamaa neighborhood, and hired some local staff. Now, in July, she was returning with Manal to help her officially open the office. Then she would return to the United States.

Aid groups were often criticized for descending on third-world countries with a Western "we know best" attitude, which Women for Women counteracted with a rule that each country's office have only one foreign staff member—the rest had to be from the community. In Iraq, Manal was that foreign staff member. The other dozen were all Iraqi.

Manal liked that Women for Women was small, since it kept her close to those she was trying to help. In the multibillion-dollar aid world of Washington, D.C., Women for Women International was tiny, with only $13 million in individual donations and grants each year. Most of these came from American women who paid twenty-seven dollars a month to "sponsor a sister," which amounted to a personal letter-writing campaign to boost women's self-esteem and offer encouragement. Each year they had about 23,000 women "sponsors," mostly from California, Texas, and New York, who exchanged more than 40,000 letters with women from third-world countries.

Part of Manal's mission was to set up the letter-writing program in Iraq. She and her staff had spent the first few weeks traveling from Basra to Mosul, looking for women suitable for their program and identifying areas of need. The mixed effect of the war was clear across the country. Baghdad had been devastated by the looting, and much of its infrastructure was leveled. Yet in southern Iraq, the Shia heartland that spanned almost half the landmass of Iraq, Iraqis were happy because Saddam was *halas,* finished.

For three decades, Saddam had brutally oppressed these southerners. During various uprisings, more than 100,000 Shia had been executed, Manal had heard, although no one knew the real figure. When

Manal arrived in June, widows were hunting for the graves of their miss-ing husbands and sons. They found only remains, buried in mass graves just miles from their homes. The sad scene had brought tears to Manal's eyes. Bent over dusty piles of bones, skulls, and fragments of clothing, widows in black abayas would pound the ground and reach their hands to the sky, tears rolling down their cheeks. Saddam's repression was worse here than anywhere else in Iraq, and many Shia women kissed Manal and told her to "Thank Mr. George Bush." These images made her genuinely reconsider her antiwar position. The sense of liberation was intoxicating. When she thought of those women, she felt an obliga-tion to put politics aside and help the Iraqi women to succeed.

CHAPTER FOUR

CELEBRATIONS ROCKED ZIA and Nunu's neighborhood for weeks, but during that time the mood veered violently between joy and anarchy. Trumpets, horns, and gunfire could be heard until dawn, releasing decades of pain and anger. Buildings were set afire, bullets flew everywhere, and storefront windows were smashed. As Baba had predicted, as soon as the government was overthrown, mobs of young men from the neighboring Shia slums had flocked into the commercial district to take advantage of the chaos: looting stores, breaking into unoccupied homes, and combing greedily through the wreckage of Saddam's family's palaces. The looters flaunted their crimes openly, as though each act of destruction hammered home the dissolution of Saddam's repressive state.

Thousands flocked to the mosques, where fiery sermons heightened anti-Saddam passions. A wave of emotion swelled across Iraq, with those repressed by Saddam determined to erase any remnants of his rule. After the statues had been disfigured and the murals chipped down, a bloody thirst for revenge took over. Saddam had escaped, as far as anyone knew, but many from his ruling Ba'ath Party and his inner circle remained. They were stopped in their cars, pulled from their houses, hunted down, and executed. Soon, bullet-riddled bodies were an all-too-common sight, with former government officials crumpled on the streets or slumped over in their BMWs. The ubiquitous looters followed, driving away their cars and picking through the closets in their houses. Poor families and squatters moved into the empty bedrooms, the taste of justice making up for the absence of even a single working lightbulb.

The drive to destroy anything connected to Saddam's state mixed with the greed and opportunism of those who had lived in poverty for years. After the big-ticket items had been stolen—arms caches, jewelry from the palaces, Saddam's Arabian horses from the Al-Jadriya equestrian club—looters returned to steal hospital machinery, priceless museum artifacts, school desks, copper from electrical grids, and piping at power plants. For weeks and weeks, no one stopped the looting. The Iraqi police and army were terrified of being seen as defending Saddam's government. They hid in their houses. The U.S. soldiers stood by and watched.

As days and then weeks went by, Zia's happiness turned to concern. "Why aren't the American soldiers doing anything?" she asked Baba, but he had no answer. Women unaccompanied on the streets were being kidnapped and raped, Mamina had heard. She, Zia, and Nunu felt as if they had no choice but to stay inside the house, though the cramped two-bedroom apartment afforded little privacy. Confined there, they began to worry that the much-longed-for liberation had morphed irretrievably into sheer anarchy.

From the front gate, Zia could see Humvees passing on the main avenue, followed by gangs of children waving and trying to play with the American soldiers. She was glad the troops were here, but she was growing angry that they weren't policing the streets, arresting thieves, or enforcing traffic laws. We must be patient, Mamina assured her. Difficult times will be followed by peace.

THE PHONE SERVICE had been knocked out during the bombing, along with the electricity supply, so even the doorbell didn't work. One day, Mamina heard a neighbor's voice calling Baba's name from outside the gate. She quickly fetched a scarf to cover her head and bustled around the simple apartment, making sure it was tidy for the guest. By May, the sisters had been trapped inside for almost two months, and were glad for some small relief from the tedium of their days, even if it was just a visit from a neighbor. They disappeared into the kitchen for tea and a bowl of sweets as Baba went to the door.

Umar, an old friend of Baba's, greeted the family warmly and settled comfortably onto the sofa across from Baba. The two men heaped sugar into their teacups as they exchanged the latest news, a blend of radio reports, eyewitness accounts, and unsubstantiated rumors. By May 2003, Bush had declared "Mission Accomplished" and much of the looting had ceased, but the country was in shambles and it was still unsafe for women to be outside on their own. Umar confirmed reports that most of the hospitals, universities, and government ministries, except for the Ministry of Oil, were looted beyond recognition or outright destroyed—including the Ministry of Education. Mamina, a teacher, slumped onto the couch, devastated by the news. Employment, health, and salary records for the nation's sixteen thousand schoolteachers had vanished? How could the Americans ever fix that?

Baba and his friends blamed Saddam, not the Americans, for the insecurity and mayhem that had replaced Saddam's tightly controlled police since the invasion. Saddam had intentionally placed antiaircraft missiles in schools and residential neighborhoods, they said, to provoke Americans into attacking civilians. He'd encouraged the looting and ordered the oil fields torched, the bank coffers emptied, and the universities unguarded, with the nefarious intention of leaving the country bankrupt, impossible for the Americans to manage.

"Saddam had ordered his defense minister to encircle the city and destroy it, but the minister refused," Umar confided knowingly, though it was just a rumor. The men settled back into the couches briefly, shaking their heads at Saddam's cruelty. Zia clenched her teeth in familiar hatred.

Umar lightened the mood. The headquarters of the Mukhabarat had been bombed, he said. Saddam's laws banning free speech and foreign travel were being ignored, and the UN sanctions that for a decade had sealed Iraq away from the rest of the world were as good as lifted. The borders were wide open and the highways were packed with truckloads of incoming goods—satellite dishes, cellphones, computers, CDs, DVDs—the likes of which few Iraqis had ever seen.

"The *ajnabi* are living in Saddam's palace," Umar added, using the Arabic word for foreigners. "Sleeping in his bedrooms and walking in their boots in his dining room." At this, Baba raised his eyebrows. The world ought to see Iraqis in the palace, not Americans. As happy as he'd originally been to have the Americans arrive, he now felt a twinge of shame at the idea of being rescued from Saddam by foreigners. But he pushed his pride aside. The truth was that Iraqis had needed the Americans to get the job done, and now they must tolerate their presence until the mission was complete and peace was restored.

Umar had been to the palace to see the Americans, he said, announcing that he had already met a captain and landed a contract to do the unit's laundry. The foreigners don't understand Arabic and need translators, he said. Suddenly, Umar nodded thoughtfully toward Zia and looked Baba in the eye.

"My friend, I am signing the laundry contract tomorrow and I would feel more assured if I had an English-speaking translator with me," he suggested.

Zia's heart rose in her throat. She spoke English fluently: her recent degree from Baghdad University was in English translation. This was her chance to get out of the house, meet the mysterious Americans, and maybe even land a job with them that paid in U.S. dollars.

Across the living room, Baba was still. Zia was certainly the cleverest of his children—and his brothers' children, as well. In school she had easily risen to the top of her class and earned acceptance into a gifted school, and he was secretly delighted when she graduated with honors and announced she intended to become a doctor. When the Ministry of Higher Education refused her medical-school application, because most spots were reserved for the spoiled sons of Ba'athists, and instead assigned Zia to the translation program that was nothing but a training ground for dead-end secretarial positions, he knew how crushed she had been. Here was an opportunity for her to prove her worth and make her training useful. He wanted her to be happy, and knew she had determination and an urge to succeed that was at least as strong as that of any young men he knew. "Zia equals seven boys," Mamina often said, and Baba agreed. Although he seldom expressed emotion, he had always been proud of Zia's intelligence and spirit. It made him chuckle to see the way she put her uncles in their place with a steely look and a quick retort. Baba didn't encourage her rebelliousness, but he never reprimanded her, either. He was sorry she was not a son. "You'd make a much better boy," he always told her.

Now, though, as Umar and Zia looked at him expectantly, Baba shook his head.

"No, it's too dangerous." He took out a Pine cigarette, lit it, and inhaled slowly. "We will not be quick to judge the *ajnabi*. They are people of the book, they have prophets, and they saved us from Saddam. For this, we will support them. But we must not act hastily. The ones here now are soldiers, and Zia doesn't know their ways. Wait until the civilians arrive." Soldiers were young, aggressive, uneducated men, he believed, and he couldn't expose his daughter to such dangers.

Across the room, Zia sighed, not daring to challenge her father but barely bothering to conceal her disappointment in front of his guest. Still, once Umar was gone, Zia disappeared sulkily into her bedroom. She was angry and feeling more confined than ever before, during what everyone had expected would be a period of great freedom. She threw herself onto her bed and pounded the pillow with her fists. One thing at least was certain: if she *had* been a son, Baba would have made a different decision.

A FEW DAYS later, Mamina pushed open her daughters' bedroom door, carrying a Pepsi and a banana on a silver tray, two delicacies that had been unavailable during the sanctions. It was small consolation, she knew, for her despondent daughter, but it was the best comfort she had to offer right now.

"Will Umar come back to ask for me?" Zia asked her mother, hopefully.

"*Habibti,*" Mamina said gently, meaning "my dear." "Be patient. Perhaps soon Baba will change his mind."

Baba had always tended to be more liberal than other Iraqi fathers. He didn't expect his daughters to wear the Islamic headscarf, the hijab, and didn't consider them un-Islamic or indecent if they wore T-shirts that exposed their bare elbows and wrists. He even let them wear American-style pants and sneakers, while most of their girlfriends had to wear traditional loose skirts that concealed the outline of their legs. Zia and Nunu had grown up listening to Baba complain about the cruel and corrupt ways Islamic strictures were enforced upon women in Iran, Saudi Arabia, and under the Taliban in Afghanistan. For a brief moment, therefore, Zia had thought her father might say yes to Umar's offer, but it was hardly a surprise when he said no.

Mamina padded into the room in her slippers and nightgown, and rested the tray on the wooden dresser littered with nail polishes, lipsticks, and eyebrow pencils. The bedroom's thick velvet curtains were always drawn closed over the windows to the courtyard. A tray filled with gold rings, bangles, and earrings glittered from the bedside table, and a few undisturbed university texts were scattered on the bed. She sat down beside her eldest daughter and, placing Zia's head in her lap, gently stroked her hair until she felt Zia's body relax. Mamina's perfume mingled with kitchen scents of cilantro and onion, and her thin gold bangles clinked softly as she moved. Mamina believed gold increased the blood flow through a woman's body, so she rarely took off her bangles and necklaces.

As her mother and sister talked, Nunu skipped around the room restlessly, full of pent-up energy. "If you go work for the Americans, you will meet a prince charming!" she teased. "But Zia, imagine how people will talk."

"So what?" Zia said. "Go ahead and let them."

Mamina quietly agreed. "Working for the Americans would be a good thing. Your father worked for a German company and those were the best jobs. But we must give Baba time to get comfortable with the idea." After all, it was easier for him to work with them because he was a man, and it was different to send a twenty-one-year-old girl into that kind of unpredictable environment. As she soothed Zia, Mamina reminded them how damaging such contact between men and women could be for a girl's reputation. Hadn't the sisters just gone to a lot of effort to help Nunu's classmate Defaf carry on a secret relationship with her cousin? Defaf and her cousin were deeply in love, but their courtship had to be hidden because he had yet to formally ask her father's permission. If her family had caught her meeting him alone before they were married, the consequences would have been devastating—no matter that he was a trusted member of the family. They might have beaten her and withdrawn her from college. But the family never found out, and, in Defaf's case, it all ended happily: shortly before the war, the cousin proposed formally, and they were married. In all of this, Mamina had freely co-conspired with her daughters and the young lovers. She detested the old-fashioned belief that a couple should meet at the altar, as most do in Iraq. "It's good for you to know his personality before you marry him so you can be relaxed with him," she always said.

So few of these stories like Defaf's ended happily, however, when women challenged the cultural norms. Mamina told them a story that had happened in her Basra neighborhood when she was a teenager, when a man down the street murdered his wife and daughter. Mamina heard later from neighbors what had happened: the young woman was married, but on her wedding night, her husband discovered that she wasn't a virgin; furious, he returned her immediately to her father. Eventually she confessed that she had lost her virginity to one of the young men in the neighborhood, and her father flew into a rage and killed her. When he found out the mother had known about it, he killed her as well.

Sixteen-year-old Mamina had been aghast. Nothing in Islam condoned this sort of barbaric practice, these so-called honor killings, yet some tribes still encouraged them as a way to punish and control women. Most of the neighborhood hated the father, both for the killings and because he orphaned his other children. But the father was not charged with a crime, and nothing happened to the young woman's lover or husband. The double murder sent a chilling message to all the girls in the neighborhood. This was a lesson to be careful, because justice still favored men.

Zia and Nunu had heard horror stories like this before; they nodded as Mamina talked. Though she wasn't trying to scare them, she emphasized how careful young Iraqi women would have to be about any contact with the American soldiers, since the pressure for these honor killings was even greater if the lovers were from different backgrounds. Mamina told them about the man who had rented their home in Basra from them after she and Baba married and moved to Baghdad. He was fifty-five years old and was always in poor health. One day, he told Baba his story:

Many years ago his cousin had fallen in love with a man from a different tribe. But the family forbade the relationship because any sons produced in the marriage would go to the husband's tribe. The two teenagers, however, continued to meet secretly. Eventually, she lost her virginity to him and got pregnant. When the family found out, the father, brothers, and uncle were livid. "She must be punished!"

But although all the men in the family agreed she must die, no one wanted to execute the gruesome task. They stayed up for hours discussing this, shouting at one another and wailing over the tragedy. The next day, they took the issue to the tribal elders, where there was a brief effort at reconciliation.

"Will someone from the tribe marry her?" the tribal leader had asked. But not even the old men wanted such a loose woman as a second wife, and no man would agree to raise another man's baby. There was nothing left to do.

"Then who will slay her?" the tribal elder asked the brothers, uncles, and cousins. Everyone had an excuse. Finally, this man accepted the task, because he was young and needed to prove his strength. He told Baba he slit her throat, but spared him any more bloody details.

"I killed my cousin with the acceptance of my tribe and the family," he confessed miserably to Baba. "But my whole life I've felt guilty and regret what I have done."

Though Baba felt his remorse was sincere, he took no pity on him. "How could you have dared to do something like that?"

"I was young and I didn't know better. Now after many years I realize I should have handled the situation differently. I could have married her."

"Yes, you should have. You were young but you had a mind. Your soul should have rejected the idea of killing her. It's too late now. You killed her and the baby inside her."

The man stood up heavily and walked to the door. "It's a curse that runs after me."

Zia and Nunu were silent, thinking about their father's righteous anger, and about the boy who had killed his cousin to prove himself to his family. It was sobering to think that killing young women could be an heroic act to some people. But they felt sure that Baba, for all his stern façade, would never let anything like that happen to his own daughters.

"But Mama, everything is different now," Zia said, her voice rising. The Americans were bringing a whole new kind of society to Iraq—full of freedom and opportunity like nothing she and her sister had seen before. She wanted to be a part of making that happen. She just *had* to get the job, and she couldn't bear to wait while things were changing out there, without her.

"We have suffered thirty years of Saddam. What is a few more weeks?" Mamina said. "Have patience. If God wills it, you will have this job." Lying on the bed, safely out of Baba's earshot, the women fell into their routine of conspiring quietly to get what they wanted, a strategy played out in women's bedrooms across the Arab world.

OVER THE NEXT few weeks, Mamina approached Baba again about the job for Zia. Her plan was to wear down Baba's resistance gently, never telling him what to do, just pushing him persistently.

"Why not let her go for one day?" Mamina would suggest spontaneously as they were sitting in the living room.

"We don't know what's going to happen." Baba sighed. He had heard from friends that Saddam's secret police lurked around in plainclothes, keeping track of those who helped the Americans and intending to punish them after the Americans left. "We should wait and see."

The power dynamic between them was a precarious one. Mamina knew not to openly demand her way or challenge his authority. When Baba felt she was too bold, he was not above opening up their marital squabbles to her brothers, who acted as a second level of authority. In such cases, the male bond was stronger than that of family—a wife simply had to obey. Mamina loved some of her brothers, but a few were controlling and bossy. Still, she couldn't stand up to them, as that would bring shame on her and her daughters. Mamina's standing in the family was important not only for her own honor, but also because her extended circle of aunts and sisters-in-law acted as informal "matchmakers" in finding Zia and Nunu husbands. If Mamina was bold, the logic went, surely her daughters would make disobedient wives.

Baba, however, felt he had good reasons to worry, and not to send his daughter out among the Americans. Not only was the city unsafe, but Baba was unconvinced by the Americans' plans for instant democracy. Maybe they would take Iraq's oil and leave. Or perhaps they would change their minds, as they had in 1992. "Maybe they're here now, but maybe the next day they will grow tired of Iraq," he reasoned. "America is a great nation that knows democracy and freedom, but they don't need Iraq. They're rich and content with themselves. They come when they like and will leave when they like."

Mamina pressured him by turning this argument around. "That's why we must support them," she said. It was true that, on the streets and in the cafés, Baba recognized a strongly pro-American mood. People talked with excitement about a Baghdad renaissance. So Mamina kept chipping away at Baba's resistance.

"If things go wrong, you can blame me. If it goes well, you can take the credit," she argued.

A few more weeks passed as they performed this gentle back-and-forth, with Zia and Nunu waiting eagerly in the wings. Eventually, Baba ran into Umar, who had just bought a new Japanese television and made clear that he was on his way to becoming a rich man.

"Don't waste this opportunity," Umar said. "The civilian contractors are here now. I spoke to them. They need translators, and they pay very well. But there are hundreds of men like us lined up outside the palace."

After he saw Umar, Baba returned home to the apartment and thought for an hour. Perhaps he believed Iraqis should help the Americans; perhaps he was interested in the business connections Zia could drum up; or perhaps he was old and tired of listening to Mamina's nagging. In the end, he never gave Zia a reason. He just said, "Go for one day and then we'll see."

CHAPTER FIVE

LESS THAN A month after the troops toppled Saddam's statue, reports came in to Heather's unit about a group of black-clad, gun-toting vigilantes who'd taken hostage several UN-run food warehouses in a Baghdad ghetto called Sadr City. U.S. troops had set up bases and begun patrols in Baghdad, but random gunfire still echoed across the city and dead bodies kept turning up on the streets. Heather felt gutted by the slow pace of law and order, but she had resigned herself to the army's crushing bureaucracy and the complicated nature of reconstruction. She struggled to keep her spirits high.

This morning's mission was to retake the warehouses, which housed a UN program that had been distributing food baskets to tens of thousands of needy Iraqi families since the sanctions of the late 1990s. "Get the food to the people" was the order. The baskets contained beans, flour, rice, soap, and a few other basic staples—and were essential to survival for many families. Distribution had been first disrupted when the Iraqi government's Ministry of Trade, which operated the program, had been looted and burned. Now they had the armed gunmen to deal with. Swathed in red-and-white-checkered headscarves, they carried AK-47s and looked "like Al Qaeda," according to other units who had seen the men outside the warehouse. But since few of the U.S. soldiers spoke Arabic, they could only speculate as to whether these guys were Saddam's men, foreign jihadis, or local teenagers with guns. Debate ensued as to whether they should arrest them immediately, or try something more friendly.

"Let's offer them Coyne as a second wife," a soldier had suggested, to hoots of laughter.

"Ha-ha, guys," she said, hardened to the teasing, but no less annoyed by the implied sexism. "Why don't we try and talk to them?" Despite the importance of communication, Lieutenant Coyne was the only soldier in the unit who spoke Arabic. Her battle-roster position was "Chief of Linguist Team" (though she *was* the "team"). She couldn't wait to leave the claustrophobic base and meet the Iraqis she'd been thinking about for so long. She yearned to let them know that her unit was there to help.

Still, she kept her finger near the trigger of her M16 as her two-Humvee convoy made its way toward Sadr City. The situation had definitely deteriorated since her last tour of the streets. Through her black sunglasses, she self-consciously scanned the flat rooftops, the shaded windows of passing cars, and the crowds of Iraqi men who watched the convoy race past, kicking up dust. Soldiers from her unit had removed the door of the Humvee—it was not armored anyway—so they could lean out and take aim, if need be. At any moment, her commanding officers warned, a soldier could be caught in the crossfire of a disgruntled Iraqi Ba'athist or Al Qaeda operative. It was nerve-racking, but she had to admit she also thrilled at the idea of being in a rough neighborhood and on a dangerous mission. That was why she had given up her job at the White House to be a soldier. She wanted to be on the front lines and out in the world, getting her hands dirty, doing good, and she recognized little contradiction in delivering the message of goodwill from behind the barrel of a gun.

As the Humvee flew along, the frenzied commercial center of downtown Baghdad gave way to a vast, flat desert of mud-brick houses, broken sewage pipes, and patches of trash-strewn land where young men kicked around a deflated soccer ball. Sadr City, she knew, was the city's largest and poorest Shia neighborhood. Built in the late 1950s to provide housing for rural peasants, the neighborhood had long operated as a center of political resistance. What began as a Communist stronghold against the Ba'ath Party soon became an organizing base of religious Shia who opposed Saddam's Sunni regime. In revenge, Saddam had neglected the neighborhood for decades. Heather saw schools without windows, roads uneven from running sewage, and residents dumping their trash in empty lots. Her convoy had to be careful not to trample the barefoot children who weaved into traffic hawking rose-colored packets of tissues or mint bubble gum.

The convoy crunched to a stop, at last, in front of the warehouse, where a group of sullen-looking men banded together. They wore sweatpants, sandals, and oversize Western T-shirts; the older men wore short-sleeve collared shirts and thin leather belts with shiny buckles. Only about six of them had weapons, but what unnerved Heather was that, while most Iraqis waved and smiled at passing convoys, these men stared blankly.

Lieutenant-Colonel David Jones, the unit chaplain who was serving as the team leader for this mission, led the way out of the vehicle and greeted the crowd. Heather stepped out behind him, trying to look friendly. After a few brief words, the young guards ushered them into the warehouse and told them they would meet with the group's sheik, a religious leader. The food warehouse was a cavernous building, like an airplane hangar, with trash, piles of rags, and stripped pieces of metal equipment. A couple of tiny windows let in streams of sunlight, although they were blanketed in dirt.

Up close, Heather saw the militiamen were not Al Qaeda, but simply teenagers. She couldn't tell who, if anyone, was in charge since they all dressed in street clothes, and all seemed eager to follow anyone who offered direction, even the Americans. The sheik had not yet arrived, so everyone stood around for a few minutes. The mood lightened as the guards' youth and curiosity got the better of them. When they realized Heather was a woman, they whispered and pointed at her. In their poor English, they addressed her the best way they knew: "Hello, mister. How are you? Good, good."

Heather smiled to herself. If they were meant to appear threatening, they must have forgotten.

"*Salaam aleikum*," she said, using the standard Arabic greeting of "Peace be upon you."

"*Wa aleikum salaam*," they replied, surprised by her Arabic. "And peace be upon you."

"You speak Arabic?" They pulled crinkled cards from their pockets to show Heather laminated badges with their photos, their signatures, and

Arabic calligraphy. The group's name was Al Houza, but that meant nothing to her.

"We're in charge of protecting the warehouse," one said proudly. Ali Babas had come to steal the food and we saved it, they said. "The food is for the people in our neighborhood."

Heather laughed with relief. She had expected a hostile army, not some sort of a Muslim aid agency with photo ID badges, even if they did have guns. She told them she was impressed at the speed and organization that had enabled them to issue ID cards in the middle of a war.

"Your energy and self-motivation are exactly what your country needs to rebuild itself." She smiled at them, sounding more formal in the foreign language than she intended. She assured them that the U.S. military wanted to help them guard the warehouses. They nodded enthusiastically.

"Bring your tanks next time!" one shouted.

The more she spoke with them, the more fascinated—and concerned—she became. These weren't just armed opportunists who'd seized the warehouse to steal food. These foot soldiers represented a complex political organization with a serious agenda, and they intended to use the aid as a way of building a power base. Although relieved the meeting would not turn violent, she worried that her unit had been dropped into the middle of a situation they didn't understand. *We're way out of our league,* she thought.

Suddenly, just as she was making headway with the guards, one of her superiors—a civil affairs major from a different unit, who acted as if he knew everything on all matters Iraqi—appeared at her side and demanded to have a word with her. A small, bossy man, his voice was scolding.

"Lieutenant Coyne, in Islamic cultures men would be offended by your trying to talk with them. I advise you to keep quiet."

Heather was taken aback. "Sir, I have interacted with Iraqis and I have never had any problems in any other situations—"

They were interrupted by the arrival of the sheik, whose already impressive height was exaggerated by a grand white turban fastened with a black, twisted piece of twine and a long robe that trailed behind him. Reverently, the crowd cleared and let him pass.

"Lieutenant, don't mess up this relationship," the major warned her. "Keep quiet and stand back."

In light of his higher rank, Heather had little choice but to follow orders. Chaplain Jones was leading the day's mission, but he had been planning to pass the ball to Heather, since she could address the crowd in Arabic without a translator. But now Heather watched the major elbowing his way to the middle of the room to greet the sheik. Clearly, he intended to dominate the scene, even though he needed a translator to make himself understood, and even though he didn't completely understand the situation yet. What galled her the most was his lame effort to invoke Arab chauvinism to justify his own. Her face reddened from the heat and the surge of irritation.

Addressing the sheik and his men, the major then launched into a diatribe, telling the sheik exactly what was going to happen—his militia would have to turn over the warehouses to the Iraqi Ministry of Trade, and in return, the vigilantes would receive "certificates of appreciation" and ten dollars each. In return, "Iraq will be a strong, vibrant democracy in which each citizen participates to the fullest. We are gonna redo everything," the major announced.

The sheik eyed the major, looking unimpressed. He would not be bought off so easily.

"Guarding the warehouse is my duty. I have ninety-two men. They need jobs." As the two leaders talked, the sheik's voice began to rise in anger and he spoke so quickly that his translator could only emit short phrases. "Why didn't the Americans protect the city from looters? Hospitals finished; schools finished; ministries finished," he said, wiping his hands together to indicate demolition.

Heather knew by then about the heavy damage, as it had been on the news every night. As the sheik continued, she had a sinking feeling in her stomach, since she knew her unit lacked the resources and expertise to handle all these problems.

But while the sheik was focused on practical matters that directly affected his men and the people he was defending, the American major didn't seem to get it, talking instead in big-picture platitudes about democracy. As Heather stood there fuming, listening to the conversation go nowhere, she recalled advice she'd read somewhere from Madeleine

Albright: "Learn to interrupt," Albright had encouraged young, ambitious women, "because no one will ever turn to you and ask what you think." Heather desperately wanted to intervene and get the negotiations back on track, but as a new soldier, it was far from easy. Female soldiers who voiced their opinions were considered outspoken, opinionated, and "bitches"—while those who remained silent were stereotyped as passive, quiet, and "weak." Furthermore, as a lieutenant, she could be reprimanded for "pushing back" against a higher officer.

As she struggled with how best to handle this brewing crisis, one of the original group of young guards approached her. The sheik had observed her conversing in Arabic.

"The sheik would like to speak with you."

She scooted over to the sheik.

"Salaam aleikum," he said.

"Wa aleikum salaam," she replied. She didn't extend her arm for a handshake, but put her palm to her heart. Careful to observe the cultural niceties, she expressed gratitude to the Iraqis for their hospitality in receiving the Americans.

"Tell me," the sheik asked, "what do you think of Iraq?"

So much, she thought. "Iraq is a country with great riches and history," she started in Arabic. "This is the home to the world's first civilization. It has been my dream to come here for fifteen years."

The sheik nodded in approval. "Yes, yes, we have much, but there is so much devastation from thirty years of Saddam, a bastard son."

She nodded. The sheik spoke in fast, classical Arabic, and she was struggling to keep up, but she was thrilled to be given the chance to negotiate. The sheik's patient demeanor and friendly expression made her think he appreciated her Arabic skills, however elementary.

"When you Americans arrived, you protected only the oil ministry," he went on. "The warehouses were being savaged by looters. My men came in and protected these warehouses."

The sheik seemed to imply that the Americans were encouraging the looting as a strategy to weaken the country.

As Heather struggled to digest this, she didn't know how to respond. She needed to convince him that they were serious about fixing his country—that they were not trying to destroy it. She couldn't exactly explain the appalling levels of bureaucratic dysfunction that she had seen during mobilization, the insufficient troop levels, and why, frankly, the soldiers hadn't taken the looting more seriously when it first started happening. Standing in front of the sheik like this, she suddenly got a taste of the magnitude of the task ahead, and the gulf in expectations between the occupiers and the occupied.

"Your men did Iraq a service by protecting the warehouses," she started. "This is the kind of participation that will make Iraq strong again. However, the situation has stabilized now, and we believe the warehouses should be returned to the government ministries, not to a religious group. We are rebuilding the ministry, and we won't be putting Ba'ath Party members back in control."

"Al Houza has a list of Ba'ath Party warehouse employees who are Ali Babas and corrupt," the sheik said. "We won't accept their return. Do you not care that the Iraqi people were being cheated by Saddam's corrupt Ba'athists?"

"Sir, that is why I am in Iraq."

He fell silent.

"We're also worried about these problems," Heather added enthusiastically. "You have to come to us if you hear about corruption. Report the people to us so we can investigate them, absolutely."

She pulled out a notebook and jotted down notes of the meeting. Out of the corner of her eye, Heather was gratified to see the crowd's attention drifting toward her and the sheik and felt a swell of victory at the connection she was making. She invited the sheik to attend a follow-up meeting at UN headquarters, and promised to arrange a peaceful transfer of control of the warehouses from the militias back to the government ministry in which few would lose their jobs. She tried to make only small, specific promises, and swore to herself she would keep them.

Although nothing concrete had been accomplished, in the end there was a sense of good feeling in the room. The meeting wrapped up with a chorus of thank-yous and "peace be upon you."

Before Heather left, she asked one of the guards if this sheik was their leader. They shook their heads. "No, our leader is Muqtada al-Sadr." A cheer went up. She scribbled down this name, too, not having ever heard it before. When she returned to base, she intended to write a lengthy memo of the meeting to send up the chain of command, explaining the sheik's needs and alerting them to the fact that politically motivated religious groups were armed and were organizing the men in the neighborhoods. Best to involve them in our efforts, Heather thought, than to make enemies. She recommended that the military coordinate rebuilding efforts with Muqtada al-Sadr's men to restart the warehouse. As she understood, army civil affairs was prepared to handle the reconstruction effort with the help of NGOs and the State Department. Heather and her unit were gathering information for them. Someone important would read her memo, she believed, and a sensible path would be acted upon.

That was the Bush administration's postwar "plan," as she vaguely understood it, and she had no reason to doubt that everything would go smoothly.

CHAPTER SIX

SADDAM'S CONCRETE, UNADORNED palace stood before Zia like an impenetrable fortress, the symbol of so many of her nightmares. It was the black hole into which Iraqis disappeared, never to be seen or heard from again. "Don't even look at it," Baba had always warned her and Nunu.

But Umar was already confidently crossing the front lawn, walking swiftly toward its entrance as a helicopter whirred overhead. *"Yella,"* he shouted back to her, Iraqi slang for "Let's go."

Yet Zia felt rooted to the spot. Saddam had dozens of palaces in Iraq, but this, the Republican Palace in the center of Baghdad, had been the seat of his whole government. The palace grounds occupied several square miles, and included a neighborhood of mansions for top government officials, a park, and military parade grounds. Zia had never seen any of it before. Iraqis considered it unwise to approach the palace, for fear of attracting the suspicions of Saddam's secret police. Most considered it unsafe to even look in its direction.

Rumors of the evil that occurred inside sent shivers down Zia's spine: many believed that Saddam kept practitioners of black magic from Babylon in his dungeon to read people's minds. Others whispered about the wild parties thrown by Saddam's maniacal son Uday, in which he got drunk, raped women, and had once beaten a guest to death. Long denied a free press, Iraqis had heard only whispers about Saddam's cruelty over the last decade, but now, with international human rights groups canvassing the country and the arrival of satellite television, evidence was emerging of Saddam's atrocities—and it turned Zia's stomach.

Mass graves uncovered in the south produced evidence of tens of thousands of Shia men, slaughtered. Human rights activists were estimating Saddam killed as many as 100,000 Kurds in the north, in some cases gassing entire villages. Thousands of victims' bodies would never be identified, but such physical evidence was not necessary. It turned out that the Ba'ath Party had kept meticulous records of every crime, including torture and execution of women and babies. Those searching through the offices of Ba'ath Party headquarters found execution orders bearing stamps from ministry officials and Saddam himself. Until now, Iraqis had only suspected these atrocities. Now, they and the world were learning the full scope of Saddam's cruelty.

Though Zia and her family had been fairly certain there had been such crimes, the confirmation of their details and extent had still come as a shock. For years, Saddam's bullies had intimidated all Iraqis, and now the Americans had made them run and hide like cowards. But that wouldn't be the end of it, Zia knew. Saddam hadn't acted alone. Tens of thousands of Iraqis had propped up the Ba'ath Party, either as passive supporters like her in-laws in Hit or as active members of his government, spy network, and secret police. They'd be back. And when they came back, the hundreds of thousands of mostly Shia Iraqis who had suffered humiliation and torture, and whose families had been killed by the Ba'ath Party, would be waiting for them. Iraqis were going to make them pay—them and their children and their children's children. Underneath the celebration of the liberation was a thirst for revenge. As Zia walked nervously toward the palace doors, she began to tremble. The violence was far from over, she suspected.

WHEN SHE FINALLY followed Umar to the doors, she was stopped by an arriving SUV. A serious-looking band of muscular Western men jumped out and jogged past, in tight T-shirts and bulletproof vests, wearing bulky black wristwatches. Guns were strapped to their sides. She wondered who they were, but was soon distracted as she almost tripped up the steps entering the palace. The ceilings soared high above her, and the marble floor shimmered before her like an endless ocean. Chandeliers lit the hallways, and a few silk-upholstered chairs with carved wooden armrests sat in front of large murals.

"Look how he lived while we suffered," she said softly.

Umar was laughing. "This is all fake," he said. "The gold is paint; the chandeliers are glass. The man had no taste!"

Umar found a circle of Iraqi friends, also waiting for the Americans to interview them for jobs. They were all dressed in short-sleeved work shirts and with mustaches, and were there to provide the foreigners with whatever they needed: translators, cleaners, photocopies, food, drivers. When Zia heard the fees they intended to charge, she was stunned. Hundreds of dollars! But this was a pittance to the rich Americans, they assured her. Standing amid the luxury, they mocked Saddam and his family. "Saddam is hiding and we are standing in his palace!"

"That son of a bitch," another said. "He didn't know his father and was trying to compensate for that by building these giant palaces."

It was one of her first days out in the city since the invasion, and Zia quickly looked around them to see if anyone was listening. She was normally quite outspoken herself, but not about Saddam. This kind of talk made her nervous, particularly given where they were. Maybe the palace was bugged, or Saddam would use black magic to hear them and find them. A lifetime of fear was not easily overcome.

After an hour of waiting with the men, she summoned her courage and wandered off to explore the palace. She didn't think anyone would mind, or even notice her—surprisingly, they didn't seem concerned about security of any sort.

The Americans had been in the palace about a month, and the place was messy. Empty plastic water bottles littered the floor, and she wrinkled her nose at the stench of sweat, leftover food, and disinfectant. In addition to the soldiers, she saw American civilians for the first time. They wore white shirts, khaki vests with lots of pockets, and baseball caps. Many looked to be in their fifties, with shadows of beards, haggard looks, and patches of sweat on their shirts.

She explored deeper down the labyrinth of hallways, discovering bedrooms, private offices, and kitchens, although most rooms were empty of treasures, probably cleared away by looters. A ballroom had been converted into a sleeping space with hundreds of bunk beds. With a small Kodak camera her uncle had sent her from Jordan, Zia snapped photos to show Baba, Mamina, and Nunu the floors and the ceilings, the murals and even the palace bathrooms, which had Western toilets, with real brass fixtures, instead of Turkish-style ceramic bowls on the floor. She imagined Saddam walking these same halls. Zia pressed on through the massive palace, driven by curiosity but terrified of what she might find.

When she got back to the group, Umar hadn't noticed she'd been gone. She told him how nervous it made her that they were all just standing like this in Saddam's palace, but he laughed again.

Don't be afraid, Umar reassured her. Saddam is *halas,* finished.

But I have been afraid my entire life, she thought.

THOUGH SHE HADN'T been given a job on the first trip, with Baba's permission Zia returned again with Umar to the palace the next day. Umar eventually found the captain he was looking for, and they signed the laundry contract. When Zia finished translating, the captain turned to her.

"Your English is perfect. Do you want a job here?"

Zia felt her heart soar as she nodded. He scribbled down a name, Captain Michaels, on a piece of yellow sticky paper, and told her to go find him at the rotunda. When she got there, she saw dozens of Iraqis standing around waiting to be interviewed by one soldier, who was sitting on a plastic chair and using another plastic chair as his desk. After a few minutes, Zia lost her nerve and left. *He's busy,* she thought. She convinced Baba to allow her to return to the palace over the next few days with Umar, and tried again. Finally, she caught Captain Michaels during a slow moment and approached him. In his rumpled fatigues, he looked up at her with a bemused expression.

Zia could guess why. She had felt pangs of self-consciousness that morning, and, suspecting the Americans held stereotypes about "dirty" Arabs, she had countered that in the extreme: wearing a white pantsuit with a short-sleeved jacket, a crisp green shirt, and polished white shoes, with her hair blow-dried several inches above her head. She had piled on her gold rings, bracelets, necklaces, and earrings, and wore thick eyeliner and eye shadow and dark lipstick. As she hobbled in high heels past the barbed wire and across cracked sidewalks into the palace that morning, the sweaty, unshowered Americans turned to stare at the movie star in their midst.

The soldier looked back at his papers. He took her résumé, which had a small passport photo clipped to the upper right corner. Pleasantries were brief.

"Are you a Ba'athist?" he asked.

"No," she said.

"What about your father? Was he a Ba'athist?"

Zia was taken aback. "No," she said, emphatically.

Then he smiled. Zia couldn't help but notice he was tall and handsome, with tanned skin, black hair, and big arms. He wore a platinum wedding ring, and under the plastic laminate that held his badge, he had put a photo of a woman.

"You're way too pretty to work for the military," he said. "You belong in an office with air-conditioning and a desk. I'm sending your application over to the civilian side."

"Okay," she said, elated at the thought of actually landing a real job with the Americans.

As Zia returned home that day, the setting sun cast rays of orange and pink across the sky as the taxi crossed the Jumhuriya Bridge spanning the Tigris River. Below her, rickety wooden boats ferried passengers across the black water. Green reeds undulated along the river's edge. Seagulls flapped and squawked overhead. Looking out the window, she felt that everything suddenly seemed brighter, and she could see from the faces of people in the street that she was not alone—people laughed and smiled and their attitudes toward one another seemed open and welcoming. For the first time in years, her future looked bright, and her fears of Saddam were forgotten. *Maybe I will rise to become a diplomat and work in the palace,* she imagined. *Or maybe I will marry a foreigner, and serve as the Iraqi ambassador to his country,* she thought, giggling to herself. Anything felt possible.

A few days later, she explained her new life enthusiastically in an email to an uncle in Jordan. "Saddam's palace is now a magical place. You can say what you want and take the job that you want. Life is difficult. We have no electricity yet, and no clean water. The security is not good. But people are happy. I am happy."

. . .

WHEN ZIA RETURNED home from the palace around seven p.m., Nunu was still sitting cross-legged in front of the television in the same bathrobe she had had on when Zia left that morning.

"Nunu!"

"I'm addicted!" Nunu laughed, cuddling the remote control. "TV is my new best friend."

Baba had recently joined the throngs of families buying satellite dishes, piping in hundreds of channels. Baba preferred CNN, Al Jazeera, and the BBC, but Nunu's favorites were American sitcoms and talk shows.

As Zia's world opened up, and she found her way out of the house and into a job, Nunu's life seemed to be moving in the opposite direction. The lack of a strong police force meant the streets were too dangerous for a nineteen-year-old to move around in freely; and while university classes had resumed, they were sporadic, due to traffic jams, lack of electricity, and general chaos. Nunu had whined about the restrictions until she discovered *Oprah*. Now, every evening on MBC 4 she got her daily dose, and her big sister knew better than to stand in the way.

Nunu loved the new flood of information and excitement from the world at large. After ten years of UN sanctions that kept Iraqis in isolation, satellite dishes, Internet cafés, cellphones, political magazines, and newspapers all blossomed across Iraq, seemingly overnight. Under Saddam, Zia's family had only two television channels, controlled by the Ministry of Information. Foreign news had been banned. Although they occasionally showed pirated Hollywood movies from the 1980s, most broadcasts had been of Saddam's speeches, parades, ceremonies, and government sessions, which Nunu had always found either boring or terrifying.

By contrast, everything about Oprah's show enthralled Nunu, even when the topic was entirely disconnected from her Baghdad living room. She loved to watch the episodes about women with credit card debt, Hollywood celebrities trying to get pregnant, fashion faux pas, and the dizzying array of fad diets. The idea that *these* were the problems American women faced! Each episode focused on women's issues from some angle, and was infused with positive messages and encouragement. What Nunu loved most were the personal survival stories, like when Oprah brought on women who had been molested or had suffered under an abusive spouse. In Iraqi culture, problems such as rape or sexual abuse were taboo, because the shame for the crime rested with the woman. Nunu was fascinated by the idea that not only did American women also suffer from these problems, but that they would confess them in front of an audience. And Oprah opened her heart to them. She asked questions and told them it wasn't their fault, and to be strong. Such emotional sharing was unheard of, in Nunu's experience. Each episode was part entertainment, part inspiration, and part therapy. American television was always so uplifting, and it motivated her to write in her journal, a secret pastime that even Zia and Mamina didn't know about.

"Oprah always says 'follow your dream,' " she had written once. "In my society, girls are not supposed to have dreams. But I do have them. Probably they are dreams that the American girls would think are silly. I dream of being a good housewife who would obey her husband and keep the house tidy. I dream of having children and a rose garden."

Lately, Nunu was always writing about what Oprah said. She came back to certain sayings: "If you want a positive life, you need to think positively and act positively. Don't compare yourself to others, because what one person has may not be destined for you." Nunu filled her journal with such emotional missives. "We are human, from flesh and blood, so it's okay if we cry and hurt." Nunu loved that one. Iraqi society could be harsh, she felt, and women's emotions were usually dismissed and denigrated by men. Feelings were shared among mothers, daughters, and sisters, but were never to be aired publicly. Oprah said that women's feelings mattered—so much so that she gave them a platform on television. Nunu felt she was slowly learning the vocabulary with which to express herself and that she was becoming aware that she had some right to do so. The kind of encouragement that Oprah gave was unheard of in Iraqi society.

As her sister walked in, she looked up from the television with a smile. While Zia was outside the house, learning about the broader world through work and career, Nunu was receiving no less of an education by having that world beamed into her living room.

"Oprah wants to be the mother of all people," she told Zia.

"Nunu, come," Mamina was saying, as she set a steaming platter of dolma—rice and ground meat wrapped in grape leaves—on the table. Nunu reluctantly turned off the television.

She moped at the table, explaining that one of her favorite series had ended. "I miss them," she said about the actors. "I feel like they were my friends and now they are gone."

Zia laughed at Nunu as she glanced longingly toward the television.

"Nunu, you should do something else, like read books. Watching television all the time is not good for you."

"Yes, it's true," Nunu said. "There was a report that says television weakens the mind and reduces the human's ability to concentrate." Then she paused. "I heard about it on television!"

Everyone laughed. Nunu held out her hand to give Zia a high five. Baba reached across the table for bread, and Mamina heaped spoonfuls of dolma onto everyone's plate.

While Nunu ate, Zia filled the room with chatter about the Americans she had seen and met that day. "They have women in the military," she told Nunu. "I saw one sitting on a tank with a gun. No one says to them, 'You should be at home doing housework.' "

Plus, Captain Michaels was so much kinder than other bosses she'd known. "He didn't shout and he dealt with his workers humanely," Zia added.

Mamina beamed proudly as her daughters laughed and told their stories. Their futures at last were looking brighter and brighter. After all these years of struggle, her girls were going to be able to reach for their dreams again.

CHAPTER SEVEN

INSIDE BAGHDAD'S CONVENTION center, Manal was watching bedlam break loose at a meeting of Iraqi women organized by the U.S. military.

A few Iraqi women, in flowery pink headscarves and high heels, sat patiently in the front. But a much larger group in black headscarves, black cloaks, and black gloves sat with their arms folded, glaring hostilely at the soldiers. They had arrived with a list of complaints, and the long lines at the three security checkpoints outside the convention center only added to their fury.

"Where are the policemen?" a middle-aged woman shouted, her face flushed with anger. "My daughters can't even go outside." Women complained that their husbands were unemployed, their children's schools were closed, and the crime, looting, and gangs in the streets were dangerously out of control.

"We haven't had any electricity since Saddam fell months ago!"

Standing in the front of the room, looking uncomfortable, was Sergeant Jody Lautenschlager, a petite soldier with long dark hair and baby fat around her cheeks. She looked about nineteen years old. Lautenschlager had organized the meeting ostensibly to reach out to Iraqi women. Manal knew her as a Civil Affairs officer detailed to work in the Humanitarian Assistance Coordination Center (HACC) and to handle Iraqis with "immediate needs."

"Okay, we do have a number of financial grants from the U.S. State Department that will be available for Iraqi women to boost female participation in the private sector," Sergeant Lautenschlager told the crowd.

Silence descended as the translator spoke in Arabic. Then, quickly, the shouting began again.

"We don't care about women in business. Our husbands need jobs! When will salaries start again for the men?"

As the room dissolved into shouting, Sergeant Lautenschlager looked helplessly around for support. *Sorry, sister,* Manal thought. She wasn't going to bail her out. Most of the Americans working on women's issues inside the palace were Bush Republicans, and they had consistently refused to associate with Manal because she had protested the war. Indeed, the only reason Manal had attended this meeting was to keep an open mind. She wanted to do what was best for Iraqi women, and perhaps there was a chance the military had some good programs. Instead, though, the meeting was confirming her worst expectations. Despite the promises made to liberate Iraqi women during Bush's campaign for war, little had happened since. Sergeant Lautenschlager's program had been one of the first times Manal had heard the U.S. authorities mention women's rights since the war began, and clearly the program was ill-conceived and these soldiers—however well-intentioned— were unprepared and inexperienced. Did the U.S. Army really believe a few business grants would buy them off?

The celebratory mood toward Americans had begun to nose-dive over the broiling hot summer months since Manal had arrived, as unabated violence and looting continued, and basic services such as police surveillance, water, and electricity, and reliable government salaries, hadn't returned. One local women's group was claiming to have documented four hundred cases of women who had been raped in Baghdad in the months since the war began. Human Rights Watch (HRW), a well-respected New York agency, verified twenty-five cases of sexual violence against women. They found that, in the chaos of war, there were no police to protect these women, no hospitals to treat them, and no judicial system to bring the perpetrators to account. Many victims didn't even go to the hospital after they were raped. The social stigma against rape victims was strong, and there was little point—the hospital equipment had all been looted. Manal's limited exposure to the Americans in Saddam's palace, thus far, revealed they had no clue what was going on in the streets. Either that or they genuinely didn't care, because they were just in Iraq for the oil or to play out some democracy fantasy cooked up by the Bush administration, Manal thought angrily to herself.

The meeting was getting nasty. In the front row, several well-heeled Iraqi women with coiffed hair and manicured nails collected their brief-cases and stormed out. Their seats quickly filled with old women in black abayas showing only their eyes, nose, and mouth, and small blue tribal tattoos on their rough hands. A few women clutched framed black-and-white photographs of male relatives who had disappeared under Saddam. Others waved more recent photographs of men they claimed the Americans had detained without reason, leaving no infor-mation about their whereabouts. "We will starve without my husband," one woman cried. These women were livid, jabbing the air with their fingers, their faces bright red, some crying openly and cursing the Amer-icans in Arabic.

"Okay, okay," Sergeant Lautenschlager was saying in a besieged voice. "We will send your questions up the Civil Affairs chain of com-mand. Come back next week and we will have another meeting and we will invite the police to hear your concerns."

As the crowd was left to stew, Manal listened in to hear what the Iraqi women were saying.

"The *ajnabi* humiliate us in our own country," they said, referring to the "foreigners."

"How do they expect us to trust them when they don't trust us?" an-other said. "We had to go through so much security to get to them."

Sergeant Lautenschlager's Iraqi translator was trying to placate the women. "Everyone gets searched this way to enter the convention cen-ter. I go through this too."

But they stared disbelievingly at the translator.

"Why are you working for them?" one asked, accusatorily.

"They got rid of Saddam," she reasoned. "They are going to help us."

The women shook their heads. Many of them came from the poor Shia neighborhood of Sadr City, where Muqtada al-Sadr had be-gun delivering fiery Friday-night sermons accusing the Americans of spying for Israel, selling alcohol, and defiling women. In the absence of any real personal contact with the Americans, many Iraqis believed him.

"Tell the truth. Tell us the real reason why the Americans are here."

MANAL STEPPED OUTSIDE the convention center into the blinding sun. She adjusted her headscarf and put on her knockoff designer sunglasses. Her loose flowing pants wafted dangerously close to the spiky barbed wire as she exited through the U.S. military checkpoint, toward her car. After the Americans occupied Saddam's palace and the nearby convention center, they allowed Iraqis to enter both freely. But in the last month or so, there had been a few attacks against U.S. soldiers, and the response had been swift. The perimeter of the palace was surrounded with concertina wire and heavily armed guardsmen, and no Iraqis were allowed in or out without a U.S. escort. The convention center was established as the place for the Iraqi public to enter if they wanted to, say, actually speak with the people now running their country, but they had to endure pat downs and metal detectors to get there. The Americans were calling their few square miles of new headquarters in central Baghdad the "Green Zone," because of all the lush parks, imported trees, and man-made lakes. It was the poshest section of the city, and it was now more off-limits to the Iraqi public than it had been under Saddam.

No, she shouldn't have attended the meeting. She instinctively did not trust the military, which she saw as a bunch of trigger-happy, macho eighteen-year-olds, pumped up on violent video games. Although the war had begun with propaganda about "hearts and minds," stories had spread from village to village about aggressive soldiers who kicked down doors and arrested men in the middle of the night. Presumably, they were looking for Saddam and those who supported him, but in doing so, often detained dozens of innocent men and left the crying families with no information about their fate. Manal had heard all detainees were being taken to Abu Ghraib prison, but even she couldn't get any information. She had to stay separate from the military, she thought, as she was a humanitarian and an activist and she had to be wary not to allow herself to be used for propaganda.

Her aid friends back in San Francisco, understandably, would find this "liberation" appalling.

The very creation of the Green Zone flew in the face of every lesson the aid world had learned over the last thirty years: If you want to help the populace, keep things grassroots—small, close to the ground, using personal contact, and let the locals do it. Don't seclude yourselves and run the country by remote control—don't topple a dictator and then move into his palace. *Don't they realize the message this sends?* Manal wondered. Of course, few in Manal's world actually believed this *was* a liberation. It was a war to control Arab oil, clear and simple, that those now in the Bush administration had been pushing for years. Many Iraqis suspected the same. It was no surprise that the U.S. military's lame efforts to do aid work were greeted skeptically by Iraqi women who had lost their husbands or had had their houses destroyed.

By late summer 2003, the Americans had established a governing body inside Saddam's palace, calling itself the Coalition Provisional Authority (CPA). The CPA held all legislative, judicial, and executive powers in Iraq. It was led by Ambassador J. Paul Bremer, a Yale graduate and a former ambassador to the Netherlands under President Reagan, who had more recently held various high-ranking counterterrorism posts in the government and the private sector. A loyal Republican and devout Catholic, Bremer was photogenic, clean-cut, and touted as Bush's "man on the ground," despite speaking no Arabic and having no experience of Iraq. Bremer's staff was mostly Republican. They made clear that political loyalty was a requirement for participation in the new Iraq. To Manal, they had little interest in women's issues, beyond media stunts. When the CPA planned a women's conference on July 9, Manal was politely told "not to come" by conference organizers, who accused her of having ties to Code Pink, the radical San Francisco women's group. "We saw your website says 'war is harmful to women,' " the organizer told her, meaning she must be anti-Bush. Manal didn't mind. The conference was held inside the U.S. headquarters, by invitation only. Few Iraqi women attended or even heard about it.

The cheery conference ended. The Washington, D.C., women flew home. The media moved on.

Four days later, on July 13, 2003, Bremer announced his selection for Iraq's first new government, the Iraqi Governing Council. Despite high hopes by Women for a Free Iraq to get half the seats assigned to women, none of the council were members of Women for a Free Iraq. Only three of the twenty-five government members were women. Of the eighteen provinces that made up Iraq, there were no women serving as representatives. Furthermore, the committee selected to draft Iraq's first post-Saddam constitution did not include a single woman.

If this is the best the Americans can do for women, we're in trouble, Manal thought. The three Iraqi women appointed to the new government were Songdul Chapouk, an engineer and a Turkmen minority from Kirkuk; Dr. Raja Habib al-Khuzai, the director of a maternity hospital in the southern city of Diwaniya; and Aqila al-Hashimi, a former international diplomat under Saddam's government. There were eighteen cabinet positions open, and only one went to a woman: Nesreen Berwari, a Kurd with a graduate degree from Harvard University, was named the minister of public works.

They all struck Manal as impressive women, but they were unknowns in Iraq, and seemed shocked by their new jobs. Dr. al-Khuzai said she was "delivering babies by candlelight" when the Americans contacted her, and openly admitted she "had no idea why she was picked." Suspicions were aired that the more powerful women were pushed aside by even more powerful Iraqi male politicians, many of them tribal leaders, who had put pressure on the CPA. They wanted female fill-ins to rubber-stamp their decisions, and the Americans weren't willing to stand up to them on women's issues. The selection gave a public impression that women and different regions were represented, yet they would present no real challenges to the other members, and be kept out of the inner power circle.

Even more troubling than the lack of women was the choice of men: two wore the black turbans of Shia clerics, and two wore the flowing robes and headdresses of tribal sheiks. Some of Iraq's most conservative, religious Shia parties were included in the council, including the

Supreme Council for Islamic Revolution in Iraq (SCIRI) and Islamic Dawa, both of which had ties to Iran—a country known for its oppression of women. Religion and politics had been kept separate in Iraq under Saddam and before his reign. What good would it serve women to remove Saddam and replace him with mullahs?

This was not a good start, Manal thought.

CHAPTER EIGHT

NOTHING WAS GOING as smoothly as planned, Heather worried.

By July, the fourth month of the occupation, Heather's unit had moved from its temporary barracks at the airport and set up camp inside the Green Zone in what she imagined were some of the fanciest barracks in all of military history: two grand residences alongside Saddam's Republican Palace, formerly occupied by ministers. Other than the blown-out windows and scattered M16s, the living accommodations were nicer than most of the soldiers' homes back in the States, with the exception that they were shared by more than a dozen soldiers. The military had divided the house up by rank, and Heather and Lieutenant Idong Essiet were the only two females in a house of nearly a dozen male officers.

These idyllic barracks were hardly representative of the situation at large, however—it was more like an oasis. In the last month, a couple of random attacks on soldiers had prompted the top brass to tighten security. The latest report showed thirty-seven soldiers killed in May and thirty killed in June. Though that was a low casualty count by military standards, given the 140,000 troops on the ground, no one wanted to let their guard down, even if probably half were accidents, illnesses, or maybe even suicides, Heather guessed. Given the amazing advances in communication—soldiers were watching CNN, surfing the Internet, and getting daily security briefings—the tale of just one dead soldier could chill the efforts of an entire unit. One story, in particular, had made the rounds: At Baghdad University, a young soldier had been accompanying some American education officials on a tour. He had walked off to buy a soda at an outdoor kiosk when an Iraqi walked up, shot him in the head, and ran away. This was the first story she'd heard of a soldier attacked not in battle, but while doing reconstruction work—exactly the kind of work that Heather and her unit thought was winning over hearts and minds. Naturally, this made many soldiers wary of all Iraqis. Since the warehouse mission in which the Iraqi militiamen had laughed with her and told her to "bring her tanks next time," she had begun to let down her guard to chat with the locals, kick around a soccer ball, or buy ice cream on the way back to base; some soldiers even had tea with Iraqi families. Heather was careful not to stereotype all Iraqis as dangerous.

But perhaps she should be more careful now.

In response to that shooting, and other scattered incidents in recent months, such as roadside bombs and rocket-propelled grenades fired at Humvees, the army had tightened security rules. Now, any soldier who left the base had to be in a convoy of two Humvees, with three soldiers in each. And at least one of the Humvees had to have a Crew Served Weapon (CSW), which was the big circulating automatic weapon atop the vehicle. Heather's entire unit had only two CSWs for one hundred troops, and only a couple of soldiers were trained to use them. This meant that the decision to heighten security, while perhaps logical in theory, meant logistical nightmares for the soldiers. With no electricity, operating schools, or running water in Baghdad, Heather's Civil Affairs unit had more on its plate than it could handle. Now, the entire unit had to coordinate each day's activities, sharing just two vehicles and dragging soldiers off their own important reconstruction missions to accompany others on theirs. It was the kind of poorly thought out bureaucratic decision that infuriated Heather—something much too small to be reported in the press, yet significant enough to doom the entire mission, in her opinion.

For example, negotiations with the sheik to return control of the warehouses had, frustratingly, stalled. She missed their last prearranged meeting when she couldn't get a third Humvee. The phone network had yet to be restored. She had no idea if the sheik used email, and she couldn't type in Arabic anyway. Setting up another meeting became impossible because she had no way to get in touch with him and her unit was quickly distracted by all the other things that needed doing. She had dutifully typed up her memo and sent it up the chain of command, but she never heard back.

Heather didn't want to leave the growing list of problems to the sheik's militias but her unit simply didn't have the manpower or expertise to run every aspect of Iraqi society. She and others tried to scale down expectations, telling Iraqis, "These things take time," or "We need your support to get the ministries up and running." But the Iraqis would say, in broken English, "Ministry *halas!*" with a smack of their hands. The ministries had been burned down or looted. The problems were only getting worse, and instead of making even small progress the Americans seemed to be falling further and further behind, on all fronts.

After all, the sheik had approached them with an open mind, but the Americans had not delivered. She imagined him waiting around, getting angrier and angrier, and finally giving up on her. He would go back to his community, and to his leader, Muqtada al-Sadr, telling them that American promises couldn't be trusted.

BEFORE HER FRUSTRATIONS began to snowball, Heather jumped off the couch.

"Morning, sir," Heather murmured to Major Norcom as she crossed the marble floors to the palace kitchen, rummaged through a care package for some breakfast bars, and flopped onto the ornate patterned sofa, resting her dusty boots on the glass table.

"Sir?" she said, finishing her snack and approaching the major, who had a map and clipboard in his hand. "I've got to inspect some potential sites for the town halls in the morning. What else do we have going on? Can I get a private and Lieutenant Essiet to go along? Who's free?"

Major Norcom looked through his thickly rimmed, square glasses at his list like a stern grandfather. The day's agenda was set either by orders that came down the chain of command, or by requests from soldiers tasked to specific areas. Captain Sumner oversaw the zoo and the museum; Captain Edwards took care of the National Library and the World Food Program; Major Norcom worked on the preservation of religious sites and community sports. Heather did humanitarian issues, such as the food distribution program.

For months now, the military had been leading the effort to piece back together a country damaged by looting, sanctions, and Saddam's negligence. While Heather expected her civil affairs unit to do reconstruction, it was hardly an appropriate role for combat soldiers. Where was the wave of experts from the State Department, USAID, and private contractors with plans to build up civil society? Wasn't the job of rebuilding the country supposed to be done by Ambassador Bremer's CPA? Heather was beginning to wonder what the CPA was up to. From brief observations, its members seemed even more clueless about reconstruction work than the soldiers.

Heather and Major Norcom looked over the map together and traced the convoy's plans for the day to maximize their time and resources. They'd begin with assessing and clearing buildings to serve for Iraq's new local advisory councils—that was a priority that came down the chain of command. With Saddam's dictatorship obliterated, steps were being taken to replace it with a democracy. As Heather understood it, a temporary government of Iraqis had been appointed to work alongside the Americans in the CPA, and Iraq's first national elections would be held the following year.

On a local level, each of Iraq's eighteen provinces would have its own elected representatives, like U.S. congressmen. Neighborhoods in urban areas such as Baghdad would also have their own advisory councils, modeled after American town-hall-style local government. In order to create this kind of democracy, U.S. soldiers would eventually work with officials from the State and Defense departments, as well as private U.S. companies who had multimillion-dollar contracts. One such company, Research Triangle Institute (RTI), had a $187 million Pentagon contract to set up 180 local councils across Iraq. Together, they were to explain to the Iraqis the machinery of democracy, from its philosophical underpinnings to the nuances of campaigning and elections to the importance of civilian participation.

There was a lot of enthusiasm back in Washington, D.C., and the task of creating democracy had all sounded very romantic and wonderful to Heather when she first learned about it. However, confronted with the minutiae of its implementation, installing democracy by fiat was not so easy, she was learning. For example, both RTI and the National Democratic Institute (NDI) had a "woman component" to increase the number of females participating in the councils, but Heather never saw enough women involved. Once, when she asked, an Iraqi told her that women were comfortable taking positions of authority in government, but the problem was the presence of U.S. soldiers at the meetings. Husbands or family members forbade the women from being in the same room with military personnel, as soldiers in Iraq had a reputation for being uneducated and aggressive men. This kind of cultural barrier was something the planners in Washington had not even begun to consider.

This particular morning, Heather's role in creating democracy boiled down to emptying squatters out of a few buildings in Baghdad that had been designated as advisory council headquarters. Securing real estate was a tiny task on the "building democracy" checklist, yet it was another change that had become harder to implement than Heather had ever imagined. No one had anticipated that, as soon as the invasion ended, thousands of rich Iraqi expats would return to the country, along with thousands of Western journalists, aid workers, and businessmen, all looking for houses to rent. Baghdad real estate prices had skyrocketed to beyond those of Washington, D.C. A furnished three-bedroom house, the sort of thing they were looking to convert into office space, could easily rent for a whopping eight thousand dollars a month—a result of market forces and savvy Iraqi landlords squeezing the foreigners.

There were hundreds of empty residences and offices belonging to Saddam's government, however, and during the war, squatters had moved into many of the empty mansions. Heather didn't know whether to call them squatters, war refugees, homeless people, or just real estate opportunists, but she was in charge of "clearing" them out so the buildings could be used by civic groups. Since the police had not yet returned to their posts, and the national army had been disbanded, this was another unexpected "building democracy" task that fell into the lap of the U.S. troops.

THE CONVOY ANTICIPATED taking an hour to get to its destination, which was less than ten miles away. The terrible Baghdad traffic was due to the absence of traffic police, traffic lights that couldn't work without electricity, and the number of cars, which had quadrupled since the borders had opened. Deeming it unsafe to be stuck in traffic, military Humvees didn't wait in the long lines—they drove against oncoming traffic or up onto the sidewalks. Still, convoys often got lost in the complicated Baghdad street system, which didn't really use street names or house numbers. Heather didn't understand how Iraqis got around. Back when city planners mapped out Baghdad—in the twelfth century—there was no use for grids, she guessed.

From her mounted perch, she waved to some kids. As the weeks turned into months, the Iraqis' mood still seemed welcoming, but when they approached Heather, it was usually to complain about the poor security, the lack of electricity, and the looting. At least the kids still waved, Heather thought. Children were always a bellwether of the public mood.

When they arrived, they found several families that had moved into the first building that needed clearing, the former headquarters of the Mukhabarat. After twenty minutes of cajoling and mild threatening, the old women and dirt-smudged children collected their few saucers and rags, and shuffled out of the house and down the street.

Heather sighed. "They are probably moving into the next empty building that we'll be clearing tomorrow," she said.

"No, I feel good about this mission," Lieutenant Essiet said, taking a swig from her water bottle. Her face glistened with sweat. She had been working to get homeless families into refugee-style camps in the city. "We are making a difference, slowly."

Heather looked away. A month earlier she might have gregariously agreed with Lieutenant Essiet, but lately she was having her doubts about whether they were making any kind of difference. Programs were implemented ad hoc, overseen by young soldiers with no direct experience, and not coordinated with any Iraqi ministry or local tribal leaders; they often didn't work out as planned. So she and her unit had cleared the building for the day—so what? Heather saw herself returning to base that afternoon and typing up her daily memo. "We cleared the building for the advisory councils," she would write. "But we don't know where the squatters went, and they'll probably return if we leave it empty for a couple days."

No one was reading her meticulously thought-out memos, she complained to Lieutenant Essiet, who disagreed. The friends had driven past a looted bank earlier in the week, and had sent a memo requesting that electricity be restored to it. The lights were now back on.

"See," Essiet said. "Someone read our memo."

Heather shook her head. "No, it's a coincidence. No one is listening to us." Heather had heard other soldiers asking the same question: Where was the wave of expertise that was supposed to arrive on the heels of the soldiers and begin reconstructing the country? Once, recently, she had showed up at the Baghdad Museum to follow up on an assessment she had sent in weeks earlier, only to find another Civil Affairs unit doing its own assessment! Weren't any of the commanders talking to one another? she wondered. And was anyone in the military coordinating with the civilian side in the palace?

BACK IN THE convoy, they checked their grids, their maps, and the GPS and mapped out the next mission. Heather stared out at the city. Baghdad felt ugly to her; like one big, low-class suburb of totalitarian architecture with an occasional tasteless monument or statue decorating a desolate traffic circle or public square. Instead of the paired, spiraling minarets attached to an open vaulted hall that she had so admired in Egypt, Baghdad's minarets were bleakly phallic towers set next to a dome covered in tacky cheap tiles. She was disappointed even by the famed Tigris River, as Saddam had constructed artificial banks of ugly brick, making it look more like a canal than a body of water considered the source of life for the earliest of human civilizations.

Not surprisingly, her convoy hit a traffic jam on the approach to a bridge over a highway. The bridge had been bombed, and there were only two lanes open for cars. They were blocked by a nasty line of honking vehicles, facing each other.

It was a classic "prisoner's dilemma," which Heather had studied in her game theory classes at Bryn Mawr. If both sides of the bridge were to cooperate, everyone would get what they wanted, to get across. However, if each side assumed the other wouldn't cooperate, they would both rush forward to be the first to get across, jamming the one lane. Both sides would lose.

"Oh, Lord," Essiet said, staring at the mess. The soldiers turned to one another, and the same question was on everyone's mind: Do we get involved? As they constantly told the Iraqis and themselves, traffic was not the military's problem. Whether or not to intervene was a constant question.

Just the other week, their unit had driven past a dead man on the side of the road. Heather had opened her mouth to suggest they stop, but another soldier said, "Lieutenant Coyne, you stop, you own it." Taking care of a dead body could suck up the day; they'd have to fill out reports and wait around at the morgue. Heather had heard that another unit had kept a dead body in the back of the Humvee for three days because they picked it up and didn't know what to do with it.

Heather's commander made the call to clear the bridge. They needed to cross, and if it could be done quickly, they'd gain some points from the locals for helping. They pulled over and drew a plan in the dust of the Humvee's hood. Heather and two others were told to cross on foot to the other side of the bridge with radios and clear the trucks so cars could pass. "Let's do it!" someone shouted. A few minutes later, a soldier radioed over to them. "Traffic's cleared, exit's ready. Send five cars over," he said.

Heather pointed at the most inconveniently situated five cars and sent them over. But as soon as she stopped the sixth car, a minor riot ensued.

"Why can't we go?" they demanded.

She struggled to explain in Arabic the logic of her traffic patterns, and as she was doing so, a driver scooted into the space she'd so carefully cleared for the oncoming traffic. She yelled at him, but the car behind him had already inched up so he couldn't reverse. She had to walk far down the line of cars, and get each one to back up. No one wanted to go backward. Every time a space opened up, a car would rush into it.

As Heather stormed around telling drivers to back up, a group of pedestrians took her distraction as an opportunity to cross the bridge on the roadway, despite the open pedestrian walkways. Even more gawkers appeared, pooling in the open spaces and congesting the area, and trying to engage her in chitchat. Horns blared, dust rose, and a group of young men circled Heather and winked playfully at her. Ten minutes passed, then half an hour, and then an hour. She and Essiet alternated between yelling and pounding on hoods and smiling and thanking profusely anyone who helped. Heather tried to pick out the people who seemed to best understand the situation and assign them a task:

"You keep pedestrians off the bridge.

"You keep the bystanders out of the street.

"You tell that truck to back up."

But they would enforce the task only once, and then return to the more interesting job of watching this female American soldier trying to organize their country. Gangs of men gathered, pointing and laughing at her. She couldn't understand what they were saying.

"They're not listening to us," Essiet muttered. Heather's frustration mounted. An elderly woman clad in black had been hanging on to her arm for twenty minutes, begging help for her sick husband, who was in one of the cars. A pregnant woman was also in the crowd. Heather drew a line in the sand with her heel, and instructed everyone to stand behind it.

"Miss, miss, the bus driver refused to go backward," one of her helpers informed her.

Exasperated, she approached the bus and made a move for her weapon.

The driver backed up.

Finally, the road was clear enough to usher through a car with the sick old man. Essiet had just signaled the next bunch of cars to move when one huge truck sneaked forward onto the bridge, just in time to block the oncoming bunch in the middle of the bridge. Instantly, cars filled the lanes behind it as far as the eye could see.

Finally Heather clicked on her radio. She was sweaty, red-faced, and parched.

"Sir, it's Coyne. We've had enough," she said. "We can't control this with the number of people and radios we have. We need barriers and guards a hundred meters down the street to channel the incoming traffic. We did our best, and some of these people know what needs to be done. We can't stay here all day."

The other soldier had come to the same conclusion. Heather crossed the bridge. She spotted an Iraqi police car, and tried to recruit the officer. He threw up his hands. The other soldiers were furious.

"Why the fuck don't they get it?" one was muttering. The situation was a little embarrassing: *If the all-powerful U.S. military can't clear a bridge, how the hell will we run a country?*

As they climbed into their Humvees, Heather looked back at the heaving, angry mob in exactly the same situation she'd found them in two hours earlier. One man called out to her, "Hey, you can't leave. Where are you going?"

CHAPTER NINE

BEHIND THE CAMERA at the press conference, Zia rolled her eyes with exasperation. This American reporter was asking such irrelevant questions.

Since meeting with Captain Michaels six weeks earlier, Zia had landed a job with the Americans in the convention center. Her job was in a new Iraqi-American media company called Iraqi Media Network (IMN). It was run by the Pentagon, and was supposed to be Iraq's first independent source for radio and TV, like an Iraqi BBC or PBS. "By Iraqis, for Iraqis" was the slogan.

Zia was hired as a translator, tasked with accompanying the mostly American reporters and doing any necessary Arabic translation. Today they were interviewing the American "senior adviser" to the Ministry of Finance, which was a misleading title: the Iraqi finance minister had disappeared and his ministry had been seized by the military, so this American was hardly an adviser—he was Iraq's de facto minister of finance.

Zia paced impatiently as the IMN journalist threw him easy questions about how much progress was being made. She wanted to shout out, *Hey, we're desperate for real information here!* Government workers like Mamina hadn't received a dinar since before the war, Zia knew. Everyone was terrified by rumors that the Americans would change the currency and all their notes would be worthless. Banks were closing, people were exchanging their dinars for dollars. This reporter didn't seem to have the first clue that there was panic in the streets. Zia couldn't stay quiet another second.

"Many Iraqis haven't received a salary in months," she interrupted, ignoring the surprised look on the journalist's face. "Tens of thousands of Iraqi government workers all want to know: Why haven't you paid them yet?"

A hush fell over the small pack of journalists gathered to interview the American official.

He cleared his throat. "Ministries are going to start paying their employees tomorrow, and they'll go two at a time."

A murmur ran through the Iraqis in the crowd. This was big news—thanks to Zia's question. That night, the broadcast would be shown on national television. She swelled with pride, but also wondered: *Will I be fired tomorrow for interrupting?* Under Saddam, such insubordination could lead to imprisonment.

Instead, when the IMN program manager, John, saw on camera what she had done, he promoted her. "Good job! You're too talented to be translating," he said. "You're a reporter now."

When Zia shared the news with her family, Baba was worried. "You will be moving around Baghdad a lot now. You must take care who sees you working with the Americans."

But Mamina and Nunu drowned out his concerns. "You are rising so quickly!"

The three of them were all delighted by this new world in which independent thinking—even by a twenty-one-year-old young woman—was not punished but rewarded. Zia couldn't stop smiling.

THE IMN CHANNEL had debuted in May 2003, two months after the first troops arrived, with the goal of spreading as much information as possible about the situation to the local Iraqis. It was a shoestring operation at first: broadcasting had begun out of a tent, with the whole project operated by just a handful of Americans. By the time Zia was hired as a translator in June, the staff had grown to 130 people and included a radio station and a newspaper. With her promotion she joined a team of twenty-five reporters.

Before she started the job, Zia's expectations for the program, and for the Americans' organization of it, were high. After all, the Americans flew invisible planes and had highly precise bombs and an endless supply of tanks, helicopters, and military gear. Amid the poverty of Iraq, U.S. troops carried tiny camcorders, iPods, laptops, and fancy sunglasses. She was stunned, therefore, to discover that IMN was a third-rate operation, nothing at all like the rich, modern, and organized one she had imagined. IMN headquarters in the Baghdad convention center was little more than a rank, disheveled room with cables snaking along the floors, where harried-looking Americans pushed past one another, shouting. Instead of being new and glossy, the technical supplies consisted of Saddam-era equipment brought over from the now-defunct Ministry of Information. Staff meetings were held on a stained king-size mattress in the middle of the room that no one had bothered to remove. The employees, she was disappointed to see, didn't even have phones.

Still, what the Americans lacked in expertise, they made up for in enthusiasm. They were always talking excitedly about democracy and freedom and how they were creating the first-ever free and independent television channel in Iraq, one that would finally give the people access to real information about their country and their government, completely propaganda-free. They just needed time to get started, they said. Zia was eager to believe them.

They were also incredibly hard workers. They didn't sit around at desks, stamping papers, filing, and waiting for instructions, the way you did in most Iraqi jobs. They worked thirteen-hour days and were always "on deadline," racing in and out of the building, interviewing people in the palace, or driving around the city making reports. After a few painful days in her business suit and high heels, Zia gave up and switched to sneakers, T-shirts, and jeans—shockingly informal, she felt, but she reminded herself that the Americans cared only about getting the job done.

The chaotic environment created ideal opportunities for Zia to prove herself, though, and as time went on she did. IMN aired every evening, and producers were desperate for material to fill the airwaves, which meant that within weeks, Zia was making videos, interviewing subjects, reading the news, editing, and making judgments on what was or wasn't suitable to broadcast. Despite the haphazard nature of the days, the job was fast-paced, high-profile, and packed with glamour. Zia had constant access to top American officials inside the palace, and a front-row seat to the Americans' billion-dollar efforts to rebuild Iraq. Plus, it was fun. IMN flew Zia around the country in a helicopter to make reports on reconstruction projects, and she even got to cover the World Economic Forum in Jordan. The United States, the most powerful country in the world, had long loomed large in her imagination; she never dreamed she would be working alongside Americans for the good of her own beloved Iraq.

The more time she spent working on the broadcasts, though, the more clearly she saw how carefully the stories were picked and shaped for presentation. When visiting reporters expressed doubts about whether IMN was truly independent, Zia was carefully diplomatic. She was growing more skeptical about the rhetoric, but was ultimately willing to accept it for the greater good of seeing America's plans in Iraq succeed.

One or two of her American colleagues complained about the CPA's "message management" and the apparent lack of resources for better equipment. But, for the most part, they were fueling her dreams of a long-term career. "One day, we'll all leave and you and the Iraqis will have to run IMN," they told her. This vision of the future was intoxicating.

THERE WAS JUST one problem: she was no longer safe.

In the mornings, as Zia stepped cautiously beyond the courtyard gate to wait for the bus that would take her to work, Nunu watched quietly from the window as her sister glanced nervously up and down the street. Baba had been right: they had better not tell anyone about Zia's glamorous job with the Americans. When she accepted the job back in May, she was the envy of all her girlfriends for landing employment inside the Green Zone. By late summer, the whole family had heard rumors that ex-Ba'athists had begun attacking Iraqis who worked with the Americans, accusing them of being "collaborators"; they were even harsher on the women who chose to work among the foreign men, in "shameful" defiance of most Iraqis' social beliefs. It was too dangerous.

The secret was getting increasingly difficult to keep, though, especially since the Americans sent a bus to pick Zia up in the mornings. The Green Zone bus was the idea of IMN's security personnel, who were inconvenienced by Iraqi staff getting held up at security checkpoints and employees missing work for lack of transportation. The bus was a simple solution for IMN management, but it made life very complicated for the Iraqi women trying to hide that they worked for the Americans. The Americans just didn't get it.

It was impossible to keep secrets in Baghdad's close-knit neighborhoods. When Nunu returned to campus that summer to finish the classes that had been interrupted by the invasion, she was besieged by young women all wanting to know, "Did your sister land a job with the Americans?" "Is she in the palace?" Some had brothers working in the palace who had seen Zia. Such jobs were coveted and controversial, and Nunu couldn't help but brag about her daring big sister.

Though she longed to get out of the house and travel the way Zia did, what she wanted more than ever was simply to feel safe, and for life to be normal again. But it was starting to look as if that wasn't going to happen for a while.

When Zia was home at night, she told Nunu stories about what was happening inside the palace, and what gossip was going around the city. One rumor, roundly believed, was that Saddam was driving around Baghdad in disguise in a taxi. Some said the CIA and Saddam were in cahoots and that they had hidden Saddam in a safe house in Tel Aviv; others had heard that extra U.S. soldiers were sent to Iraq to marry Iraqi women—Nunu and Zia giggled at this. Zia's friends in the Green Zone were sure that the soldiers' sunglasses gave them X-ray vision to see through women's clothing. When Zia pointed out how impossible this would be, the other girls remained convinced. "American technology can do anything. If they can make air-conditioning inside their clothing, they can make X-ray glasses." Based on the locals' disbelief that the Americans could withstand Iraq's scorching temperatures, a rumor had spread that the soldiers' clothes were air-conditioned.

Nunu loved the descriptions of the soldiers that Zia and her colleagues worked with every day. The soldiers seemed like knights in shining armor. Rugged, tall, rich, and modern, they had done what Iraqi men had failed to do: they had overthrown Saddam and freed Iraq. They were liberators, and they were also *huge* flirts. Every girl had a story of a soldier winking at them, complimenting them, smiling or waving at them. Nunu told Zia her own favorite story, about one of her university friends, who had dared to wave at a soldier right behind her father's back. When her father turned around just as the soldier was returning the wave, Nunu's friend was terrified. But her father just smiled and waved back, assuming it was for him. The girls thought this was hysterical.

Nunu often daydreamed about marrying one of these soldiers, though Zia often had to remind her about the darker side of all of this. There was a broadly accepted stereotype that cast the Americans as sex-obsessed, godless, violent, and aggressive, which meant that simply working alongside them could be dangerous for the reputations of young Iraqi women. Zia told her that even the male workers inside IMN whispered such rumors to one another: *The Americans have sex all night in Saddam's palace.* One of Zia's Iraqi male colleagues said that if a man could get into a room alone with an American woman, she would have sex with him. Nunu was wide-eyed, but Zia assured her it wasn't true, or at least, she didn't think so. Even so, Zia had to be careful about her associations: she was just one of hundreds of Iraqi women working for the Americans, but, because of her ambition and ability, she was pushing the boundaries of what society would allow, and, as Mamina had warned, her reputation was now at stake.

Watching Zia stand there waiting for the bus, Nunu scanned the still empty street and thought about how quickly evil rumors could spread. The worst gossips were the spinster sisters across the street: hateful, bitter, bored women who spent their lives perched in their window, gazing judgmentally down upon Zia and Nunu and all the other girls in the neighborhood.

Nunu had once been a rambunctious tomboy who rode her bicycle, played in the streets, and beat up the neighborhood boys. But such freedoms ended as she blossomed into a young woman. In the late 1990s, Iraq was becoming more religious, and suddenly there were so many things young women couldn't do. If Nunu ran around in the street, the neighbors would *tsk tsk* her. Walk slowly, they reprimanded her. If she shouted, an uncle was always on hand to *shhhh* her. Speak softly, they said. In the classroom, a girl who showed more exuberance or natural intelligence than her male classmates was frowned upon. Mamina tried to shield her from these messages, but she, too, was vulnerable to society's expectations, and was sensitive to criticism that she was a loose mother.

After a girl turned twelve, bicycle riding was forbidden, because a young woman couldn't be seen with her legs apart in such a way—all the boys would stare and the spinster sisters would whisper, "What a dirty girl." Her bicycle rusted and eventually she gave it to a younger cousin. As Nunu became a teenager, the message of shame intensified. If she wore jeans, they would say she was "wild." Should any young woman dare to be seen standing with or talking to a young man who was not a relative or a fiancé, word would spread that she was "on a date," and no other man would propose to her. All these actions were *haram,* shameful, and should a potential suitor come to the street and ask around, as was the tradition, he would certainly be counseled against associating with such a loose girl. Zia herself already stood out, with her sharp tongue and free-flowing hair, and although Nunu tried to be as obedient as possible she knew that she, too, was considered unacceptably liberal. Nunu and Zia were lucky, though, that Baba let them be themselves—Nunu had friends whose families guarded their reputations so fiercely that they were not allowed to leave the house without their brothers or fathers. No doubt that was the only kind of woman the spinster sisters approved of. Nunu shook her head in frustration and walked into the bedroom to get her diary.

Outside, Zia was thinking similar thoughts. She lifted her chin, looked up the road, and huddled her jacket closer to her, keeping an eye on the spinster sisters' window across the way. What did they think when the bus arrived in the mornings? Did they know where she was going? *Well, they will have to get used to the idea,* she tried to tell herself. It was like her American colleagues at IMN said: this was a new Iraq now. They were free. They had democracy. This was the time for women. If she was pushing society's expectations, that only made her proud. One day, she imagined, her granddaughters would look back and say, "Zia's generation changed things for us." The old ways were over. Iraqis were going to act and think like Americans now.

Yet as the sun rose, the dawn chill evaporated, and the neighborhood fell into its daily routine, Zia observed that little had changed in her neighborhood of Karrada.

The Americans could give them satellite television and democracy, but what would it take to change people's minds on an issue like women's rights? A young boy on a donkey meandered slowly past, picking through trash for anything useful. The fruit vendor set up his rickety cart to display summer fruits and vegetables such as okra, watermelon, and purple grapes. Soon, the art galleries would open their doors, along with the butcher, the cobbler, the pharmacist, and the goldsmith. Later in the evening, Baba would gather in a semicircle of plastic chairs in front of an art gallery with his six friends to hash over the day's events. The men were mirror images of one another: wrinked, with bald scalps, wisps of hair on the sides, mustaches, and spectacles. They smoked cigarettes with one hand and drank tea with the other; several newspapers lay on the table. So consistent was their presence, the tea seller rolled his cart from a block away to be closer to them. There was Abu Hassan, an agricultural engineer who was also a painter. He lived across the street. Abu Enwar, an artist and a Christian, who had a shock of white hair that matched his mustache; Abu Kamran, a Kurdish merchant; Abu Hussein, a professor, with small round spectacles and a salt-and-pepper beard. There was also Abu Jawadi and Abu Thafir, who lived in another part of the neighborhood.

Like Baba, these men were already modern in their thinking. They were educated in European countries in the 1950s. No matter what Saddam did, he couldn't get them to change their minds about politics. When Zia did overhear them, they were usually reminiscing about days when Iraq was a monarchy, or when General Kassim was in power, in the 1960s, or making jokes about religious extremists. When they tired of politics, they exchanged gossip: who was engaged; who was sick; who had a new job; who had moved. Abu Hassan's wife nicknamed them the "Reuters of Karrada," after the popular French news service, because they always knew everything happening in the neighborhood.

Mamina and the other wives teased them for being so set in their ways. With the arrival of the Americans, sunglasses had become popular in Baghdad, and Abu Hussein showed up one afternoon in a pair. "Nice glasses," Baba had said. Soon, all the others wanted the same. They agreed, the following day, to go to the same store and buy the same sunglasses. Baba drove. Since then, whenever the sun shone brightly, they all sat around enjoying their sunglasses. When they read the papers, they all changed their sunglasses for clear spectacles.

Maybe, just maybe, these men would accept greater freedoms for women. But she wasn't so sure about the rest of the country.

THE BUS TURNED the corner and stopped in front of her house. As she boarded, she quickly checked around the street to see if anyone was looking, but today, at least, she saw no one.

In the front row, Zia's friend Suhaad patted an empty seat.

"Shlonich?" Zia said, Iraqi slang for "What's up?"

"Koolesh Zein al-Hamdulilla," Suhaad replied. "Everything's great, thanks be to God."

Zia slid into the bus seat next to her. Zia knew Suhaad from college. She and her brothers all worked at a ministry that had been looted and destroyed in the war. Because she spoke English, she had accepted a job as a translator, where she earned ten dollars a day. Her brothers refused to work for the Americans, and Suhaad complained that they screamed at her and threatened her for doing so, even as they took her salary.

Hind, another young woman sitting near them, had taken a job so she could leave her abusive husband. Hind's father had married her at sixteen to the son of his business partner, who promised to allow her to attend college. At first, Hind was proud to be married before all her classmates, and she had a showy wedding to make them jealous. But Hind got pregnant immediately, and then her husband refused to let her go to college and forced her to veil. If she was defiant, he beat her. Many men believed that the Quran condoned beating women, but Zia and her family disagreed. Even under Saddam, Islamic classes taught a hadith in which the Prophet said, "Women are like glass, so treat them delicately. Don't hurt them." But it didn't stop Hind's husband from abusing her. Now, after work, she hid inside the Green Zone for as long as possible. "He knows he can't touch me here or I'll tell the soldiers," she had confided to Zia.

As the bus lurched through the clogged city streets, other young women boarded, several of whom Zia had gotten to know over the first month of work. During the ride to the Green Zone, the women always chattered endlessly. There were few other people, beyond their own sisters and the women on the bus, with whom they could discuss their exciting new lives.

As a group, the women felt intoxicated by the messages of freedom and women's rights emanating from the palace, although some took their freedoms too far, in Zia's opinion. Many left their houses in one outfit, and then changed into short-sleeved T-shirts, jeans, and hot pink lipstick on the bus. "We can wear what we like now," said one woman in painted-on jeans. One restroom in the convention center became infamous as a changing room: young women went in wearing veils and Islamic dress and emerged looking fit for a nightclub.

"C'mon, this is a job. You have to be professional," Zia pointed out, but no one paid attention. The overall mood was exultant. They were businesswomen like the prophet's first wife, Fatima—many of the young women were earning more than their fathers. They had exciting jobs that would make all their girlfriends jealous, despite the fact that none of them could know about it yet. The layer of intrigue added to the adventure. No one said it, but they all felt it: they were the envy of all the young women in Baghdad.

Partway through the morning ride, one of the girls who boarded brought some major news: an Iraqi woman, working for the Americans, had married a U.S. soldier.

"What!" Zia was stunned. "Was he Muslim?"

The girls laughed. "Of course not!"

"Even if he did convert, it would not count because it would be for convenience, not for true reasons," another pointed out.

Zia was speechless. It was one thing to flirt—she and Nunu made jokes about that all the time—but to actually get married to an American soldier?

Under Saddam, women were frowned upon for marrying foreigners because nationality could pass only through the father. But surely the Americans could dismiss this law. Still, there were tribal restrictions and customs, particularly in the rural areas. Most Iraqi marriages were arranged by the families between cousins, or at least within their tribe.

"Did he ask her father?"

No one knew.

In Iraqi tradition, the suitor had to bring many relatives and friends to the house and formally propose, to prove to the bride's family that he had a good reputation. The young women on the bus doubted the soldier had done so—what Iraqi father would accept him as a son-in-law? Still, they were enthralled by the story.

Zia and her friends raked over the details endlessly. The bride's name was Ehdaa. Some had heard she was a doctor, while others said, no, she was the receptionist at the Rashid Hotel (which was more believable because everyone was convinced those women were prostitutes who had worked for Saddam's lascivious son Uday). The soldier had fallen in love with Ehdaa the minute he met her, and a month later he proposed and they were married. The girl telling them the story had seen the wedding photos on the Internet: he was in his army fatigues, bulletproof vest, and buzz-cut hair; she was smiling, her wavy black hair falling softly around her shoulders. They kept their marriage a secret while the bride applied for a visa to the States.

The gossip was tinged with envy.

"She is not beautiful!" someone complained. "If you brought her to the home of any Iraqi man, he would say she is less than average."

Everyone concluded that the Iraqi woman had married the soldier because no Iraqi man would have her.

OVER THE NEXT few days, however, Ehdaa's fairy-tale romance took a grave turn. Email was a new phenomenon in Iraq, and Internet cafés had spread across the city. Young Iraqis loved to chat with one another on Yahoo Instant Messenger, spending hours and hours on the site. Before long, Zia didn't know anyone who wasn't gossiping about the marriage between Ehdaa and the soldier.

"They say she's a *kafir*," Suhaad said on the bus one morning, in a low voice. *Kafir* meant "infidel" or "pagan," and was the most derogatory term imaginable. Some extremist Muslim groups believed Islam sanctioned the execution of kafirs. The wedding photo had spread beyond Baghdad and had been picked up by Islamic websites across the Arab world. For those looking for examples of Americans' nefarious presence in Iraq, this photo of a U.S. soldier and an Iraqi woman said it all: *The Americans are here to steal and dishonor our women.* To many, even those who were glad to be rid of Saddam, this was a reminder that America was still an invading Christian army, which many believed to be controlled by the Israelis. The Quran is very clear on this point: Muslim women cannot be allowed to marry a non-Muslim. Women in Islam are considered sacred symbols, responsible for upholding the honor of the religion; they are so precious they must veil themselves to prevent another man from being tempted by them. The job of the man is to protect his women, and hence protect Islam. Zia knew there was no more striking symbol of the ultimate conquest than for invaders to have sex with Islamic women—and if the woman does so willingly, there is no greater betrayal.

She's a dead woman, Zia thought, horrified.

Eventually, someone who recognized Ehdaa weighed in with her full name and address. The Western press got wind of it and British and American reporters wrote about it. Each day on the bus, Zia heard new, increasingly frightening developments.

"Men are outside her house demanding she be killed," Suhaad said. "Her family locked her in to punish her." The soldier was going to be kicked out of the military.

They debated her fate. "Her brothers will kill her," Suhaad said. "No, her father will!" someone else chimed in.

"No," Zia assured them. "Think about it. If she was from that kind of family, they wouldn't have let her work at the Rashid in the first place. I bet the family knew. I bet they approved the wedding with the intention of covering it up until she was out of the country. They're only punishing her now because the wedding was exposed."

But they still might have to kill her, Suhaad worried.

"She didn't think it through," Zia agreed, shaking her head. "She'd better get out of Iraq with him, or she'll never survive."

CHAPTER TEN

THE JADRIYA POLICE station was a run-down stone building with only a folding table and a few chairs scattered across glass-littered floors. The station had been occupied by U.S. military police after the invasion, but in the six months that had passed, some of the Iraqi police officers had started trickling back in to duty. When Manal arrived with Ahmed and Mustafa, two of her male Women for Women staff members, there were mustached Iraqi policemen with AK-47s milling around one side of the front office, while a couple of MPs in army fatigues stood on the other side. Both groups of men looked surprised as Manal swept in, in her headscarf and long skirt. One of the Iraqi policemen let out a low wolf whistle.

"Sorry, uncle, I don't think so," she said in fluent Arabic as she and her escorts pushed past. "I'm here to see the girl," she announced in English to the MPs.

"The girl," Muntaha, was a prostitute Manal had been contacted about by Sergeant Lautenschlager. Some MPs had been patrolling a Baghdad market when they saw a man brutally beating a young woman, who was screaming for help. The soldiers intervened, but then had no idea what to do next. With no Arabic speakers in the unit, they couldn't understand what had happened, so they brought her back to the police station, put her in a cell, and contacted Sergeant Lautenschlager at the Humanitarian Assistance Center.

"Can I see her?" Manal asked.

The chief of the Iraqi police walked over, looking dubiously at Manal. "Why would you get involved? This is a family matter."

Exactly the problem, thought Manal. When a young Muslim woman was caught in prostitution, the family punishment was most often a so-called honor killing. Prostitutes in Iraq were considered less worthy than stray dogs. To restore the family honor, the men had to decide whether to stone her publicly, suffocate her, burn her to death, or stab her.

Manal didn't bother trying to appeal to the sympathy of the police chief, as she doubted he had much. "Then murder will be your problem to handle."

He shrugged. Under Saddam, such a death would not legally have been considered a murder. He looked pointedly at Ahmed and Mustafa, and they returned his look of exasperation.

Great, Manal thought.

Within a few months of her arrival in Iraq, Manal had hired a dozen more staff members, mostly women. Working sixteen-hour days, she also had several programs up and running, including the letter-writing exchange between American and Iraqi women, a weekly class to train the women in their rights, and another class that trained women in basic business procedures. She also organized and trained dozens of Iraqi women's rights groups that had formed since the war began.

Ahmed and Mustafa had been hired by Manal's boss, Zainab. Manal didn't trust them; they didn't seem to take women's rights seriously. Nor were they above making chauvinistic comments, tinged with sectarianism.

"When they said an American woman was coming to run the office, we thought, 'Yes! *Baywatch,*'" they had joked, obviously disappointed by Manal's veil and conservative dress. "But, instead, look what they sent us—a Wahhabi woman!" they had continued, comparing her to the extremely conservative Sunni group. Manal had ignored them, since she knew Women for Women needed some male employees. Today she had asked them to accompany her to the police station as protection, knowing postinvasion Baghdad was unsafe for single women and hoping a male presence would earn her a warmer reception among the Iraqi police.

Yet it didn't seem to be working. Ahmed pulled her aside. "Hey Manal, what are you doing working with prostitutes? Our jobs are hard enough," he said. "This will make us enemies quickly."

"Someone has to stand up for these women," she said. But Ahmed just rolled his eyes.

"We can help," she insisted again, but this time mostly to herself.

MUNTAHA WAS CURLED up in a corner in her cell. She was skinny. She looked younger than her seventeen years, and her long dark hair fell loosely, in tangles, around her soft face and doe eyes. She was refusing to speak to anyone, but years of aid work had trained Manal in what to do. She introduced herself, and said, in soothing Arabic, "I don't care what you've done." She continued as the girl looked up. "I know you are a prostitute and, you know, I just want to make sure you are okay. I don't want you to continue this work, and I can help you find a job, but if you do continue, I have access to condoms, and can get them for you."

Manal doubted she would be providing birth control, but wanted to show the frightened girl that she understood and was there to help, not judge. It worked. The Iraqi took an instant liking to this curious, veiled young American. Soon, they were chatting freely, and she told Manal her story.

When she was fourteen years old, Muntaha's father had forced her to marry a hideously ugly cousin. Though she hated her husband, Muntaha had no say in the matter. She was to cook, clean, and satisfy his sexual needs. School was not an option. When the Americans arrived, Muntaha and her girlfriends predicted that everything would change. Squatting barefoot in the front courtyard washing pots, they watched soldiers passing through their neighborhood. They giggled and fantasized that the soldiers were there to liberate them. The fall of Saddam and the talk of freedom were intoxicating.

But months passed and life only worsened, except for one change: Muntaha's father-in-law bought a satellite dish, which brought a feast of American programs into their home. The shows were about sassy women, none of whom had brothers or uncles telling them what to do. American girls always talked back and expressed their feelings. For most of the young women on television, fathers didn't seem to have control at all over their lives.

Before long, Muntaha and her friends began to wonder about life beyond their neighborhood. The television had opened Muntaha's mind, yet also deepened her resentment and frustration about her situation. On the news, the Americans talked constantly about democracy and freedom, and she began to feel a sense of entitlement. She relayed to Manal how her feelings had changed. "I should be able to do what I want now. This is democracy."

Manal nodded from her side of the cell, but her heart began to sink as she listened to how "democracy" had unfolded in Muntaha's mind. One of the most popular new television shows was *Star Academy*, a version of *American Idol* produced in Lebanon. When Muntaha and her friends saw the young Arabs singing and dancing in front of a panel of judges, they declared that this was their destiny.

"I knew I could win if given the chance," she told Manal. "A great talent lives inside me and I want to show it to the world."

Manal sympathized: Muntaha was so hungry to express herself, to be recognized as an individual, to free herself from her role as servant in her arranged marriage. Across the Arab world, shows like *Star Academy* served as an outlet for women's repressed dreams. It wasn't entirely clear to Manal what happened next, but Muntaha said she hatched a plan to run away. She had somehow befriended an older woman in the neighborhood who offered to hide her and help her make plans to go to Dubai to audition for *Star Academy*.

Manal knew where the story was going, but said nothing. Aid workers were all too familiar with stories about young women whose dreams of moving to Kuwait to become a model, or to Beirut to be on a reality show, led them into danger. In many cases, these women were being lured into human trafficking and sexual slavery by other women who offered them shelter from abusive husbands or families before betraying their trust.

A few months after Muntaha first saw the U.S. soldiers in her village, she ran away, to the home of the older woman. The first few weeks of her liberation were the most fulfilling and carefree of her life, as she described them to Manal. The woman took Muntaha to clandestine "jeans parties" where all the girls shed their abayas and put on denim pants like they saw in the American movies. They danced around and showed off their jeans to one another. Later, the woman introduced

Muntaha to pills, which eased her fear that her family would find her. During the day, Muntaha slept or hid in the house in case they were looking for her.

Then one day the woman turned to Muntaha and said, "I have cooked for you and fed you and taken you to parties. Now you owe me a thousand dollars."

Muntaha was shocked. "I thought you adopted me," she told her. But the woman said she had never agreed to that.

"You can't go back to your family, now that you've run away."

She told Muntaha she would have to work off her debts through prostitution. Muntaha cried. She was trapped, although she tried to console herself with the idea that it would be no worse than when her own husband forced himself on her. The woman offered her a deal. "Look, as soon as you finish paying me back, we can go to Dubai."

"That's why I became a prostitute," Muntaha explained to Manal. "I had no choice."

Muntaha then pulled out a small, wrinkled wedding picture from her wallet. "Look at this," she said, pointing at the photo. Manal drew in her breath. Next to the willowy, swanlike Muntaha in her white wedding dress was a stumpy old man, a full foot shorter than his bride, with a face so grotesque that Manal thought he was deformed.

"Now you see what they made me do," Muntaha said, angrily. "Would you agree to marry this man if you were me?"

Manal was speechless.

"Yes, you see," Muntaha said defensively.

Manal took the wedding photo. "Wait here. I'm going to help you."

THE SUN WAS beginning its slow descent as Manal returned to the front office. Like most Iraqis, Manal was fasting for Ramadan, the Muslim holy month; since she hadn't eaten since sunrise, she felt weak and irritable with hunger. She had already been in the police station for almost two hours, but now the situation seemed only to be getting worse.

"The family is outside," the police chief warned her as soon as she emerged from the cell block. Manal's heart sank.

Her phone rang. Ahmed, who had left the station to fetch Muntaha a change of clothes, was now circling the station in his car. "Manal, this is bad," he said. "One of the police officers must have tipped off the family. How else would they know she was here? There's a leak."

She could hear Mustafa also fretting. "Now look what's happened. She can't leave. If they find out who we are, they will come after Women for Women."

Manal peered out the window and saw a line of cars beyond the barricades and barbed wire the soldiers had erected around the station. Inside each vehicle were several men, whom Manal assumed were Muntaha's brothers, cousins, husband, and father, waiting like tigers to pounce. Had the situation been addressed quietly, without the public knowing, the family would have been more likely to sweep it under the rug, and even to deny it to the neighbors. However, the convoy outside the police station meant that in this case the family was very publicly admitting the situation, which would make it harder for them to back down without "restoring" the family's honor by killing Muntaha. Had the military police not been in the station, Manal was certain the Iraqi police would have let the father barge in and take Muntaha.

Eventually, Ahmed and Mustafa entered the station. Manal briefly shared Muntaha's story with Ahmed, and showed him the photo of Muntaha and her husband. Ahmed visibly recoiled at the image. That, more than anything else, made him more willing to help.

They vacillated on what to do. "Let's wait," Manal suggested, but another hour passed and the standoff continued. Manal went back and forth to talk to Muntaha.

Finally, the sun set, and Manal was desperate to break her fourteen-hour fast. She could hear her stomach growling and was desperately thirsty.

She approached a couple of the Iraqi policemen. "Do you have any water?" she asked. "I'd like to break my fast."

"You are fasting?" asked one of them, visibly surprised.

"You're Muslim," the other observed, handing her the water.

"Of course I'm Muslim," she said, laughing and pointing to her hijab.

"We thought you just put on the headscarf to see us, like the other *ajnabi* women," the policeman said.

"No. *Yanni*, I'm Muslim." *Yanni* was a colloquialism popular only in the Iraqi dialect. They chatted in Arabic, and after a while, the police-men warmed to her. Soon the police chief joined them.

"Look, let's just talk to the family and give her back."

"They'll kill her," Manal said.

"Don't be dramatic. They won't kill her," he replied.

But Manal wasn't convinced. They continued to wait, and chatted into the evening. Eventually Manal convinced the police chief to keep Muntaha in her cell, just for one night. Ahmed had been monitoring the situation outside, and by nine o'clock the cars had left, and they decided it was safe to go. As a precaution, a soldier escorted them to their car. They edged around coils of barbed wire and across the blocks of concrete and shattered glass to her beat-up old car. Manal was exhausted, and as she looked up at the soldier's haggard face, she realized he was tired too. He was in his early sixties, and had been one of the troops who had insisted on rescuing Muntaha from the market. It suddenly occurred to her that he and Sergeant Lautenschlager had both gone out of their way to help this girl.

"You know, you most likely saved her life," she said to him.

"Hey, it's okay, ma'am. I'm happy to help," he said. "Now I have something to say when my granddaughter asks me what the heck I'm doing in Iraq."

THE NEXT MORNING, Manal awoke at four, shortly before sunrise. Wearily, she roused herself out of bed in the pitch black and made her way to the kitchen to prepare a meal. She knew that across Iraq, and across the world in different time zones, millions of other Muslims were also waking to pray and eat. The sense of unity fought off her fatigue. She cooked a couple of fried eggs, took some pita bread and silver-wrapped triangles of cheese out of the refrigerator, and sat in the kitchen chair in her robe. As soon as she finished eating, she would go back to sleep for three more hours.

As she ate, she thought about Muntaha. The girl had only one choice, really: she had to reconcile with her family, however improbable that seemed. Unlike in the West, women here couldn't start over, with a job and an apartment, by themselves. Muntaha had little formal schooling, didn't drive, and had no work experience outside the house. Even if she had an income-producing job, the stigma against young women living alone was fierce, mostly from female neighbors, who wouldn't want a pretty, unsupervised young woman in their midst. Traveling abroad would be just as difficult. She would be hassled every step of the way— by border guards, customs officials, hotel desk managers, real estate agents, taxi drivers. There was, in effect, an all-male conspiracy against the unaccompanied woman in the Arab world, even in so-called modern countries like Jordan, and Muntaha didn't have the strength to stand it. She would be lonely, ostracized, unprotected, and would always feel hunted by her family.

Manal sighed. Reconciliation was always possible, she told herself, even given the extremity of Muntaha's crimes. In her experience, families rarely wanted to kill their daughters, and many looked for an excuse, or an alternative, that could still save their honor. However, for this to work Manal needed to find a place for Muntaha to stay while the family cooled off, like a House of Ruth in the States. Manal had heard that one or two such shelters existed in Iraq, but she didn't know where. They were extremely controversial, so they had to operate clandestinely, like a secret underground network for abused women on the run. Manal imagined they survived by the goodwill of a few survivors. Local women helping one another—that was how so much true aid work was done in the world.

While Manal's upbringing couldn't have been further from Muntaha's, she did recognize a common thread, which made her even more determined to save the girl. Manal had been pushed twice toward a marriage she didn't want, and had struggled to find her own voice. Although she had grown up with the freedoms of the West, she had had to balance her family's Muslim traditions with the desires of a young woman exposed to glitter and instant gratification. It hadn't always been easy.

Raised in South Carolina, Manal was the daughter of Palestinian intellectuals who had moved to the States shortly before she was born. She was raised speaking Arabic, and learned about international politics and activism from her parents' weekly debates over Palestinian politics. Manal's family were secular Muslims, and her mother raised her to believe the veil was a symbol of oppression. When Manal became a teenager, she devoted the feminist energy she had learned from her mother and grandmother to American issues; she joined the debate team and was a lively orator, with strong opinions and a penchant for leadership.

By the time Manal entered middle school, her parents had moved to the D.C. suburbs, and they enrolled her in a private, highly prestigious Islamic school in Virginia, run by the Saudi Arabian government. Manal attended along with other Arab students and even a large handful of African American Muslims whose parents had joined the Nation of Islam during Malcolm X's time. In those halcyon days before Al Qaeda, the only thing most teenagers knew about Islam was that the singer Cat Stevens had converted, so Manal loved being surrounded by other smart, diverse young Muslims. This was her chance to explore her faith more deeply. She had always felt drawn to Islam but was wary of the stereotype of veiled Muslim women as docile, quiet, and obedient, since she was so gregarious. Could she reconcile these two identities?

In high school, Manal came to see her mother's anti-veil attitudes as old-fashioned. Times had changed since the 1960s. By the 1990s, the generation that had thrown off the veil as an act of female liberation had been superseded by a wave of young people concerned that Islam was being abandoned. As is often the case with immigrants, the need to identify with the motherland was strong. Manal decided when she was sixteen that she, too, would don the hijab. She was the only young woman in her class to take the veil, and the decision earned her respect at school, as several girlfriends followed suit. The decision was a serious one for her; once she put it on, she didn't intend to take it off. That first morning Manal came downstairs from the bedroom in a hijab, her mother was furious.

"You're not going to school like that," she said. For the next six months, they argued.

"We fought so hard for our rights," her mother had shouted during one of their regular fights. "You've shut the door on everything we earned for you." All of her mother's friends, who Manal called "hard-core secularists," laughed at her and started a bet as to when she would back down and remove the veil.

"The most important thing is to be truthful and honest and God-fearing," they told her. "It's not the physical scarf."

"I believe that, but they're not mutually exclusive and I need a reminder," Manal said. Temptation surrounded young people in America, as it didn't in the Middle East, she said. Boys expected physical contact at parties, and young people frequented dance clubs and drank alcohol. By putting on the hijab, she was drawing her lines in a public way.

Once the veil was wrapped around her head and pinned tightly behind her ear, Manal knew she had made the right decision. It was an extremely visible sign of a faith she was very proud of, and it made her feel more deeply committed and closer to God. She also decided to follow the other tenets of her faith by eschewing alcohol and pork, refusing to date or have any physical contact with boys, and praying regularly. Rather than lead a stoic life, though, Manal felt she had as much fun as, perhaps more than, her Westernized counterparts. Feminism had become trendy in U.S. universities as Manal headed off to college in the early 1990s, and many young women showed their allegiance to women's rights by chopping short their hair, dressing in flannels and baggy pants, and disguising their femininity. Manal felt her way was better: the hijab served the same purpose but was considered feminine, even attractive, to Muslim men. Socializing came in the form of all-girl dance parties, in which the veils came off, and they danced together in circles and showed off their best hip-swaying, shoulder-shaking moves to Egyptian and hip-hop songs. Free from the pressures of male attention, girls' confidence soared and their friendships deepened. People wouldn't judge her by her breast size or hairstyle, Manal thought; they would be forced to get to know her and talk to her.

When Manal didn't take off the veil, her mother eventually became resigned to the idea. In return, Manal promised herself to honor the battles her mother had fought for women by being a forward-thinking Muslim woman. She wouldn't crawl under a shell and become submissive. Rather, Manal argued, she was charting a different path for Muslim women: being deeply committed to the requirements of the faith but also strong, outspoken, and equal to men. To prove her point, Manal continued playing on her town's girls' basketball team—elbowing for re-bounds and hustling up and down the court with pants under her shorts and wearing a hijab. After a while, the stares she received only made her feel more special for bucking the stereotype.

Although confident beyond her years, Manal was still young and could have bouts of insecurity about her unusual identity. The year she graduated from the Islamic Saudi Academy, on a trip to Jordan to see her family, a cousin proposed to the then seventeen-year-old Manal through her father. No one saw this as unusual, not even Manal's mother, as arranged marriages were the norm in Palestinian society. Many of Manal's classmates had returned to their Arab homeland and gotten married. However, Manal was aware that she was no longer going to be able to maintain her two identities, as an American teenager and a Muslim daughter. After much deliberation, she opted for the latter. When her father asked her opinion of the marriage, she remained silent—a statement equal to acquiescence. It was an inconsistency in Manal's personality that would plague her for years: while she was outspoken about women's rights in general, she swallowed her voice when it came to herself, calling to mind the Arab phrase "A carpenter's door is never fixed."

The engagement was set and Manal returned to the States, where she agonized silently for months before finally stepping up and express-ing her unhappiness. Her parents would never force a marriage on their daughter, and they called off the engagement shortly thereafter.

A few years later, while she was working toward a master's degree in Arab studies at Georgetown University, she attended a protest against the sanctions that were destroying Iraq. At the protest, she met an Iraqi man, a Muslim eleven years her senior, who quickly proposed. Even as she married him at twenty-five, part of her felt she was not ready, that he was too conservative, but another part was reacting to decades of silent messages that she *ought to* be married by twenty-five, that she *ought to* be the quiet, demure wife that Arab men preferred. She regretted it even as she was going through with it, but she married him anyway.

Manal would realize what a mistake this was on the first night of her honeymoon. The couple had consummated the marriage, and though it was Manal's first experience, she had barely bled. Her husband, who, unbeknownst to Manal, had already grown suspicious of his wife's virtue, became even more so. One evening, in an Internet café in Santorini, Greece, Manal uncovered an email he had written to an online doctor asking how a husband could know if his wife truly was a virgin. Manal was furious. Of course she was a virgin, and his suspicion not only called into question her entire identity as a Muslim and Arab woman, but it revealed an enormous gap in trust between the newlyweds. (The doctor's response had been "The best way to know would be to ask.") Yet her husband told her she ought to be grateful he didn't divorce her right away, due to her "defect" of not bleeding.

Manal stayed in the marriage, believing she *ought to* suppress her feelings. In the next year, he grew more controlling, while Manal tried harder, assuming the whole responsibility for their happiness until she found herself spontaneously bursting into tears for no apparent reason. He wanted her to be slimmer, to cook better, to do more laundry, and even implied she should ask permission to leave the house. Theirs was not a partnership. She was to be subservient to him.

During this time, Manal continued her studies at Georgetown. She committed herself to exploring what the Quran and the hadiths truly said about women, as well as the history of women in Islam. She read books by Islamic feminists such as Fatima Mernissi, whose groundbreaking book *The Veil and the Male Elite: A Feminist Interpretation of Women's Rights in Islam* popularized the idea that many of the most conservative aspects of Islam were in fact incorrect translations of the Quran or false recordings of the Prophet's words. This "Islamic feminism" was a break from the feminism of Manal's mother's generation. Rather than calling for a repudiation of Islam, Mernissi and others used the Quran to challenge the very patriarchy that clerics claimed it legitimized, disputing the myth that the Prophet had said, "Those who entrust their affairs to a woman will never know prosperity." Over the centuries, this hadith had been repeatedly evoked to forbid Arab women from voting or any kind of political participation. Scholars like Mernissi claimed that the way to challenge inequality in Islam was not to move away from religion, but to push for a correction of its teachings. They argued that the Prophet was a great defender of women's rights, and that practices such as honor killings were perversions of the sacred texts.

This position appealed greatly to Manal, and yet she realized her marriage was a contradiction of it.

The marriage finally reached its boiling point on the docks of the Potomac River. Her husband became enraged at a friendship she had struck up with her rowing coach, and, upon seeing them talking by the river's edge, he had launched into a public tirade. Manal was horrified—not so much by the embarrassing spectacle, but by the look of pity on the coach's face. *What must he think of me?* she wondered. She had chosen the veil to challenge Western misconceptions of Muslim women, but now, instead, she was confirming the worst stereotype of the belittled wife.

So, after less than two years of marriage, Manal left her husband and filed for divorce. She knew divorce would bring a stigma, and that her chances of remarriage were slim, since she'd lost her virginity. She felt the disapproving glares from her relatives when she visited them in Jordan. The period was a painful one for her, yet ultimately liberating. She survived and got to know herself better, and grew stronger, to the point that she barely recognized the young woman who'd allowed herself to be pushed into marriage.

She knew that Muntaha wouldn't have all the opportunities she herself did, to bounce back from such difficult situations, but she saw pieces of her own story in the girl's plight, and understood intimately that sense of being trapped. She was determined to help her in any way she could.

AT SEVEN, MANAL awoke with an idea. She would use Muntaha's case as an opportunity to push for the funding of a shelter as part of the new Iraqi Ministry of Labor and Social Affairs, which was still under the supervision of the Americans. After a morning of phone calls, she tracked down the office and drove over to meet with the ministry officials.

"She's under eighteen, and she's in your jurisdiction," Manal said. "You should place her in a protective shelter at least until we figure out what to do."

The minister's deputy listened, and then said that he didn't consider Muntaha a minor because she was a married woman. "Look, if this was my daughter, she would be dead," he said. "I think you should give some thought to letting justice take its course."

"If you were not forcing girls to get married at fourteen you would not have to deal with this," Manal responded curtly. Others suggested putting Muntaha in an orphanage, which soon came to seem like the only solution.

When Manal went to the police station to transfer Muntaha to the orphanage, she found the girl in an excited state.

"Look, I can get out of this myself," she said. "One of the policemen offered to take me to Dubai and be my pimp. I will get clean there, save up money, and then find a job."

"No, no, don't do that," Manal insisted. "I have a better solution."

The orphanage, however, was filthy. Inside a dilapidated house, several disabled children roamed around unsupervised, their pants soiled. No one was paying attention to them, and the men leered at Manal. Muntaha looked horrified.

"I'm sorry, but you're going to have to stay here," Manal said, trying to be reassuring.

Manal and Ahmed drove off in silence. They both felt terrible. "We can't leave her there," Manal whispered. "She can sleep in our office."

"No way," Ahmed said. "Manal, we are just beginning. We are already confronting many suspicions in the community about our Western agenda. We must slow down, and not push too hard, too fast."

"But she'll be raped," Manal said. "We can't leave her there!"

Ahmed turned the car around. There was only one other group that could help Manal: the U.S. troops. She asked Sergeant Lautenschlager to take Muntaha for a couple of days while she tried to find a suitable shelter so the family could cool down. Lautenschlager agreed, even though doing so could plunge her into serious trouble if a commanding officer found out.

Muntaha spent two nights in the small château that Lautenschlager's unit occupied, as Manal ran around looking for a solution. The most promising seemed to be a shelter called ASUDA: Organization for Combating Violence Against Women. It was several hours' drive north, in the city of Sulaimaniya in the Kurdish region. She inquired about transporting Muntaha there. However, the next time she visited Muntaha, the young woman had had a change of heart. She had phoned her family and learned that her sisters were being punished for her crimes. She wanted to go home.

"I don't believe my father will hurt me," she promised.

Manal reluctantly returned with her to the police station. The police chief had spoken to the father, who had told him that Muntaha had been "troublesome" from an early age. The father had been eager to get her off his hands as soon as possible. He was a wealthy man, who paid a large sum of money to the ugly cousin to marry her. When Muntaha ran away, the cousin complained to the father that he owed him a replacement wife. If Muntaha wasn't returned to the husband, the tribes would get involved to settle the situation. Most likely they would demand that the father compensate the husband with one of Muntaha's sisters.

"I made a mistake and my sisters are going to have to pay the price. I can't let that happen," Muntaha said. Manal had no choice, but at least she wanted someone to negotiate the return. She looked at Ahmed.

"You're going way too far if you think I'm going to negotiate," he said. "Manal, I'm from another tribe. I have no position in the community. Who would I be to dare approach the family?"

The police chief put his hand to his heart. He was an avuncular old man who Manal had come to respect over the course of the past forty-eight hours. She trusted his word meant something. "I will negotiate," he offered.

The next afternoon, Muntaha disappeared out the police station door and into the back of a car. A month later, Manal ran into the police chief, who said he had visited the family and that Muntaha had survived, but Manal was never sure what really happened.

The experience left Manal with mixed feelings. Perhaps she had saved Muntaha's life—perhaps—but doing so had had repercussions. The U.S. military police had undoubtedly made enemies of Muntaha's extended family. The police chief had risked his own skin. Women for Women had put themselves in jeopardy and had antagonized the Ministry of Labor and Social Affairs.

She didn't expect women's rights to be handed to her—she knew she would have to fight for them. But the situation was very, very complicated. It wasn't always easy to know when you had done the right thing.

CHAPTER ELEVEN

WITHIN SIX MONTHS of the Americans' arrival in Iraq, Zia's career path had far exceeded even her wildest dreams. She had gone from being a harassed, lowly secretary at the Egyptian embassy to a *manager* of a U.S.-contracted company inside the Green Zone. She had authority, respect, and a big salary to prove it. Men listened to her, and career opportunities seemed endless. Despite the ongoing violence, life was much better than under Saddam and they had hope for the future. In her closet, she had hung an image of George Bush printed out from an IMN computer. Each night, Mamina said a prayer of blessing for him. When her grandmother visited, she kissed the picture. "If I could die now and give this man my extra years, I would."

Zia's promotion from reporter to transition site manager had occurred shortly after she had challenged the U.S. senior adviser with her question about when salaries to Iraqi government officials would resume. Her promotion boosted her salary to five hundred dollars a month, with an extra month's pay as a signing bonus. Rather than report, she would take on managerial duties, such as overseeing budgets, handling construction projects, and dealing with personnel matters. Her father also benefited, winning a $120,000 contract to build a security fence around the perimeter of IMN's new headquarters. She also landed an internship for Nunu, but after a few weeks, Nunu complained the pace was too fast. Zia had taken to her job like a racehorse finally let out of the gate, but Nunu couldn't break free of the role she had been groomed for so long to play, as the meek, subservient Arab girl. She cringed when given a task without specific instructions and was too shy to talk to the American men. When a few Iraqi employees received threats for working with the Americans, Nunu decided to quit, and Zia agreed it wasn't worth the risk. But Zia never once contemplated quitting. She loved her job. Each day, she felt more and more like IMN was her family.

But the situation inside the Green Zone was changing, too, as time went on, and not always for the better. By early fall, a group of Americans had begun arriving to work for the CPA who were very different from the ones she'd been meeting and working with in those first few months. They were civilians whom Zia came to know collectively as "the contractors," and they were not exactly, as Zia put it, "high quality" people. Until then, most of the CPA staff had been college-educated government employees from the State Department and the White House: young, ambitious, and deeply loyal to President Bush. Around the office, they posted copies of the Bill of Rights, and compared Paul Bremer to Thomas Jefferson. They spoke passionately about improving Iraq.

The contractors, though, didn't seem to care about Iraq. Muscular, tattooed guys with mirrored sunglasses, five-o'clock shadows, and a hungover look, they carried guns and swaggered around like they owned Iraq. They had been hired on temporary contracts by corporations such as Bechtel and Halliburton for technical jobs: setting up Internet systems, logistics, radar, supply, maintenance, truck driving, and security details. Many were older divorced men whose every other word was *fuck* and who boasted about working in a country that had "the highest virginity rate in the world," they estimated. When Zia left the office late, she saw them grouped around a picnic table, beer cans piled high and whiskey bottles on the ground, making raucous jokes.

Zia had no choice but to work with them. Some were nice, like Pat and Pappy, two retired Vietnam vets in their sixties who had been hired to provide security at IMN's new Salhiya site. At least they were respectful; most of the contractors treated the Iraqis as though they were inferior. A lot of the Americans were like this, Zia had noticed, even the ones who knew a lot about Iraqi history and spoke some Arabic—she still detected a condescending tone when they talked to her.

The female contractors were the rudest. Sailors in Basra didn't have mouths as foul as these women's, Zia told Mamina. In the evenings, as Zia left work, she saw the women spilling beer on their tiny tank tops and sitting on the men's laps. Zia's Iraqi male colleagues were obsessed with these women, convinced that they needed only to wait for their turn, presumably, to have sex with them. Once, Zia overheard a woman named Meghan openly bragging about sleeping with a different guy every night. *So it's true,* she thought. The sleaziness all came to a head over the summer, when photos surfaced online of an American camera-man for IMN sitting bare-chested at Saddam's pool in the palace, with Iraqi women in bathing suits balanced on each of his knees. Everyone gossiped that he was running a prostitution ring inside the Green Zone, hiring Iraqi women to have sex with the contractors.

Other, equally worrisome changes were happening at the IMN channel itself. The insistence that IMN was "independent" had always been fairly ridiculous to Zia, since the Americans were constantly doctoring the news to portray their efforts in a positive light. The programs they ran had clearly been pieced together by the military. Bremer's spokesman, Dan Senor, was constantly coming and going, directing story ideas and angles, and rounding up reporters for interviews with specific officials in which they suggested the questions. Iraqi journalists were told to refer to the military as the "forces of liberation," although Al Jazeera and most other channels called them "the occupation."

"Do they think we are stupid?" Zia wondered over lunch with her Iraqi colleagues.

"No one knows propaganda better than Iraqis!" a friend joked.

They were still trying to run the channel on the cheap, too, and sometimes poor conditions made it difficult to get the job done. Zia's and the other Iraqis' complaints about the problems fell on deaf ears, but, luckily, they weren't alone. Leading the criticism was the IMN program manager, Don North, a cameraman for U.S. news channels who had reported from Vietnam. He was so frustrated that he threatened to quit. Ahmed Rikaby, an Iraqi expat from Sweden who had been news director, had already quit in August.

Zia was disappointed that things weren't going better for the channel she'd become so devoted to, but the good far outweighed the bad. She reminded herself that for every sleazy American on the staff, there were two good ones, like her buddy Daniel, who worked as a cameraman, or Don North. Her Iraqi colleagues felt similarly.

"At least it's not Uday," pointed out one female reporter, who had worked for Saddam's channel. Saddam's son had run Iraqi television and was known for raping the pretty reporters.

"Yeah, it's still better than being a journalist under Saddam," said Zia's friend Susan. "All we did there was read a piece of paper into the camera."

Zia agreed. And if IMN overdid it in projecting the positive side of the story, it was only fair; Zia felt the mainstream media tilted the other way, showing only criticism of the U.S. effort and publicizing the increasing number of attacks on the soldiers. Zia attended many big press conferences with Ambassador Bremer, and the questions from the American and British media were more like accusations, often beginning with "Wouldn't you say . . ." or "Isn't it true . . ." The CPA worked hard, and was making some achievements; at least IMN showed that. Zia still believed in the project.

And now, as a manager, Zia felt like she might be able to make a difference, and she knew her decisions affected others. Aware of her heightened position, she always had lunch with the Iraqi staffers and tried to stay on their level. When Ramadan came around, she gave them envelopes of cash—money from her own pocket—as was the tradition. She felt a real emotional investment in the office. Despite her problem with the channel's content, as the fall wore on she could see all her efforts bearing fruit as the office came together.

Another thing that kept her feeling happy about her work was a new friendship she'd developed inside the Green Zone. Ironically, it was with one of the contractors. Keith was a forty-eight-year-old senior network engineer for a U.S. company, hired to set up the server in Zia's office. He was more than six feet tall, with a broad chest, sunburned cheeks, and flecks of silver in his brown hair. They called him the "tech guy," and everyone liked him. He made jokes at the meetings. When everyone else was rushing around on deadline, Keith liked to say "Take it easy," which he explained was a popular phrase from back home in California. Although Zia knew he drank alcohol, he cursed a lot less than the other contractors and, most important, he was respectful to Iraqis. He treated the staff as equals, made friends with everyone, and asked lots of questions about the country.

He flirted, too, particularly with Zia. Whenever he came into the offices, he smiled at her. She couldn't deny being flattered.

Over time, they got to know each other. Keith rushed into a friendship, letting all his emotions and stories and opinions hang out, but Zia tiptoed much more cautiously. Islam didn't condone such friendships, since they opened the door to sexual temptation. (The Prophet taught, "When a man is alone with a woman, Satan is with them.") But Zia decided there was nothing wrong in spending time with Keith in the company of others.

Eventually, he asked to eat lunch in her office, and she agreed—as long as they left the door open. Keith's manner was easygoing and nonjudgmental, and Zia found herself speaking openly about her opinions of IMN.

"Iraqis have satellite television now. They can watch dozens of other Arab channels, and no one is watching IMN. Iraqis call it 'a mouthpiece for the occupation,'" she worried.

"Hey, they've got a hundred million dollars, and it's not exactly going to the channel," he said.

"What do you mean?"

Keith explained that IMN was run by one of dozens of U.S. corporations with multimillion-dollar Pentagon contracts to reconstruct Iraq. "Look around you," he laughed, gesturing at the bare room and the equipment left over from Saddam. "Where's the money going?"

Zia had always thought that they were making do with a low budget.

"Do you know what Americans get paid to be here?" he asked.

"What?" Zia asked, not sure she wanted to hear.

"Some get a thousand a day, plus meals and housing and transportation."

She felt stung. Most Iraqi workers, Zia knew, were paid only six dollars a day.

Conversations with Keith made Zia's head spin. He came from the contractor world, but he talked to her like they were equals. He never tried to sugarcoat the situation, like the CPA people or the White House people. He was honest and forthright. When she danced around questions about the background of the contractors, he laughed.

"Zia, if these guys had any kind of normal life back in the States, why would they leave it and come all the way across the world to work in a war zone? Half these guys are running away from alimony payments." He laughed again. "Not exactly the best and brightest."

They talked and talked. Even though Keith broke down some of her idealism about the States and IMN, he also shared her hope. For all the corruption and sleaze, neither of them doubted that, in the end, the USA was going to succeed in Iraq. And for all his frankness, Keith was no cynic—quite the opposite.

He told Zia the story of taking an Iraqi man atop the convention center to install an antenna. From the rooftop they could see all of Baghdad, and their gaze fell upon the nearby zoo. The Ferris wheel was broken, the cages were empty, the boats in the ponds sat on mud, and the grass was dead. Keith's Iraqi companion teared up, and pointed in the distance to a mosque under construction. It was the size of several football stadiums; Saddam believed he could impress the Muslim world by building the largest, most expensive mosque in the Middle East—even if Iraqis starved, they died of simple diseases, and their children begged on the streets. "I used to drive past that mosque and hate Saddam. We were starving while he was building that. Now I stand here and look at Baghdad and I actually feel there might be hope for the future," the man had said.

As Keith told that story, tears welled up in his eyes. "It rips me up to see things like the zoo. Those places should be filled with green grass and families having picnics and children laughing."

Zia was touched by his concern. No other American seemed to care in such a heartfelt way about her country.

"Why don't you let me take you *out* to lunch sometime?" he suggested once, casually.

"No, thank you," she said.

"Why not?" he asked.

"What, like on a date, with you?" Zia said. *Iraqis don't date,* she thought. "Um, you're a friend who I work with, and that's it."

Keith pretended to pull a gun out of a holster at his hip, and aimed it down. "Bang!" he said, grinning.

"What are you doing?" she asked.

"I just shot myself in the foot. Any woman says to you, 'You're a friend,' that's it. It never goes further. That's the kiss of death in our country."

Zia laughed, but she couldn't explain how different things must be here from his world in California. In any case, she had to admit that Keith was fun to be around, and she found herself thinking about him more and more.

CHAPTER TWELVE

IN LATE SEPTEMBER, Aqila al-Hashimi left her home, body-guards in tow, and began her morning commute to the Green Zone. An Iraqi mother who had just turned fifty, with bobbed black hair and owlish glasses, al-Hashimi held a PhD from the Sorbonne, and was one of only three women appointed in July to Iraq's new interim government. She was regarded with hope as a proponent of women's rights.

But that day she never reached her government office. Only a few blocks from her home, gunmen ambushed her car. Five days later, she died of her wounds. The news of the assassination reached Heather as she had just begun working on a project to promote women's rights in Iraq. Instead, she found herself overseeing a memorial and consoling sad, terrified women, many of whom had known al-Hashimi. "Was she being punished for pushing women's issues?" they wondered. Her attackers got away, and no one knew for certain the motive. Some speculated that al-Hashimi was punished because she didn't wear the veil. Heather didn't know how to respond.

After a summer juggling dozens of different reconstruction projects (none of which came to fruition), Heather had changed gear. When her unit, 354th Civil Affairs, prepared to return to the States at the end of the summer, following their six-month rotation, she had requested to stay, with whatever organization would take her. She was assigned to the CPA to work on governance in the Baghdad region. Although she'd still be in fatigues and army boots, and carrying a weapon, she was detailed to work mostly with civilians from the State Department and aid organizations. She was thrilled. Her dream job had always been to help the people of Iraq, and the army had just been a way of getting here. Besides, she was ready to move on. The U.S. Army might be the best in the world in warfare, but had been a nightmare of disorganization when it came to rebuilding and running a government. Every project fell apart in the details. The soldiers were tired, confused, hot, and overstretched, and were feeling like their work belonged to the CPA. In the last few weeks, kids had stopped waving and attacks against soldiers and Westerners had increased. By far, the biggest blow to the reconstruction effort came in August, when terrorists blew up the UN headquarters in Baghdad. About a mile away, Heather had felt the living room of her villa shake, and minutes later, concerned emails began pouring in. Unable to leave the Green Zone for security reasons, neither she nor her comrade—a trained paramedic—could rush to the scene. Twenty-two people were killed, including the much-beloved head of the mission, Sergio Vieira de Mello, who had survived for hours under the rubble before dying. How had terrorists slipped past 140,000 troops to blow up the UN building in the middle of occupied Baghdad? Morale sank. The United Nations withdrew its operations immediately. After a long hot summer of disappointments, most soldiers in her unit concluded that implementing democracy was merely a fantasy: mission impossible. The sense of adventure and purpose with which they had started the mission had worn away. She was sick of the greasy food, her grimy, salty army hat, and her grubby, hot Kevlar vest. Most of all, she was exhausted by the army's increasing fixation on its own bureaucratic rules rather than on the deteriorating situation, as evidenced by the many memos emphasizing the importance of wearing the uniform correctly, fastening their seat belts, and passing the physical fitness test.

Heather's had been the lone voice arguing it was not the Iraqis' fault; that this wasn't working because the army was bureaucratic and inflexible. Soldiers weren't trained in nation-building; most were trained to blow things up, not build them.

Many soldiers had been shouted at by Iraqis who they were trying to help. "If those *hajjis* had any balls they would have overthrown Saddam themselves," they responded. *Hajjis* was the derogatory nickname for Iraqis, taken from the Arabic word *Hajj*, which is the annual pilgrimage Muslims make to Mecca.

Even Major Norcom, who had worked around the world, was calling democracy in Iraq a fantasy. "Coyne, it's in the Iraqis' DNA to be ruled by a strong man. They don't get democracy."

Heather was glad to be at the CPA, among people who still believed. This was the "wave" that Heather and her unit had expected would be coming in on the heels of the troops, back in April. The mood behind the palace walls was energetic and optimistic. Everyone was willing to work from 7:00 a.m. until 11:00 p.m., and over dinner they talked of nothing but their big plans to rebuild Iraq. Few had spent much time outside the palace, working with Iraqis, Heather observed. But she was as keen as they were to believe that all their grand plans would succeed if they just worked hard enough. Inside the palace, the UN bombing was viewed as an "isolated incident" committed by Al Qaeda terrorists, not an albatross signaling worse acts of resistance to come.

Heather sensed disorganization was still widespread, and there were aspects of the CPA that bothered her. New arrivals crowded the cafeteria and lines of tiny, white trailers rose up behind the palace to accommodate them. Although they were thousands of miles from home, the dynamic inside the CPA was becoming as insular and incestuous as in a small high school. Cliques formed, with status bestowed on those closest to Bremer's inner circle. Romances flourished, although they usually died quickly. The sense of adventure and danger mingled to create a strong sexual energy that led to endless one-night stands, much gossiped about, in locales as exotic as Porta-Johns, Saddam's poolside, and behind tanks. Although the hedonism would be shocking to an outsider, Heather rationalized it with the explanation that they were away from home for months, if not years. They were only human. She herself was no angel, although she had gone to great efforts to keep her flings private. Most in the CPA thrived on a mix of intense workdays and just-as-intense partying. But what Heather didn't approve of was those who cared only about the latter. As the Green Zone became its own self-contained city, hundreds of corporate contractors arrived to fill jobs that had more to do with sustaining the CPA than helping Iraqis. Heather knew them as corporate contractors, and the most offensive were those assigned to the security of officials such as Bremer. They brandished their weapons and had a reputation as trigger happy when an unlucky Iraqi passed in their crosshairs. Their self-image as wild cowboys was backed by the absence of any law with which to restrain them. They operated under immunity from U.S. or Iraqi prosecution, and they knew it—occasionally getting themselves into late-night, drunken gun battles on the streets of the Green Zone. Heather steered clear of them and surrounded herself with those who believed in the mission. There were plenty of other groups to associate with. Tasks were massive, and CPA employees that she met described with awe their responsibilities, though no one doubted their ability to pull them off.

Heather was hired to be a civil society officer in the Baghdad region; her job was to "build up civil society," a nebulous goal that included supporting grassroots Iraqi organizations, developing local councils and community outreach, and supporting women's groups. She was to oversee training and development for all the Iraqi civil society organizations; to support the local advisory councils, which were the building blocks of Iraq's new democracy; and to take up Colin Powell's call to bring women's rights to the country.

SO FAR, HEATHER discovered, U.S. efforts on behalf of Iraqi women had been scattered and disorganized. Her friend Jody Lautenschlager was getting all the humanitarian groups together each week in the convention center. Bremer's office had assigned women's issues to the office of Judy Van Rest, a former regional director for the Peace Corps who had worked in D.C. under the Republican presidents Reagan and Bush senior. Her office was pushing women's issues through its "democracy initiatives," aiming to increase the number of women participating in the local advisory councils, but few women were even showing up for those meetings.

Over a few weeks, Heather made friends with other U.S. aid workers interested in women's issues. There were also people she met inside the palace who expressed interest: the hardworking State Department bureaucrat Stephanie Kuck, who was appointed to work on democracy and women's issues in Judy Van Rest's office; the handsome globe-trotting ex-soldier Sloan Mann from the Office of Transitional Initiatives

(OTI), an arm of USAID; and the wryly cynical Eastern European aid worker Ester Lauferova—all had come up as people informally interested in the subject, but there was nothing connecting them, and they, like Heather, were swamped with other projects.

One morning, though, at a staff meeting, her boss, Ted Morse, told an anecdote about a female engineer he had met the other day, on a trip to Baghdad's electrical switching station, who had been prevented from rising in her career by Saddam's government. (Heather had already realized that if there was one thing the CPA loved, it was anecdotes about how Iraqis had suffered under Saddam.)

"Very few women are in technical or managerial positions in Baghdad's municipality, yet Iraqi women are competent and highly educated," he said. "How can we utilize women in terms of rebuilding civil society and in restructuring Iraq and get them into government, education, and politics?"

Someone else mentioned a proposal that had been submitted a month earlier, suggesting that they build a series of women's centers in Baghdad.

"I like that idea," Morse said. "Let's do it! Where's the proposal? Who can we give it to?"

Inside the world of the CPA, Heather had been shocked to observe how massive decisions involving millions of dollars were made quickly, handed over to people with no experience, and yet few doubted that the outcome would be successful. No one was surprised when he turned to her.

"Um, okay," she said.

The budget was soon decided on: $1.4 million for the first of nine centers. For her, that was a massive sum, but in comparison with most other projects, it was a drop in the bucket. And just like that, Heather became in charge of the largest U.S. project on behalf of women in Iraq. She knew that many Iraqi women had been pushing for more to be done, and was excited to announce her program at one of Sergeant Lautenschlager's meetings. Then al-Hashimi was killed. After a few days of grieving, the women seemed ready to return to the issues, but Heather noticed that the crowd was smaller and quieter.

. . .

WHEN IT CAME to Iraqi women's rights, Heather didn't want to meddle much in the substance of the issues. Sure, the hijab would irritate the heck out of her—it looked hot, and Iraqi women were always fiddling with it—but whether they wore it was their choice. She didn't have strong feelings on how Iraqis should view abortion rights, marriage, children, or divorce, either, nor did she get involved in individual cases. She wanted the legislative processes in place so women's views were represented equally. What those views were was entirely up to them.

Heather had not come to Iraq specifically to promote women's rights, and she didn't know much about doing so. In that respect, she was a classic American postfeminist. Born in 1972, she was raised with an awareness of the feminist battles that preceded her, but she felt that the battles had all been fought by the time she came of age. Equal rights were something she took for granted. "Glass ceiling" was not part of her lexicon in high school and college. Work hard, and you'll get ahead just like men, she had assumed. Any woman still talking about "feminism" was just part of a special interest group.

But the older she got, the more she saw subtle signs of discrimination, small and large, although it wasn't until she enlisted in the army that she really experienced blatant sexism. In the airplane to Kuwait, she had leaned forward to remove an item from the overhead container. A commanding officer slapped her on the ass. Heather had chewed him out so loudly she doubted he would ever try that again, but she had the confidence and experience of a thirty-year-old, and most of her female colleagues were much younger, some barely out of high school. They got harassed the most, and few stood up to the sexist banter and the occasional groping that was the norm in the military. When a woman is treated like that from age eighteen onward, she never really learns to stand up for herself, Heather knew.

AS SHE THOUGHT over her new assignment, Heather's excitement grew. She envisioned nine sunny, airy "Iraq Women's Centers" in neighborhoods across Baghdad, with computer rooms, conference tables, and an active membership of neighborhood women who would use the centers as a hub for their activities. Women would receive job training, network, organize political campaigns, and support one another. She imagined leaving Baghdad and being able to say, "I created nine women's centers." That would be a tangible accomplishment.

But she wasn't sure where to start. Did Iraq have any local women's groups, and did they already have centers? She had no idea. She emailed Sloan, Stephanie, and Ester and asked them to partner with her.

"Let's do this!" she said.

Sloan applied the brakes. He was a former civil affairs officer, like Heather, and had spent most of his twenties and early thirties living abroad and working in war zones.

"Whoaa. These things take time," he said.

Sloan wanted to flesh out the details. Heather had few contacts among Iraqi women, and little expertise in launching aid programs. Given the increasingly tight security restrictions, she wouldn't be able to get out of the Green Zone regularly enough to execute the plan. Many of the international aid organizations that she could have turned to were packing up and leaving due to the bombing of the UN headquarters— and others viewed soldiers like Heather as the enemy.

"We need someone on the ground," he said. "You should meet Manal Omar." Heather had already heard about Manal through the grapevine, and the way Sloan raved about her only heightened what was becoming legendary status. She spoke Arabic; she was Muslim; and she was living alone in a house in downtown Baghdad. (Among the hundreds of eager Americans locked in their palace offices, proximity to and acceptance by the locals carried a large measure of clout. And here was Manal, not only living like the locals, but living *among* them, socializing with them, and gaining their respect and trust. There was a popular story circulating about Manal, that, following a back operation, she was unable to attend one of the weekly meetings of Iraqi women's groups. Instead of proceeding without her, all the women moved the meeting to Manal's house.

That was influence.

Since Manal couldn't come to the palace to meet with them, because of that operation, Heather's group arranged a conference call with her.

·   ·   ·

MANAL ROLLED HER eyes as she hung up the phone. *Women's centers?* she thought. That was such a typical U.S. government project—they just loved bricks-and-mortar buildings that they could point to as accomplishments. The aid world had long moved beyond dropping buildings into communities as a way to help them. That was so 1980s. And why had a rookie soldier been put in charge of more than a million dollars, when she knew nothing about women's rights?

Sloan had promised her that Heather was not another "bright idea fairy," Sloan's term for the people inside the CPA with millions to spend, dozens of big ideas, and absolutely zero expertise. Manal could tell the soldier was intelligent and grounded, but that was hardly enough.

"We want a safe space for women to go to discuss social and political ideas," Heather had explained on the phone. "We see about nine centers across Baghdad, and we have funding for each of them."

Manal had not been polite.

"So we're just talking buildings?" she said. "Have you thought about what will go on inside them? Where's the softer side of your plan? Where's the human resources development, the capacity building, the sustainability, the community ownership?"

At one point, Heather had suggested the centers could be a place to do Internet training. Manal barely contained her exasperation.

"If you're talking about computers, you're talking about the elite," Manal said. "Most women I work with don't have electricity in their houses, let alone a computer. They wouldn't even know how to work one. What will the center do for poor women?"

Heather hadn't had an answer.

In recent months, and especially since their help with the young prostitute Muntaha, Manal had tried to soften her perception of the military. Many of the people involved had good hearts, and while as a body they represented the brutal edge of Bush's foreign policy, Manal had learned that most individual soldiers cared little about politics. Unlike the Republicans in the CPA, they got their hands dirty each day and were on the streets and in the neighborhoods, and she respected what Heather was trying to do. Nonetheless, the wall that separated aid workers from soldiers existed because the military did still shoot at people—whether they had to didn't matter. Everything they did, even rebuilding schools, was to advance a military and political agenda. Heather was doing aid work, but as a military appointee to the CPA, she still used her title, wore a uniform, and carried an M16 rifle. Whereas Manal was there to help women for women's sake—whether or not it served the USA's political agenda in Iraq.

Another reason to keep her distance was that the military, even civil affairs, wasn't trained in aid work. Just because the soldiers were good enough to pick up the slack left by the CPA's incompetence didn't mean that they were doing humanitarian work correctly. Too often they assumed aid work was about donating pencils or bags of flour, but in fact helping people was incredibly complicated and, Manal knew, usually done wrong. The field of international aid work was as old as the Marshall Plan in the 1940s, but had really taken off in the 1980s with the widespread publicity given to the famines in Africa. Billions of dollars of aid had poured into Africa, and legions of do-gooder institutions with utopian plans and millions of dollars had descended on the continent, and yet, twenty years later, the problems persisted. Some in the aid world, including Manal, had incorporated the lessons learned: now, instead of just trying to feed hungry mouths or construct buildings, aid workers were being trained to help people help themselves. Rather than descending on communities with a we-know-best attitude, aid programs now sought to empower locals, let solutions percolate up from indigenous communities, and take into account cultural and political norms. *Sustainability* became the buzzword; programs had to be able to continue after the international aid community moved on.

Perhaps women's centers sounded good on paper, but what real assistance was being delivered, how would it be sustained when the Americans moved on, and was it even really needed? How did Heather know what was needed, and how would she assess her program and readjust when necessary? None of this had been thought through, and Heather, for all her good intentions, intelligence, and organizational skills, was way out of her depth.

So Manal had just wished them luck and hung up the phone.

AS HEATHER SLINKED back to her office, she felt embarrassed. She was the deadweight in the group, she knew, even though Manal had been diplomatic about it. She knew she was just the money gal. And yet, she wasn't ready to throw up her hands.

Within hours of their first phone call, Heather had called Manal back to make her case. Manal had the expertise to create programs, the contacts to give it legitimacy, and the freedom to move around the city; Heather had the money and the power inside the CPA to get property. Together, they were the perfect team, she argued.

But Manal again refused.

"In the development world you have to let the women decide what they want to do and form their own group to do it," Manal explained. "You wait and let them lead you. It's dangerous to put faith in bricks and mortar and think they will come."

This time, Heather had another answer.

"What you're talking about is fine if we had all the time in the world. But we don't. We have a window of opportunity for women and it's closing. The first Iraqi government has been picked and there were only three women in it. Women weren't organized and they missed their chance to lobby for better representation."

Now Manal was listening.

There are more big decisions coming, Heather continued, and Iraqi women have to be prepared. The first elections were scheduled for the following year. The constitutional committee was being selected, and the ink would be dry on a new Iraqi constitution by 2005. Judges were being picked for indefinite seats. Iraq's justice system was an open book at the moment, and this was the best time to effect legislation regarding "honor killings," divorce, and the role of Islam in women's lives. Now was the time for change. They had to seize the moment. If women's groups didn't act fast, decisions would be made without them and it would be five times harder to reverse them. The window would close.

Heather insisted, "We're looking at a short time frame to get women mobilized to participate in the political process. The centers could be a springboard for them to organize."

Heather spoke of the postwar period as a golden opportunity for Iraqi women, comparable to the 1770s in America, and she imagined that if women had been sitting at the table when the U.S. Constitution was being written, perhaps it wouldn't have taken them 150 years to gain the right to vote.

Manal paused, and then repeated something she'd said earlier. "Women for Women focuses mostly on poor women," she said. "If you're talking about women in government, you're talking about the elite." She could be convinced this might be a good idea, but she certainly wasn't interested in working with the sophisticated Iraqi expats or the suits sent over from Condoleeza Rice's office.

But Heather didn't recognize the distinction. Helping get women in government would, eventually, help poor women, she was sure.

"Look at Afghanistan in 2002," Heather pushed, getting passionate. "We did it the right way, we waited for these ideas to come from the grassroots, and we missed the window. By the time they were organized, the constitution, the *loya jirgas*, the things that needed to have women's voices had already happened."

Yes, that was a good point. Manal had to consider, though, that teaming up with Heather would effectively make her a pariah in the international aid world. She was already an outcast just for being in Iraq. Working with the military on a project meant knocking down a big safety wall. Manal believed that civilians ought to feel that aid was coming from an impartial source, with no strings attached.

Still, Manal liked Heather. She spoke some Arabic, knew the history of Iraq, and struck Manal as someone with heart.

Manal also felt affected by the assassination of Aquila al-Hashimi, which Manal agreed had probably been done to send a message to women's rights activists. Women had to fight back. Iraqi women did face an unprecedented opportunity to enshrine their rights in the law and constitution, a goal that would help them all. And she certainly wouldn't be able to make such a difference alone. Women for Women was a small organization, dependent on grants and donations, working with almost no security. Manal thought of the poor women in the Shia south who needed more programs, training, and aid than Manal could offer in her current situation. Heather had $1.4 million to start building nine women's centers, with more money promised. Who would Manal be helping if she refused to get involved? Women needed these centers, and the male-dominated Iraqi government had already shown its unwillingness to help.

"You know, as much as I don't like it, and it's not the way to do this, it does make sense," Manal finally said. She had to take the idea back to Women for Women International's main office, but she was feeling convinced. "What kind of timeline are you thinking?" Manal asked. Heather held her breath as Manal's tone changed. They were going to be a team.

After six months of failed initiatives, Heather was determined to get something done quickly. She promised it would be an "instant thing." She figured it'd take two weeks to look at about a dozen sites. They already had the funding, and Sloan Mann's Office of Transitional Initiatives had agreed to renovate them. The process of obtaining the properties would take about a month, and they could start hiring in the meantime. They would be ready in time for women to use them in preparation for next year's national elections. But they had to hurry.

HEATHER THREW HERSELF into the project, immediately scouring lists of possible properties and investigating all leads. She really wanted the women's centers to work, but it wouldn't be easy. Plus, her heightened involvement with the problems facing Iraqi women—which she hoped to help address with the centers—had also heightened her staff's curiosity about her own status as an American woman. Why, they wanted to know, didn't she have a husband and children?

Heather preferred not to get into it. In the wake of her parents' divorce, years earlier, Heather had vowed to never marry or have children. She had career ambitions, and her own mother's struggles to balance career and family in the 1970s had left young Heather skeptical of the modern-day mirage that women could "have it all." Raised in Kansas in the 1950s, her mother had been an early feminist pioneer, one of the only women in her high school class to attend college. Hoping to escape the repressive Midwest, she and Heather's father moved to Berkeley, California, in the 1960s, and Lelia was one of the first four women admitted into the California Institute of Technology's PhD science program. After graduation, she became one of the first female science professors at Princeton University. When Heather came along, she raised her daughter with stories of bra-burning marches and personal battles against sexist male supervisors (one told her she couldn't enter his program because the lab had no ladies' bathroom). Heather still kept a framed photo of her mother on graduation day, rebelliously waving her diploma. She had cut her gown into a miniskirt and worn black fishnet stockings.

But as Heather's parents started a family, Lelia's career lagged as she struggled to maintain her rigorous work schedule with the needs of children, in an era that still expected women to serve a hot dinner nightly and sew their own drapes. As Lelia pushed forty, her husband was openly having affairs, often citing the "free love" language of the women's movement to justify his sleeping around. Heather still recoiled at the memory of her mother telling her and her sister, "I'm divorcing your father." It was the early 1980s, and she bore the stigma of being the only girl in her elementary school class with divorced parents.

From her mother's experience, Heather concluded that if she wanted to succeed, she had to choose between a career and a husband. By the 1990s, society sent out a more liberating message about modern women's equality, but personal observation showed otherwise. As she reached her late twenties, she saw her female friends get married, get pregnant, and struggle with their jobs and their ambitions. Despite many gains, American women were still very far from the kind of equality that her mother's generation had fought for. Heather didn't believe she could stay compatible with one person over her entire life, and had little interest in starting a family. She had thought long and hard about her choices and she was comfortable with them.

AS MUCH AS Heather tried to keep her views to herself, however, the fact that she was single and childless was controversial among her staff. Many had only seen Americans portrayed in the movies, and studied Heather with fascination. As they became more relaxed and familiar working with one another, they pried endlessly into her private life. Heather shook her head as nonchalantly as possible. But soon the Iraqis filled the informational vacuum with gossip. Was she gay? A prostitute? Or maybe she hated men. Heather's top assistant, Thanaa, kept her informed of the rumors. When security in the Green Zone tightened, people who came in for meetings would often stay over in trailers rather than travel at night. Heather could tell by the embarrassed whispers and suggestive looks on her staff's faces that they assumed the guests were sharing her trailer.

One afternoon, during lunch, a young staffer let his curiosity get the better of him.

"Excuse, Ms. Coyne. I am so curious. Why aren't you married?" he asked nervously.

Perhaps this was the time to resolve the question.

"I don't plan on getting married." Judging by the silence and shocked faces, Heather realized the impact of her honesty. She tried to explain. "People get married too easily," she said. "I think only about thirty percent of people who do get married ought to do it. The rest just do it because they feel like they have to."

Still, silence.

"Then, half of them cheat anyway," she continued. "If you can't make that commitment, you shouldn't enter into the agreement."

Thanaa, a veiled twenty-three-year-old, piped up. Heather had watched Thanaa's confidence soar in recent months as she worked her way up inside the CPA. However, Thanaa always made clear her life goal: to get married and have children, as quickly as possible.

"Yes, but, Miss Coyne, how could someone not want to get married?" Thanaa asked politely.

Heather thought she had just explained her answer. She faced enough judgment as a single woman in her thirties in her own Western culture and felt annoyed at having to justify her personal life to prying Iraqi colleagues who would certainly not ask a man such a loaded question. Yet, around the table, the Iraqis were already trying to offer her blessings. "God willing, you will get married."

"No, I really don't want to."

"But, miss," Thanaa pressed, looking increasingly distressed. "How will you have children?"

Heather said simply, "Oh, I don't want to have children."

Looking around at the stupefied faces of her staff, she tried to lighten the mood. "Children are dirty and noisy. They need to be cared for all the time."

No one found this funny.

"I'm joking," she said. "It's just that I'll always be in war zones, and it'll be too dangerous to have a child," she said.

That was a more satisfying answer, but there was one more outstanding concern.

"But, Ms. Coyne, if you don't get married, you don't get all the *stuff* that comes with marriage . . ." the male staffer trailed off, obviously referring to sex.

Heather laughed. "Well, you can get all those things without getting married!"

She hoped that would end the conversation, and—maybe—even plant the seed in his mind that women could have the same kind of sexual freedom as men. But a horrified look crossed his face instead, and he turned beet red. No, she didn't think he'd gotten the message.

CHAPTER THIRTEEN

ZIA GRABBED ON to the dashboard as Keith cut through traffic, laid on the horn, and gestured wildly out the car window with his hand.

"I'm driving Iraqi style," he joked.

She laughed. After several more weeks of Keith's relentless lobbying, Zia had agreed to have lunch with him in a restaurant downtown. Lately, she had noticed many Iraqi women sharing pizzas in the Green Zone café with contractors, or strolling down the wide, tree-shaded boulevards, shoulder to shoulder with soldiers. But such images of Iraqi women "dating" American men, however normalized inside the Green Zone, were still shocking to Iraqis. That Zia was willing to risk being seen in public with Keith was a measure of her optimism that the Americans would push Iraqi society to modernize. Zia had heard about the assassination of Aquila al-Hashimi—everyone had—but no one knew for certain that she was targeted because she was an unveiled woman. Zia was more apt to believe the rumors that Sunnis still loyal to Saddam Hussein had killed her because she was working for the Americans. Even the devastating UN bombing, which she believed was orchestrated by foreign fighters, had only fortified her resolve that the Americans needed Iraqi support more than ever. Many other Iraqis felt the same. Plus, she liked the modern idea of going out on an American-style "date." It was just lunch, but it felt like she was breaking barriers for all Iraqi women. Although, of course, she hadn't dared to tell Baba.

Scattered attacks against Americans had been occurring across the city, so to play it safe Zia suggested Keith disguise his nationality. It had taken some preparation: he ditched his SUV and borrowed a rusty pickup truck from an Iraqi coworker; he wrapped a red-and-white checkered scarf around his neck. The hope was that, from a distance, other diners might assume they were an Iraqi husband and wife, or perhaps that he was a Western journalist and she was his translator. Hundreds of foreigners were now living in hotels and rented houses in Baghdad, including journalists, aid workers, businessmen, and even the odd tourist—they wandered around souks with cameras, picking out vegetables at the markets or dining at the few restaurants that had begun serving alcohol to attract a Western clientele. Some women tried to blend in by wearing a headscarf, but they usually pulled it back to reveal their bangs, which was more the style in Iran than Iraq. And they matched their veil with khaki army-style pants and sneakers—which Iraqi women would *never* wear in public. Since few spoke Arabic, they almost always had an Iraqi driver or translator standing attentively alongside them.

Westerners seemed to feel that Baghdad was still safe enough to move around in freely, but Zia felt it better to avoid attracting attention. She preferred that no one recognize her and ask questions. Even in a city of six million, Baghdad could feel as small as a village, and Zia was always running into someone who recognized her, or who knew her father or sister. Yet, for as much as she knew she had to keep her outing a secret, she felt very cool. Here she was, on her first American "date," coming from the palace, where she worked with people from the White House. She felt special, and the risk only fueled the excitement.

At the restaurant, Zia ordered in Arabic for them both. Within minutes, colorful plates of meze covered the table: eggplant and tahini; hummus, parsley, and tomatoes; and a basket of pita bread. Sun poured through the lace curtains, and Zia could see the busy street outside, and several other tables of Iraqis nearby. They spoke in hushed tones, but no one bothered Keith and Zia.

Keith told her more about himself. His father had served in the navy during Vietnam, and Keith grew up in the Philippines, attending a Christian school, before the family moved to California. In the late 1960s, while his brother and friends headed to Berkeley to be hippies, Keith returned to the Philippines as a student missionary. He was an idealist, but he'd also gotten, at a young age, a cold, hard glimpse of what U.S. aid looked like on the ground: the prostitutes, the alcohol-fueled parties, the corruption—all masked by bullshit flag-waving patriotic rhetoric. That was the USA to Keith: some good, honest deeds, and a lot of PR. Nonetheless, Keith's father had raised his son to love his country, and he did. He carried that belief in the American way of life into Baghdad, but that alone wasn't enough. "Let's just say the corporate pay made the risk 'manageable,'" he said, laughing.

Zia loved his openness. To Zia, Keith was the complete opposite of emotionally distant, taciturn men like Baba. He spoke warmly of his emotions, shared his thoughts and feelings, and seemed genuinely interested in hers. He also did little things that she had never seen Arab men do, like open doors for her, carry her bag, and buy her sodas. *They treat us like princesses,* Zia thought.

Over lunch Zia learned that Keith had another, more somber side too. Underneath his joking manner, he was often depressed. Like many of the other contractors, he was escaping problems back home. He was twice divorced, and had a fourteen-year-old daughter, who lived with one of his ex-wives, to whom he paid hefty child support. He'd never graduated from college and had hopscotched around in his career. By contrast, his life in Baghdad offered freedom, money straight into his U.S. bank account, and a circle of guys to drink and joke around with— but even as he described it so enthusiastically, Zia could tell he felt it was a little depressing.

She had sad stories too; the pressures of poverty, the fear of the Ba'ath Party, and the time the Mukhabarat forced her to spy on the Egyptian embassy, where she worked, tapping the family's phone lines. She would have been terrified to speak so openly during Saddam's time, and doing so now felt cathartic. Keith listened with interest and understanding.

Soon, Keith and Zia's conversation morphed into sexier topics. Zia had been dying to ask about the female contractors at IMN. She was burning with curiosity about male-female relationships in America, but she danced around subjects taboo to talk about with a man, like sex. Keith, however, dived right in, in his usual frank style.

"Zia, I grew up in the sixties and seventies in California. Sex was no big deal. You meet a woman, you find each other interesting and attractive, you take her home, and you F each other's lights out. That's the final piece of the puzzle and you know if you're compatible."

Zia smiled in surprise, even though she'd suspected as much from television.

"But isn't that bad for the woman?"

"No." Keith laughed. "Women want it that way too. That's feminism. If she doesn't enjoy it, maybe she won't take your call the next day."

Keith presented casual sex as a mark of women's liberation. He wasn't about to let her take the high road, either. "You know what the problem is in the Muslim world?" he said, leaning forward conspiratorially. "Sexual frustration."

Zia thought this was hysterical.

"Here, I see this tremendous amount of sexual frustration between men and women, and quite frankly, I find it offensive," Keith said. How come men can go out and do anyone they want, but you become an outcast in the family and subject even to being killed if you go and sleep with someone?"

It was true, Zia knew.

"If you ask me, there're a lot of sexual time bombs floating around this country," he continued. "It's gotta be frustrating. I'm not a woman, but we all have those feelings, and the women have to repress them and the men get to go out and release them with prostitutes."

There was a long silence.

"It's got to make for one hell of an interesting wedding night," Keith said.

They both laughed.

"No kidding!" Zia said.

Zia told him about the wedding night of the aunt of one of Nunu's friends. The girl's family arranged her marriage to a man she didn't know. A few days before the ceremony, her mother explained what would happen, physically, on her wedding night, and the poor girl was terrified. She had never been alone with a man, and the thought of this stranger touching her made her tremble. So when they arrived at their hotel room, she locked the groom out on the balcony!

"No way," Keith interjected, wide-eyed.

The groom banged on the glass door, but the bride wouldn't let him in for hours. Finally, he promised not to touch her. But as soon as she opened the door, he beat her and forced himself on her. When her mother, aunts, and sisters gathered the following morning, as was traditional, to see the bloody sheet and hear the story of the wedding night, her bruises said it all. She told the women what had happened, and finished with a long sigh.

The grandmother frowned. "You're so stupid. You shouldn't have done it. Now you've been beaten by your husband and you'll always remember that as your first time." All the other women agreed that she had been foolish.

Keith thought that was harsh, but Zia was laughing. "I told Nunu, 'Hey, her mistake for letting him in. She should have left him on the balcony all night.' "

"But didn't she want to divorce him after that?" Keith asked.

"No way! No one would marry her again."

The check arrived, and they got ready to leave. "On my wedding night," Zia added thoughtfully, "my mom said she'll be in the room next door. That way, if something goes wrong, I'll have a place to run."

CHAPTER FOURTEEN

SOON AFTER MANAL and Heather had agreed to collaborate on the women's centers, they settled into what they hoped would be a productive division of labor. While Heather worked the political angle with officials inside the Green Zone, pushing through the paperwork and locating possible buildings, Manal hit the streets, hiring Iraqi staff, corralling women to sit on a board of directors, and determining what types of programs and events the women needed in the centers. The aid worker and the soldier made for an unusual pair, but neither could accomplish their aim without the other. The unlikely friendship that developed surprised them both. People stared when they had meetings over dinner, Manal in her headscarf and Heather in her fatigues, but they had too much work to care.

Manal saw her role as helping Iraqi women organize into groups, and then training them to be effective organizations. She had created weekly meetings with the nascent Iraqi women's groups. The first was called "Women in Government," in which she brought together women to network and to discuss strategies to get them into government, including campaigning, politicking, lobbying, and legislation. The second was called the "NGO Coordinating Committee," which was to train the women on basic strategies. On their own initiative, many had already formed groups such as the National Council of Women or the Muslim Women's Association or the Women's Alliance for a Democratic Iraq, but they had little experience in organizing. Manal taught "Robert's Rules of Order," the widely used procedures for organizing group discussions in the West; the creation of steering committees; fund-raising strategies; government lobbying; how to write mission statements; and even how to design brochures. Many of the women she dealt with were lawyers, professors, and engineers, but since the formation of a women's group had been forbidden under Saddam, these well-educated women were hungry to learn how to develop and fund their organization. Manal worked closely with Hanaa Adwar, a petite Christian lawyer in her late fifties who was from the southern city of Basra.

Getting support for Heather's women's centers from these Iraqi women ("buy in," in Manal's aid-world parlance) was key. From the beginning, they had to feel they had a stake in the process. If she and Heather did all the work, and then tried to hand over the center on opening day, Manal knew no one would take ownership and it would fall apart. The women needed to feel a sense of investment—that this was *their* center, not the Americans'.

So, sitting around a conference table covered with Pepsis, ashtrays, and fans, Manal had announced the project to a dozen or so leaders of local groups. They were ecstatic. The figure of $1.4 million put stars in their eyes—it was an astronomical sum of money in Iraq—and ideas flew: one center would have a pool, another a computer room, another a health clinic. One woman suggested opening small shops inside the centers where used items could be donated and resold at low prices. These shops could serve as business models for women, as well as provide needed items to poor people. The possibilities were endless—the women were excited, committed, and hopeful. Manal shared their enthusiasm with Heather during their daily phone conversations, and they were both thrilled.

But then came the more tricky task of actual governance. Manal wanted the women to choose for themselves a board of directors. But who would be on it? After months of unity over the summer, the local women had begun to splinter into groups based on Sunni, Shia, and Kurdish identity, as well as those who veiled and those who didn't, those who had benefited under Saddam's regime and those who hadn't. It was a dismaying trend that Manal did her best to overcome.

THE FIRST SIGN of division came during a meeting Manal held in a restaurant around August. Manal had asked the women to suggest important issues to address.

"Ending the U.S. occupation," one woman said bitterly. A murmur spread across the room.

"No, the Americans are here to help us," another woman replied. Several women nodded their heads in agreement. Yet Manal had seen support for the soldiers wane recently as stories spread of nighttime raids on homes, innocent husbands and sons detained, and rumors that Iraqis were being tortured in Abu Ghraib prison.

Manal tried to avoid taking a position, and eventually attempted to move the conversation forward, but other divisions arose. At some point a woman raised her hand and stood up to speak, when suddenly another woman across the room rose and pointed her finger. "She's a Ba'athist!" she shouted. "She worked for Saddam!"

"No, I didn't!" the woman replied.

They began to argue. Another woman suggested that any former Ba'athists should be forbidden from attending the weekly meetings, and to this many Shia women cheered, while the Sunni women sat stone-faced. Sensing an opportunity to talk through a painful subject, Manal decided to try to address the situation by allowing the women to take turns expressing their opinions. Unbelievable stories poured forth of suffering and loss, of disappeared husbands, mass graves, starving children, and widows. Women cried openly and spat angrily. Many of them wouldn't—couldn't—accept reconciliation with those who had worked under Saddam. They even shouted at the expat Iraqi women who had left in the 1980s, accusing them of abandoning Iraq during its most difficult time.

Their emotion was so raw, and its expression so new, that Manal realized a civilized discussion was impossible. And yet she could hardly exclude all women connected to the Ba'ath Party, or from Sunni families. The meeting became nasty, and order broke down. Manal, who was Sunni, lobbied to keep everyone working together and she grew close to many women. But over time she noticed fewer and fewer Sunni women attending the meetings.

The division deepened into the fall, particularly after the assassination of Aqila al-Hashimi, who had been replaced in the government by a deeply conservative Shia woman named Salama al-Khafaji from Najaf.

She wore black robes from head to toe, as well as socks and gloves, and she refused to shake hands with men. Al-Khafaji had been selected by the remaining members of the Governing Council, which was majority Shia. The Americans—who had picked the government to begin with—had chosen not to intervene, despite widespread opposition from most Iraqi women's groups to the selection of such an obvious Islamic fundamentalist. Many well-educated women vied for the position, including Rend al-Rahim, a Shia who did not veil. After she was rejected, she said that the decision was dominated by the deeply conservative, pro-Iranian heads of the Islamic parties in the Governing Council, including the Shia religious leader Abdul Aziz al-Hakim, the head of SCIRI, a pro-Iranian, deeply conservative Islamic group; and Ibrahim al-Jaafari, spokesman for the Islamic Dawa Party, another Iranian-funded Shia group.

The presence of al-Khafaji, a dentist by training, seemed only to be making things worse for those who were trying to help women. She went on television and, from beneath her veil, denounced all American and British "activists" in women's rights, as well as the female Iraqi exiles who had returned to the country. "Western-minded women who came with the occupation, carrying weird ideas and wanting to teach young Iraqis that it's their right to have premarital sex—Iraqis with all their tribal traditions won't accept these women," al-Khafaji told the press.

Manal didn't know a single activist who encouraged premarital sex. No one was talking about abortion, birth control, or whether Muslim women should wear the veil, or any such controversial issues. Up until then, women of all classes and religious affiliations had been united by the same issues: their desire to strengthen inheritance, divorce, and child custody laws in favor of women; to end honor killings; and to push for a quota of women in government. They wanted better education for girls, more women trained in business skills, and better health care. Manal had very carefully focused her efforts on training the women in the process of being a group—on fund-raising, organizing, and structuring their groups—not on their political message.

But politicians such as Salama al-Khafaji honed in on differences and stereotypes, skirting the issues that united women, focusing on divisions, and accusing Westerners in the Green Zone of lurid behavior that undermined Muslim values. Many conservative women openly disapproved of the legions of young Iraqi women working inside the Green Zone for the CPA. They remarked disparagingly about their tight jeans and excessive makeup, their unsupervised contact with men, and the rebellious ways they disobeyed their family in the name of "democracy." Some older women felt such behavior heralded a liberation and a return to the freedoms Iraqi women enjoyed in the 1960s and '70s, while al-Khafaji and others condemned it as un-Islamic and threatening to long-standing cultural traditions such as arranged marriage. Manal became convinced that al-Khafaji was a puppet for the Shia men on the Governing Council. They knew she would represent an extremist position for women, and yet should anyone complain, they could say, "You wanted a woman. Here she is." The strategy divided and silenced women.

At her weekly meetings, Manal noticed that women began to sit separately: the veiled in one corner and the unveiled in another. Manal had gravitated to the veil as a teenager as a way to stop people from judging her by her looks, but now she was finding the world of veiled women to be just as judgmental as, if not more than, the alternative. Even among the veiled women there were divisions between those who wore plain black veils or patterned, colored ones; between those who covered themselves not just with the veil but with gloves and socks, versus those who wore makeup, jewelry, or high heels under their veils. Manal's efforts to steer the veiled and unveiled women onto issues that they could agree upon, like health care, education, and participation in government, were futile.

As Manal saw it, for every self-righteous Islamist covered from head to toe there was a self-righteous secularist with a feminists-don't-veil mentality. Manal was in the middle, a progressive, liberal woman who also veiled. But her nuanced position was lost in the rhetoric. The veil was becoming to the Iraqi women's rights movement what abortion rights was in the 1970s to American women—the single polarizing issue that divided the movement in half and turned each side against the other. Without unity, we will never get anywhere, Manal tried to tell them.

Even Manal herself was not immune from the judgments, she discovered one day.

"Manal, it's good you wear a hijab but why do you wear trousers?" a veiled woman interrupted the meeting to ask. "Why not wear a skirt and be complete?"

With that, the unveiled women in trousers went into an uproar. "What does a skirt show?" said one. "A skirt is a piece of cloth. It's not religion."

When the uproar that followed finally died down, they turned back to Manal. "It is good that you have come all this way to help us," one said. "But who is taking care of your children in America?"

"Oh, I don't have children," Manal replied. The women studied her face, and Manal knew they were trying to guess her age. Clearly, she was of an age at which she *should* have children, they decided, and looked at her with suspicion: Would this women's center discourage women from having children? Manal knew she was up against Arab women's stereotypes about loose, single Western women who were "antifamily." She realized her personal life was becoming a distracting focus of controversy. Until then, she had been viewed not as an American, or a Western woman, but as a Muslim woman who looked like them, observed their customs and holidays, and spoke their language, albeit with a Palestinian accent. She didn't want to lie, but she also didn't want to hurt the burgeoning plans for the women's centers. The next time a group of women asked her a personal question, she offered a more diplomatic answer.

"Doesn't your husband mind you are here?" some woman asked her.

Manal shook her head. *"Id'eelee,"* she said, Arabic for "Pray for me."

"Oh yes, yes." The women nodded, satisfied that, at the very least, Manal agreed she *should* have a husband and children.

They promised to pray for her.

CHAPTER FIFTEEN

DAYLIGHT STREAMED AROUND the curtain's edge as Nunu watched Zia and Mamina prepare for a trip to the goldsmith's shop. Zia's $500-a-month salary was a lot of money, and the family needed some safe way of storing it. That wasn't easy to find: many families had lost all their money when the banks were looted after the invasion. So far, they had been hiding Zia's cash in a plastic Tupperware box in the refrigerator and in rice boxes in the cupboard, but, as word spread that Zia worked for the Americans, Baba worried they might be burglarized. Given the rising inflation, Baba suspected the currency would soon become worthless, and decided that gold jewelry was always a safe investment. The family goldsmith, Ali, had a tiny storefront in a neighborhood across town in Khadamiya that Mamina, Zia, and Nunu all used to visit together before the war.

Nunu didn't want to go with them today, since she didn't really feel safe out in the city these days, but she knew if she'd asked, Baba would have said no. He didn't try to stop Zia, though. It was a mark of increased respect for her, which surprised and pleased both sisters. Zia was the family's main breadwinner now, and this had boosted her status among their father and uncles. Each month, she bought the family a new gift—an air conditioner, a generator, Nunu's beloved television. "Not even a fifty-year-old man with a PhD could earn this salary," Zia proudly confided to Nunu, and she was only twenty-two. Zia would never directly disobey her father, but she did take advantage of the changing dynamic. Now when Umar visited, Zia sat in on the meeting and spoke with him as an equal, while Nunu stayed on the sidelines, where she'd always been more comfortable.

However, while she could work, drive, and financially sustain the family, Zia still could not tell Baba about Keith. Nunu and Mamina loved to hear her talk about Keith, though, and their evening ritual was to huddle in the bedroom after dinner and hear Zia's stories about her day among the Americans. Each night Zia entertained them with jokes Keith told, emails he sent, or the interesting insights he gave her into the occupation. When they heard Baba pass by the door, they lowered their voices. The three women knew there was nothing shameful about the friendship, but there was no way to know how Baba would react. In his heart, he might be okay with the idea, but society would pressure him not to accept it. Just as they had condemned Ehdaa's marriage to the soldier months ago, the shopkeepers, neighbors, and even Baba's friends would gossip and maybe even threaten the family if news spread that his elder daughter was romantically involved with an American. No one knew how Ehdaa's story had ended, but Zia assumed her family had caved in to pressure to punish her. Baba, too, would feel pressured to act. He would never lay a finger on his daughters, but he might force Zia to quit IMN, condemn her to the house, and maybe never speak to her again.

Yet, despite the possible consequences, Zia's relationship continued. Nunu loved hearing about this kind and chivalrous American—she knew that Zia secretly enjoyed the thrill of rebellion and forbidden romance. Each week, Zia and Keith saw more and more of each other. They made excuses to meet up for lunch, to take a stroll, or to pass each other in the corridors of IMN. When they didn't see each other they exchanged flirtatious emails or spoke on the phone. Zia made clear, though, that it was strictly platonic. She told Mamina that if Keith tried to hold her hand, she pulled away. He didn't dare try to kiss her, as she emphasized that Iraqi women had no physical contact before marriage. She admitted that she wasn't sure how Keith felt about this: sometimes he would say, with wonder in his voice, "This is the first time I've been only friends with a beautiful woman." This made Nunu giggle. It was clear to everyone that the unfulfilled desire only strengthened the magnetic pull between them.

Finally, Nunu began to tease her big sister.

"Ohhhh, Keith this and Keith that." She laughed. "You always find a reason to bring him into your stories."

Mamina nodded, smiling. "When you speak of him, your eyes shine."

Zia rolled onto her back and looked at the single exposed bulb that lit up the room. "He is wonderful, Mama."

"You love him!" Nunu exclaimed, delighted. Zia didn't deny it.

NUNU WAS SETTLING onto the sofa with her university books, in her favorite comfy spot, legs tucked under her, as Mamina and Zia finished preparations for the trip to the goldsmith. Mamina handed Zia a long shawl, which she draped around her head, wrapped around her neck, flipped back over her head, and pinned snugly below her left ear. Mamina did the same.

"Uh, I look like I'm from Najaf," Zia complained.

"You do," Nunu agreed from the couch. She hated seeing her mother and sister that way.

The sisters had only ever veiled when they visited conservative Iraqi places such as the holy Shia city of Najaf in the south, where it would be scandalous not to. They didn't like the pious, severe look of the hijab, and their family didn't believe the Quran mandated it. The Quran instructs women to dress modestly, saying a woman should "draw a scarf across her upper chest," but its translation is disputed; some Muslims believe that means only that women should not reveal their breasts, while others say the Prophet wanted women's bodies hidden completely under abayas. Another section in the Quran, invoked to pressure women to veil, states, "The wives and daughters of the Prophet and the women of the believers should draw a cloak close around them." But some people argue over the translation, believing that the Prophet did not say a cloak, but meant a curtain—like a door—to be drawn to give privacy to his wives when the husband's associates visit the house. Across the Muslim world, different societies interpreted the Quran differently, as exemplified by the vast array of different headscarf styles: some women show the tops of their hair and their necks, while others cover their face or even their eyes. Mamina had raised her children with a more liberal view of the veil as a symbol. "Islam is not a cloak you wrap around you. It is in your heart, and it is your character."

But since the invasion, more and more women in Iraq had donned the veil as a simple, practical safety measure. It also covered the streak of hair Zia had dyed blond years earlier. Ironically, such a symbolic adoption of Western trends was safer under Saddam than the U.S. occupation. Today, since they were traveling into volatile neighborhoods where Muqtada al-Sadr had supporters, any visual indication of loyalty to the USA was dangerous, even a streak of dyed-blond hair. Furthermore, Mamina didn't want to chance running into a gang that might try to kidnap her beautiful daughter. The anonymity of the veil, the way it hid any marker of femininity, was a layer of protection.

When they were finished, as they headed out the door, only their fingertips and faces showed.

Nunu watched them go, uneasily. "I'll make dinner," she said, waving goodbye as cheerfully as she could.

After they left, though, Nunu couldn't keep her mind on her texts. She was supposed to be studying poetry by Samuel Taylor Coleridge, and she had an exam coming. Usually Zia helped drill her, but she had been too busy lately. Nunu still felt unsettled at seeing her sister don a veil—even under Saddam they had rarely had to do so. She had certainly never imagined that women in the new Iraq would be forced to veil, and the thought frightened her.

Nunu tried again to focus on her texts, but studying felt unimportant these days—as did everything else. There was very little meaning or direction to her days. Since the new school year began, classes had been erratic. On a typical day, when not in school, she studied, cleaned the house, did the laundry, arranged the clothes in the closet, and took a nap. If Mamina and Zia went to the market, Nunu cooked. When her father returned home, he switched on the generator to watch the daily news, which was increasingly about attacks against soldiers and other Iraqis, or a helicopter downed, a building bombed. Many incidents occurred within miles of their house. The nerve-racking events unsettled Nunu.

On campus, things were changing too. When Nunu arrived in October, she was a little disappointed that everything looked the same. She had imagined new state-of-the-art facilities under construction, shiny textbooks from America, and laptops with Internet access in all the classrooms. Instead, it seemed worse than it had been before. Instead of laptops, the classrooms had no lights. The fans still didn't work, and the same wooden blackboard was on the wall; many things they used to have had gone missing during the looting. Student records had been destroyed, so confusion dominated the first few weeks of registration.

Even the joy of seeing the soldiers patrolling over the summer had faded. They visited less and less often, and when they did, they no longer waved.

"They never even look at us anymore," Nunu had complained to Zia.

"That's because the female civilians have arrived at the palace now from America, and they're prettier than we are," Zia explained.

"Oh," Nunu said glumly.

So she stopped waving at them, too, and the distance grew. Male students on campus didn't like the soldiers, and they glared at girls who waved to them.

One day recently, Nunu had been sitting on a stone bench with Noor and other friends, all in long skirts, with books on their laps, when three soldiers passed across the campus pavilion. Nunu watched them, thinking that, should robots drop from outer space, they would appear no less incongruous: their round helmets and steel-plated vests, their grenades, rifles, and ammunition, their big boots and camouflage pants, and their Humvees in the distance. Suddenly she was feeling uncertain about the military presence.

As she looked on, though, an older male student approached the soldiers and spat at one of them.

Nunu inhaled sharply, along with all the other nearby students, who froze in fear. Nunu considered running away, but she was too scared. The soldier stopped in his tracks and turned around. He eyeballed the Iraqi man, who stared back at him with hatred.

"He's dead," Nunu whispered to her friend. "The American will kill him right now."

Instead, another soldier said something and patted him on the arm. They walked away.

The story of the incident spread over the campus and the student was heralded as a hero. "The American soldiers are weak," the male students cheered.

Nunu and her girlfriends disagreed, however. "No, he didn't shoot him because he didn't want to hurt any innocent people standing nearby."

But the young men insisted. "They are afraid of us."

ZIA DIRECTED THE taxi to the goldsmith's shop in the Khadamiya neighborhood. To get there, the taxi would first pass through Adhamiya, a predominantly wealthy Sunni neighborhood that had emptied right after the invasion, as all the ex-Ba'athists had fled the country. In recent months, though, they had returned, and now the neighborhood was known among Baghdadis as a stronghold for Sunnis who opposed the Americans.

Zia settled back into her seat. Before she had left, she had been careful to empty her purse of her laminated badge that read U.S. COALITION FORCES. In recent months, Adhamiya had become a mecca for the *irhabeen,* slang for insurgents or terrorists, although the locals called them "jihadis," a more heroic term. Ex-Ba'athist families living in the plush homes, with gated driveways and inner courtyards, took in these fighters and helped organize through Syria a pipeline for arms and money to fuel resistance across Iraq. When unemployment skyrocketed after the Americans disbanded the army, government ministries, and state-run industries, the insurgency had become a kind of employment center, where a former soldier could earn twenty-five dollars for helping to lay down a roadside bomb or shoot a rocket-propelled grenade.

Zia was so busy with her job that she had spent very little time outside the Green Zone lately. Now, as she passed through the city, she felt depressed. The Green Zone always had electricity, clean streets, bottled water, and ample food. The feeling of upward momentum and progress was in the air as everyone talked excitedly about their democracy projects and the millions of dollars at their fingertips. But life outside the Green Zone, she was realizing, felt as stagnant as the brackish water pooling in the alleys. Rubbish piled up uncollected, and young men sat idly with worried faces. A trip through Baghdad that had once taken about twenty minutes could easily take an hour or two. Power outages meant the traffic lights didn't work, and many of the traffic police hadn't returned to the job. She didn't want to think that the occupation wasn't going well. It was easier to arrive early and stay late at work, safe in the bubble of the Green Zone.

Yet she had to admit to herself that even the Green Zone felt less safe lately. The growth of the insurgency was having a huge and worrisome impact on U.S. efforts in Iraq. Stories abounded of convoys attacked as they left the Green Zone, of roadside bombs and ambushes. No longer did anyone drive out of the Green Zone to have lunch or attend a meeting—that was considered too dangerous. The kind of lunch date that she and Keith had enjoyed only a month earlier might be too risky now, for fear that an insurgent waiting outside the gates could follow them and shoot into their car. Even inside the Green Zone, a siege mentality had started to take hold. Just last month, Iraqis pulling a donkey cart had launched thirteen rockets over the walls of the Green Zone at the Rashid Hotel, where Deputy Defense Secretary Paul Wolfowitz had been staying. One American colonel had been killed. Ever since then, several rockets a week were lobbed from outlying neighborhoods into the Green Zone. No one else had been hit, but the effect was unnerving.

Zia understood the enemy: tens of thousands of Sunnis still loyal to Saddam were launching the attacks, and they lived in neighborhoods like Adhamiya. They were joined by foreign fighters from Jordan, Saudi Arabia, and Syria, who had volunteered to be martyred in what they believed was an American-led Christian crusade against Islam. But few of her American colleagues understood what was going on, or even knew which neighborhood was Adhamiya. Many Americans had unknowingly hired ex–Saddam employees as translators and advisers, who intentionally gave them bad information, pointing the finger at Shia neighborhoods. New to Iraq, with no knowledge of Arabic, most Americans didn't understand the layers of Iraqi society, the allegiances, the religious loyalties, or the neighborhood affiliations. They didn't know whom to trust or what to believe. They saw only two groups: themselves and Iraqis. Us and them.

After the attack on the Rashid, the Americans had changed the way they dealt with their Iraqi staff. The insurgents who hit the hotel must have had help from the inside, people pointed out accusingly. Someone must have informed them as to where Paul Wolfowitz was staying.

The Americans decided to issue new security badges for all Green Zone employees. Zia's had a red rim around the edges. Only Iraqi employees had this red rim, she noticed. Before, there had been no difference in the badges worn by Iraqis and Americans. At checkpoint lines where soldiers used to flirt with her, now, instead, they sent her through a second round of security, emptying out her purse and waving a wand around her body. More and more sections of the palace and the Green Zone were closed off to those with red-rimmed badges. Inside the Green Zone, someone's level of security clearance denoted the importance of their job, their proximity to Bremer, and their special status. Iraqis, she realized, now had the lowest level of security of anyone— even Pakistani immigrants brought in to fill low-wage cleaning jobs had higher security.

A badge she had always worn with pride now felt like a marker. She felt humiliated.

"So they think all the Iraqis are spying on them?" she had said to Keith. "This is ridiculous. We're working here to help them. This is a dangerous job for us!"

Keith nodded, helpless. "They don't know who to trust."

EVENTUALLY, THE TAXI passed through Adhamiya and into Khadamiya. There was no sign marking the change of neighborhoods— Baghdadis just knew. Khadamiya was a devoutly Shia neighborhood, home to the shrine of the seventh imam, Musa al-Kadhim, one of the last known descendants of the Prophet. Green-and-white flags waved from homes, symbolizing Shia identity. Images of Mohammed Sadiq al-Sadr were tacked up onto shop windows, showing his black turban and long gray beard. Before he was killed by Saddam, al-Sadr was a prominent Shia grand ayatollah, and the father of the current militia leader Muqtada al-Sadr. Sunnis didn't recognize the authority of al-Sadr, and few Americans knew who he was or what he stood for, but everyone in Khadamiya knew.

Mother and daughter exited the cab and plunged themselves into the dusty open markets, packed with other black-robed figures. Mamina and Zia stayed close, identifying each other only by the white leather of Zia's purse and the gold handles of Mamina's. Dust rose from the ground and diffused the bright midday sun into a hazy glow. People pushed and bumped. Exhaust mixed with cooking smells. Spice markets displayed dozens of burlap sacks of sumac, cardamom, lentils, rice, and bulgur. Black leather sandals hung for sale on the open doors of the cobblers' homes.

Above the crowd, Zia could see the helmet and black sunglasses of a soldier moving toward them. He approached like a giant, poking through the roof of a Humvee, manning a swiveling gun, part of a line of Humvees cruising slowly down the traffic-packed streets. As they turned a corner, the gun swiveled on its axis, causing the crowd to collectively suck in its breath. Zia wanted to shout at the soldiers, "Get out of your car and talk to the people!" Zia knew lots of soldiers—she heard about their pet projects and saw photos of their families at home—so she could see them as humans, but most Iraqis saw only the barrels of their guns.

Zia didn't say anything, though, and eventually the convoy moved on. Zia heard a wake of disparaging chatter as she and Mamina hustled along the familiar route to the goldsmith.

"*Salaam aleikum*," they greeted Ali as the door chimes tinkled.

"*Wa aleikum salaam*," he replied.

Ali brought out a silver tray with three glasses of strongly brewed Lipton tea. The women heaped sugar into them as a sign of appreciation. They chatted, sharing the latest gossip and stories of run-ins with the military. Streams of Arabic were punctured by English terms like *security* and *the situation,* generalities that allowed Iraqis to complain without taking a position on who was to blame. There were worried shakes of the head. Once, it had been safe to openly endorse the Americans, but now it was better to be ambiguous, even among trusted friends.

Finally, Zia's eyes wandered across the glass counter filled with dangling gold bracelets, cuing the goldsmith to show them his favorite pieces. Her long, slender fingers danced around the jewelry, and eventually she settled on a white-gold bracelet that had grooves and a pattern that, to Zia, resembled a U.S. flag. She picked out one for Nunu as well, choosing a similar pattern, but smaller and in yellow. They settled on a price of five hundred dollars for both, and Zia paid in greenbacks.

Back outside, the women window-shopped for another fifteen minutes, and then caught one of the dozens of taxis zipping past. Dropping their packages onto the front seat, they rolled down the windows and relaxed their feet.

But halfway home, they hit a traffic jam created by a "Free Saddam" demonstration in Adhamiya. Mamina sighed angrily when she saw rows of praying men. Except for the end of Saddam's reign, his Ba'ath Party had discouraged Islam, but now they were acting like dutiful Sunnis and leading public prayer. "Look at these hypocrites," Mamina said to Zia. "They put on any mask to keep themselves in power. Why don't they pray in their houses?"

The taxi driver swiveled around. He was young, in his late twenties, with close-set eyes and a mustache over crooked teeth. "You'd better shut up. You're brainless. They're better than you and they're going to pray and you'd better be quiet."

The women were stunned, but Mamina was the quickest to recover. "You can't talk to me that way."

The taxi driver reacted fiercely, and the two quarreled until Mamina backed down, as she always did, willing to sacrifice position for peace. As the journey continued, though, the driver grew more agitated.

He told them he was a Sunni and had been a sniper in the Iraqi army until the Americans disbanded it after the invasion, leaving him with no source of income. He made general threats against the Americans. Zia, who had become used to these violent barrages, ignored him for a while.

"Yeah, I graduated from the academy and the Ba'ath Party gave me this car. I was someone important. Now I'm jobless. Soldiers are nobodies now in Iraq."

"You love Saddam?" Zia said.

"Yeah, I do. He was a real man. The Americans are bastards and soon we'll kick them out. We're working on that."

"Yeah, I love him too," Zia said, shooting a knowing look at Mamina. Her tone was sarcastic, but the taxi driver didn't notice.

"Oh yeah? That's good," he said.

The car rolled past the checkpoint outside Saddam's former palace, where a pretty, young Iraqi translator stood near the street. She was translating between the passing Iraqis and the soldiers.

"Look at them," the driver snarled. He lowered his voice and began to brag. "These translators are whores. I just killed two last week and I'm following the third. I'm just waiting for the right timing. The second one I killed while she was with the Americans. The bullet went through her heart; she was standing there translating and all of a sudden she fell down."

Zia and Mamina glanced at each other, and Zia's hand flew up to her hijab, to make sure it covered the streak of dyed blond hair. Mamina's tolerant expression was gone. She tried to keep the conversation flowing.

"Why did you kill them? They just want to make a living," she said. "You see beggars and street children and prostitutes. If they work, it's not to betray anyone. Where are they supposed to work?"

"What? Are you kidding?" he said. "A girl who works with an American? Men she doesn't know? I just can't believe it. They are dirty. Some of them get in a car alone with Americans. A girl with a man in the car—what does he do with her? They are infidels," he said.

Zia couldn't stop her hand from fiddling nervously with her headscarf. She had to get out of the car. Mamina directed the taxi driver down a side street several blocks from their house, and then they stood on the sidewalk, speechless, watching him disappear into the bustling city.

CHAPTER SIXTEEN

AS MANAL AND Heather were working to get their women's centers started in Baghdad, another U.S.-run women's center was being opened in southern Iraq, headed by a young woman who would become a close friend to Manal. Fern Holland was a blond, thirty-two-year-old attorney from Bluejacket, Oklahoma; she worked for the CPA in its south-central branch, sixty miles south of Baghdad in the Shia heartland of Hilla.

Like Heather, Fern was being given millions of dollars to build centers for women, and Manal was hoping to have Women for Women International offer a "rights awareness" program to the Hilla women through one of Fern's centers. Manal got in touch and Fern agreed to meet.

Once past the ring of polluted industry that circled Baghdad, Manal could reach Hilla in a ninety-minute drive down a four-lane highway that cut through empty desert. Hilla felt like a town ripped from the pages of the Old Testament, where families in mud-walled houses lived off fish from the rivers and dates from the palms. In places like these, national governments weren't recognized. Thousand-year-old tribes presided over legal and social matters. On the phone, Fern referred to Hilla as the "real Iraq." It wasn't the kind of place with many hotels, so Fern invited Manal to share her tiny room.

When Manal finally met Fern in person, she was taken by how out of place she looked in Hilla. She looked fresh out of an episode of *Little House on the Prairie,* with her long, straight hair, soft freckles, and a sweet dimpled smile that turned up to sky blue eyes. Her veil was not pinned tightly around her face, but pushed at least two inches back, so her bangs peeked through at the front. Fern made clear that she saw the veil as a symbol of oppression, and wore it only when she had to. She didn't seem to realize how controversial she was in conservative Hilla, or if she did, Manal thought, she used her presence to make a point.

Still, Manal was amazed at how much Fern had accomplished in just a few months. She already had a women's center up and running, and was working on a second one. In part, this was due to the freedom with which Fern could operate, since, unlike Heather, she was outside the confines of the Green Zone in Baghdad. The same security restrictions applied, but she ignored them. Fern even had her own car, and she drove herself among the small towns of Karbala, Kut, and Hilla, setting up her centers.

While they shared Fern's room, Manal noticed that Fern also worked herself to exhaustion. She returned to the room at midnight and sent email until two a.m. By dawn, she was up again. Even as she worked seven days a week, she complained about a lack of time. In addition to building a women's center similar to Manal and Heather's, Fern was also trying to put together an international women's rights conference at Babylon University. Her Iraqi coworker, Salwa Oumashi, seemed equally devoted. When she and Manal did take some time to get to know each other, Fern could be intense, accusing the Americans in the Green Zone of "running Iraq by remote control." Unlike Heather, a team player who had risen through the ranks of bureaucracies, Fern had a go-it-alone attitude. Manal learned she had worked all over the world, enrolling in the Peace Corps and traveling to Russia, Namibia, and other far-flung spots to work on legal issues. When the war started, she had volunteered to come to Iraq and take any job on offer. After a few weeks in Baghdad, she had been repulsed by the sheltered mentality inside the Green Zone, and volunteered to go to Hilla.

The day after Manal arrived, she went to visit the building Fern was renovating as her second women's center. She showed Manal the premises, and described her vision of fresh paint, desks, and new computers. Fern didn't speak Arabic, and as she disappeared inside the building, Manal chatted with two local guys whom Fern had hired to guard the site.

"Who was in this building before we took it?" Manal asked them.

When Manal heard the name, she almost fainted: Muqtada al-Sadr!

She knew that al-Sadr headed the most powerful anti-American insurgent group, the Mahdi Army, responsible for hundreds of attacks against U.S. soldiers. He had serious clout in the Shia regions. And she imagined he would be very unsupportive of a U.S.-run women's center.

When Fern returned, Manal tried to convince her to give back the building. "You don't want this building!" she told Fern. "You are in Hilla, you know, you are in al-Sadr's territory. You don't want to take a building from him."

But Fern didn't see it that way. From her perspective, women had been shunted aside for too long in the region, and she was going to put a stop to it. Why should Muqtada al-Sadr's needs take priority over her women? "It's not his building," she said.

"Fern, slow down," Manal said. "Look, you are talking about the south, you are not talking about Baghdad. And you can't constantly push—you have to build contacts and support."

Though she was very worried for Fern now, Manal admired her courage and commitment. Women's rights was something they would have to fight for—it wouldn't be handed to them—and Fern was unafraid to ruffle feathers to defend Iraqi women. Manal also admired her conviction, since she herself vacillated constantly: Were they pushing too hard, or not hard enough? Was Fern doing the right thing by putting herself out there, meeting people, and getting the job done? Or was she just going to make enemies and get herself hurt, or worse?

But when Manal saw Fern interact with the old, wrinkled widows, with small, faded tattoos on their faces to identify their tribal affiliation, almost invisible under the layers of black but for their callused, aged hands, she felt inspired. She realized that the local women had genuine affection for Fern. Around Hilla, they called her "daughter," "Barbie," and "the angel."

"If I don't stand up for these women, no one will," Fern said. Manal knew this was true.

MANAL SET UP a program in Fern's women's center, in which she sent women from Baghdad to train women in Hilla to teach classes to other women. After this, Manal returned to Baghdad, but she and Fern stayed in weekly, sometimes daily, email contact. She thought about her constantly; Manal knew how controversial a figure Fern was inside the CPA, where many people, including Sloan Mann, refused to work with her because of her disregard for security precautions. They considered her reckless, but Manal wavered on whether her new friend was courageous or cavalier. So many of the Americans were hiding inside the Green Zone; by contrast, Fern was actually spending time with those she was trying to help.

As the fall wore on, Fern's profile continued to rise. Even as she opened centers and ran programs, she had somehow found the time, by October, to head up the organization of a four-day international conference for Iraqi women. Manal again was impressed; the sheer logistics of holding a conference in Hilla were daunting.

"With no airport, how will the internationals get there?" she emailed Fern. "With few hotels in Hilla, where will everyone stay?"

Fern had taken care of everything. She organized buses from Baghdad and the regions. She convinced the head of Babylon University to allow the women to stay in dormitories and to host the conference. Fern didn't want the kind of showy media event the CPA had held in July. She wanted "real women," as she put it. She wanted to invite Baghdad dentists, doctors, and politicians, and to sit them next to poor, illiterate, and vulnerable farm women. She arranged for delegations of Kurdish women to come from the north. She arranged for buses to collect women from the Shia towns of Babil, Karbala, Najaf, Diwaniya, and Wasit in the south. The point was to unite Iraqi women of different sects, classes, and politics to work together for the greater good. Women from the group Muslim Sisters Organization, in black cloaks, gloves, and socks, would sit at tables with former expats such as Rend al-Rahim, who was about to be appointed Iraq's first female ambassador to the United States. The conference would be called "The Heartland of Iraq."

As the conference gained momentum, more and more U.S. groups attached themselves to Fern's coattails. As Manal saw what was happening, she grew more uncomfortable. The three groups hosting the event, the American Islamic Congress, Women for a Free Iraq, and the Iraq

Foundation, were the same Pentagon-backed groups that had dominated the July conference of which both she and Fern had so fiercely disapproved. Manal worried that, while Fern's instincts and intentions were clearly good, she couldn't stand up to Bremer, and she simply didn't understand the complexities of bringing this kind of change to a country like Iraq.

By the time Manal saw the agenda for the conference, she realized that Fern's initial mission had been hijacked by those more powerful than her in the CPA, whose support she needed. The conference didn't include any of the types of issues Manal felt the women needed— shelters, health care, human rights, reconciliation, or education. It focused on democracy training, and as far as Manal was concerned, that served the Bush administration's political agenda, not the Iraqi women's social one. Maybe Fern's guest list was egalitarian, but the speakers and topics were elitist. And the fact that all this would happen in Hilla, a conservative town surrounded by poor, religious, struggling farmers who worried more about their next meal than about elections, seemed a recipe for disaster. What would the local men think when they saw all this attention for women? A clash seemed inevitable, but there seemed little that could be done to prevent it.

"You need to keep an Iraqi face on this," she warned Fern, who agreed with her. But then, mere weeks before the conference, Manal heard that U.S. National Security Advisor Condoleeza Rice had prepared a video message to be shown to the attendees, and Ambassador Bremer was going to fly down by helicopter from Baghdad to congratulate the audience.

At this, Manal called Fern again. "Condoleeza Rice? Fern, I wouldn't do that. It's not going to go over well." Rice was the female face of an occupation that was growing more and more unpopular. Manal thought it inappropriate to bring together Iraqi women under the pretext of listening to them, but then involve people with specific political and military agendas. It smacked of helping them, but only on U.S. terms. Help with strings attached.

But few others saw it that way, and by then it was out of Fern's hands. If Rice wanted to speak, Fern wouldn't have been able to stop her. Manal saw that Fern, like so many other well-intentioned people and projects in this occupation, was being tugged in different directions by powerful people, and that no progress would be made.

Manal decided not to attend.

HEATHER HEARD A lot about the "Heartland of Iraq" conference as it approached, and, for all that she knew Fern was a controversial figure, she was glad to know someone was making progress on women's issues. She and Manal had gotten off to a slow start with their own centers, and Heather realized that her estimation of "a couple of weeks" to open the first center had been pure fantasy. A month had passed, Manal still didn't have Iraqi women for the board of directors, and Heather was bogged down in the process of finding a building.

There were two ways to get property in Baghdad. Either you arrived with guns and thugs and seized it by force, which was how most of the Iraqi political parties operated, or there was the correct way: go through the CPA's Office of Facilities Management, which tried to keep track of available properties—mostly former offices of the Ba'ath Party, or mini-mansions owned by Saddam's officials. The Americans now officially owned them and were trying to award them to new political parties or civil society groups like the women's center. Heather had imagined that she would simply look through the grid coordinates for available properties, visit a few, pick a building, and start renovation. However, Manal recognized that different neighborhoods were dominated by different tribes and religious affiliations, and insisted the Iraqi women have input on every decision.

"You can't just force a center on women. They have to be part of the process," Manal said. Heather knew she was right, but it took time. Given the security restrictions on Heather, and the many roadblocks and traffic jams the Iraqi women might face—not to mention the sheer difficulty of explaining directions in a city that didn't use street names or signs—the logistics of bringing everyone together at a site was overwhelming. Heather had to reserve a convoy of Humvees, then get security clearance to bring the Iraqi "site survey" women into the Green Zone, then find them flak jackets and helmets. One trip to see a building could occupy the entire day.

A few weeks in, they found the perfect building—a former Ba'ath

Party office that everyone agreed on. But then an old man suddenly turned up claiming the Ba'athists had stolen it from him. "It was my art institute," the old man said. "We thought when the Ba'ath Party was gone, we'd get our building back." He had all the paperwork. Heather gave him back his building, and started the search again.

The next "perfect" building was one that a Kurdish political party also wanted. Heather fought hard for it and won by lobbying her contacts inside the CPA. But when Manal found out that Heather had wrested it from a political party, she backed away.

"We can't take it from them," she said to Heather.

"No, don't worry," Heather assured her. "We talked to the right people and we're going to get it. It's ours."

But Manal shook her head. Perhaps Heather had the legal authority according to the CPA, but on the streets, muscle mattered.

"If we inherit that building," Manal told her, "the Kurdish party will move somewhere crappy, then they'll drive by and see us inside with our lights on and our computers and women going in and out. What do you think they'll do? Even if the leaders understand, the guards will come after us."

Heather understood that "come after us" meant physically attack the center. Would the local police department stand up to a Kurdish group to defend a women's group? Manal doubted it. Was there even a local police department up and running? No one was certain. So it was back to the drawing board. Weeks turned into months. Heather was getting frustrated.

So, when she heard about Fern's centers in Hilla, she was impressed that Fern had managed to accomplish so much. She knew Manal was not attending the conference, but had assumed she was too busy. Early in the conference, Heather joined a busload of Iraqi women on a morning excursion to see the historical sites of Babylon. Spirits on the bus were high as the women were enjoying a three-day getaway, all meals and accommodations included, with no housework or hovering husbands. This was their chance to participate in the massive changes occurring in their country, which they had only heard about on television. The women clapped and sang songs the entire trip. At one point, they turned to Heather and Stephanie Kuck, who had come with her: "American song!" they insisted. Heather chose Woody Guthrie's "This Land Is Your Land." It seemed appropriate.

When the conference started and she saw all the attendees, Heather breathed a sigh of relief. At least someone was getting something done. *Nice,* she thought, looking at the agenda. It was packed with interesting workshops, speeches, and discussions on democracy: How could they ensure women were involved in the new Iraqi constitution? How could they improve women's chances of getting elected to political positions? The leaflets distributed asked questions such as "What is democracy? Does it mean majority rule, and if so, what protections ought there to be for minorities? Does freedom require the separation of religion and state?" This was exactly what the women needed, she thought happily.

The first day of the conference, the women gathered in the auditorium of Babylon University. One of the organizers asked women from each of the different provinces in Iraq to stand up. Each group had a smattering of women either veiled in colored headscarves, unveiled, or in all-black abayas. However, when the organizer called out the Najaf province, every woman was cloaked entirely in black. Many even wore gloves and hoods, with slits for their eyes. Heather rarely ran into women like this in Baghdad, and seeing them in such force emphasized for her how vast and diverse Iraq's female population was. It was never going to be easy to do something that would need the approval of such a wide spectrum of women.

She peered curiously toward the women in black. The black cloak was an intimidating barrier to friendly conversation. How could she tell if the woman was smiling, or happy to speak with her? Without being able to see her mouth, Heather feared she wouldn't understand her Arabic, and the conversation would become awkward. *What if I run into her later, and don't recognize her?* It was easier to socialize with the Iraqi women who looked and dressed more Western. From what Heather could see, the Najaf women also stayed in a tight huddle, speaking only to one another. Sometimes she caught them staring at her, though, and she wondered what they thought. She imagined she must look unusual to them, as an American woman in soldier's fatigues.

The conference hosts were Iraqi women: Rend al-Rahim, Zainab al-Suwaij, Safia al-Souhail, Ala Talabani, and Tanya Gilly. They were mostly expats, professional women who had lived outside Iraq for a decade or more and had contacts inside the Bush administration. One of the first speakers, Rend al-Rahim, looked more like the CEO of a Fortune 500 company in America—nothing like the Najaf women. She told the audience that women's rights were impossible without democracy. "If women want government to be responsive to their needs, they will need institutions that ensure that their leaders are representative and accountable." Heather saw some women sitting attentively in the lecture seats, pens at hand and conference literature on their laps. Other women, the conservative ones, sat stone-faced in the back.

Heather drove back to Baghdad and returned the following day. She saw that the organizers had tried to overcome the women's self-imposed ethnic and religious divisions and force them into collaborative workshops on governance. Someone had brought copies of the Swiss constitution, the only one the organizers could find in Arabic. During lunch, Heather shared a table with a group of Iraqi women, and found herself transported back to high school civics class as she explained the differences between central and local government, and the separation of powers. As the question of freedom in a democracy came up again and again, Heather saw how the textbook philosophy collided with the messy reality of life in Iraq.

"Who has which freedoms?" the women wanted to know, and "Where do they end?"

Rather than welcome freedom, the women complained about it.

"Too much freedom is not good because men take advantage of this freedom and rape women," one participant pointed out to her. Many in the room nodded in agreement.

"Men shouldn't have so much freedom. They must be controlled," said another.

"Under Saddam, at least I could leave the house. Now I don't have the freedom to do that."

Heather listened empathetically. "Freedom doesn't come at the exclusion of the rule of law," she explained, adding, "We're working on that."

Throughout the meeting, she caught glimpses of Stephanie Kuck doing the same, and briefly met Fern, who was running around. Her straw-colored hair brushed loosely around her shoulders and she was harried but pleasant. She congratulated Fern on the conference, and they chatted briefly. Fern struck Heather as friendly, intelligent, and passionate about her work.

As she left the university at the end of the day, she noticed Iraqi men protesting outside the gates. They had hung banners across the doorways, but Heather couldn't read what they said.

Great! she thought. Under Saddam, no one was allowed to protest, but under democracy, they were free to express their voices. Protests show that people feel comfortable expressing their opinions freely. Protests are progress.

THE PROTESTS WERE not good, thought Zainab al-Suwaij. The conference was a disaster and the Americans had no idea.

Manal was not the only woman with strong concerns about how the conference would play in conservative southern Iraq. Zainab was one of the hosts and a speaker, and an acquaintance of both Manal and Fern. A founder of Women for a Free Iraq, she was the granddaughter of a well-respected Shia ayatollah, and had fled Iraq for Boston in 1993. She had worked with Fern to arrange this conference, but had disagreed with her idea to invite such a variety of women. What to Fern was diversity, to Zainab was a toxic mix. Bringing Sunnis and Shias together was a volatile combination, but Fern had gone out of her way to invite the most extremist and intolerant of the Shia groups—even supporters of Muqtada al-Sadr and the Fadhila Party, another Iranian-backed group.

Being new to the country and not speaking the language, Fern had little way of knowing that many of the women she had invited were from politically active families who had risen up against Saddam in the 1980s and '90s. After he killed hundreds of thousands of Shia after the first Gulf War, and enforced his police state, many disappeared into Iran to hide out and wait. Zainab thought of them as "sleeper cells" waiting for a crack in Saddam's armor, so they could return to Iraq. The Americans gave them their chance to return to power, but their political goal was not democracy. They wanted to create an Islamic state, dominated by Shias, just like in Iran. They also wanted revenge against those who had supported Saddam and killed their family members. The Americans had helped them do something they never would have done on their own—establish a Shia power in Iraq. Now they wanted the Americans out of the way.

"Fern, don't let these people into the conference. They will disrupt it," she had argued. But Fern had insisted. Unlike Manal, Zainab had agreed to attend. And now, of course, they were interrupting and arguing at every turn.

Zainab had agreed to give the controversial talk about the role of Islam in the new Iraqi government and constitution. She was firm on this subject: government and religion should be separate, to maintain the purity of the Islamic religion. Yet, when she broached the topic of separation between mosque and state, the Najaf women objected.

"Does she mean that religious men and women can't be part of politics?" shouted one black-clad woman in the crowd. "This will make us a secular society—and we will not stand for a secular society!"

Fierce agreement was expressed. "The mosque should be the state," said another. "Islam is tolerant of other religions, so it should be the official religion of Iraq," one woman said.

"*La, la,*" Zainab said, "no, no." "In Iraq, politics and religion have always been separate."

But these women seemed to have been prepped with arguments beforehand, as they stuck loyally to their line, "the mosque should be the state." She overheard them saying, "Democracy means rule by the people. That is forbidden. God must rule, not people."

She thought to herself, *These are extremist ideas from Iran.* They want a theocracy and nothing less. The Shia found the notion of the separation of mosque and state outrageous, and interrupted whenever they could.

The Western women weren't helping matters. Most conservative Iraqi women ridiculed them behind their backs.

"Why are these American women here—why don't they go home and take care of their children and their husbands? American women are against marriage and families. They abandon their elderly parents and let their children misbehave. Look at how they are dressed—they want to teach our daughters to be prostitutes. Don't speak to them!"

With each passing day, the male crowds outside the university thickened. Local residents accused the Americans of brainwashing the women. In the evenings, an Islamic scholar arrived at the dormitories, uninvited, and began to proselytize to the women, warning them of "foreign" ideas brought by the Americans. Zainab heard that young clerics loyal to Muqtada al-Sadr spread rumors in their Friday sermons that Americans in the conference were planning to offer "free abortions" to the women and "show porn" to the men.

Zainab and other women stood up to the protesters, and tried to reason with them. This is what freedom means: you have a right to express yourself, and we will listen, but now we have the right to speak too. If you believe in freedom and democracy, if you say you do, then you must let women speak.

But they didn't care about freedom or democracy. They cared about Islam.

The Americans seemed unaware of the controversies, which unfolded entirely in Arabic. And the Americans understood only Sunni and Shia—not the dozens of different, layered groups that stratified each. If they did hear of complaints or controversies, they characterized them not as serious threats but as freedom of expression—and even encouraged them.

At the end of the conference, the organizers submitted four recommendations to Ambassador Bremer, who had arrived to give the closing remarks. 1. Women should make up 30 percent of all committees responsible for drafting the new Iraqi constitution. 2. All laws discriminatory toward women should be repealed. 3. The future constitution should require that the Iraqi parliament have a quota of no less than 30 percent women. 4. Monitoring committees should be established in all Iraqi institutions to ensure women's rights are protected and promoted.

The videotape from Condeleeza Rice was shown, a huge coup for the organizers, but Rice was a woman who represented the military occupation to the local women. Zainab saw the Americans congratulating themselves. For them, the four days had been enlightening and educating—they believed that it had raised awareness, organized the women's groups, and unleashed newfound energy to tackle women's rights. Zainab, however, thought that although the conference was effective on paper, it had in fact cemented the bitter differences. To the men of Hilla the conference was a slap in the face, and they were furious. Fern would have been much better off lying low and not challenging the Iraqi men so publicly. Zainab's driver had told her that even the man Fern had hired to operate the sound system had been outside helping hang signs that said THESE ARE FOREIGN IDEAS AND THEY ARE AGAINST ISLAM. DO NOT LISTEN.

She warned Fern about one employee in particular.

"Are you sure?" she said.

"Fern, I don't know what is going on but this guy is playing double agent with you. He is showing you one face, but what he feels inside is something else. Please pay attention and be careful. You must not trust anyone here."

But Fern quickly became distracted by all the other things to do. She had a good heart, Zainab thought, but that wouldn't be enough. Fern had her vision of Iraq, and she had her vision of how this would all play out. She didn't want to hear otherwise. She listened only to what she wanted to hear.

CHAPTER SEVENTEEN

ZIA JUMPED WHEN her phone rang as she sat in her office. She hadn't forgotten the crazy taxi driver's threats, and it made her more nervous than she used to be. For the past several weeks, she had been driving herself to work, since no one took the Green Zone bus anymore. Everyone agreed publicly that their different work schedules made coordination impossible, but that was only part of the truth. A gunman had recently opened fire on a bus of cleaning ladies driving into the Green Zone. No one had been hit, but the message was clear. Zia felt it safer to drive herself.

Right now, though, she had a different thing to worry about.

"Zia, your father is on the grounds!" her friend whispered when Zia answered the phone. "He is asking around for Keith."

Oh no, Zia thought. Baba knew people at IMN because he had installed the security fence in the fall. Everyone had been gossiping about her and Keith lately, so it was not surprising that one of the workers must have ratted her out to Baba—Arab men always stuck together. She looked out her window and saw Baba standing on the grass, chatting with a circle of workers.

She knew he would be circumspect, not wanting to spread any dangerous gossip about his own daughter. However, simply by being here he was sending her and the office workers a clear message that he was aware of what was happening, and didn't approve. Zia quickly called Keith.

"Don't come over!" she said. "My father's here. He's looking for you."

"I'll come over and talk to him. We should meet," he said.

Zia drew in a breath. "Keith, no. You can't just meet my father casually. That would be very insulting."

Keith didn't understand. "What are you talking about? Let me talk to him."

"No. Keith, stay where you are. Promise me."

Zia called Mamina, who warned her, "Hide from him, Zuzu. Don't let him find you or Keith. He is coming to threaten Keith to stay away from you."

Baba stayed for an hour or so, and then left without seeing either of them. When Zia returned home that night, she waited nervously for him to say something, but Baba ignored her. She wondered how much longer she'd be able to sustain this careful equilibrium between her Iraqi traditions and her new "American" freedoms.

WHILE IT WASN'T yet causing real problems at home, by December her and Keith's relationship was starting to make things complicated at the office. They had done their best to hide their feelings for each other, but the merest hint of friendliness between a man and woman started the rumor mill going. Zia's office was next to the office for IMN security, and Iraqi men constantly came and went, peering into her office each time, and noting Keith's lunchtime presence. Closing the door would only fuel more speculation.

Some friends were happy for her, but others were nasty, and the workers who didn't know her well were even worse. Zia continued to rise at IMN and was now one of the most senior Iraqi employees; her position provoked envy from the women and sneers from her male underlings. Many of IMN's blue-collar jobs were filled by poor Iraqi men from conservative Shia neighborhoods such as Sadr City. They smiled at the Americans and said "Welcome!" and "Bush good!" But in Arabic, Zia heard them cursing their employers and speaking of the humiliation of having foreign soldiers in the Arab homeland. They called them *"kafirs"* and "traitors," even as they accepted paychecks from them.

As angry as these men were at the Americans, they were even more upset by Iraqi women, like Zia, who dressed in Western clothes. They whispered "whore," and worse, as she passed. Once, Zia passed a group sitting on a blanket on the ground having lunch, and the men leered up at her.

"When you wear those pants I can see your pussy. I am thinking of you naked and I can imagine everything."

At first, the women complained, and a few of these men were fired. But Zia feared making enemies who might wait outside the gates of IMN for her. So she said nothing.

All of this made Zia nervous. There were too many reasons for others to dislike her—her job with the occupiers, her position as manager within the office, and now her taboo relationship with an American man. Her heart, however, didn't give her much choice: she and Keith grew closer each day. In the evenings, instead of drinking with his contractor buddies, he returned to his trailer and called her at her parents' house. They talked for hours each night. Zia suspected he was falling in love with her, but he showed no signs of moving their relationship forward formally. An Iraqi man and woman wouldn't dare spend so much time together before getting formally engaged, but Keith seemed comfortable. He said they were dating.

They didn't have the luxury of waiting forever, though, even if Zia had wanted to. Events were already conspiring to bring their relationship to a head. One afternoon, a call came in from Mamina's youngest sister, a conservative, traditional woman who liked to meddle in family affairs. She was the self-appointed family matchmaker. She had found two Iraqi brothers living in London who were looking for wives, and who preferred two sisters. She had sent photos of Zia and Nunu. Liking what he saw in the photo, the elder brother had dispatched his extended family to make a formal offer. First they would propose to Zia, then, after a few months, if that marriage went well, a second offer would be made to Nunu.

When Mamina called with the news, Zia had been at the Republican Palace, entering a meeting with senior American officials from IMN. Among her new, Western friends, an arranged marriage looked backward, and she felt embarrassed at her mere involvement in it. Moments later, her aunt called, clearly thrilled with herself over the news. "Well, what do you think of this offer?" she asked her niece. Zia was noncommittal.

"I think it would be best if you gave him my email and told him to contact me first."

Her aunt was indignant at the suggestion. "Who do you think you are—Brooke Shields?" she fumed. The call ended quickly.

Judging by Mamina's face when Zia walked in the door that evening, her aunt had not let the matter drop, despite Zia's lack of enthusiasm. Nunu, by contrast, was beside herself with excitement.

"Am I going to London?" she sang excitedly.

Zia ignored her and went straight into the bedroom to have her nightly conversation with Keith. She told him about the proposal and tried to laugh about it.

"He knows only my weight, my height, and my appearance, and he wants to marry me? What, does he think I'm a cow at the market?"

Nunu had been hanging around the bedroom with a long face during the phone call. After Zia hung up, she bristled. "You're being very hasty."

"Things are different since the Americans arrived," Zia said. "We should know our husbands beforehand and talk to them."

"They're not different," Nunu argued. "You can talk with your husband after you're engaged."

Mamina arrived, closing the door and shushing her daughters.

"Zia, what are you thinking?"

"I want to marry Keith."

"Yes, *habibti*. But what does Keith say about this?"

Zia looked annoyed by the question. Mamina's joy at her daughter's heady feeling of love had recently hardened into more practical questions: When would Keith propose? Where was the ring? And what was the plan to convince Baba? Zia had given only vague answers, because that's all she had. The Americans said things would improve, and Zia believed them, and she dreamed of living in Baghdad with Keith as her husband, both of them working for the U.S. embassy.

"*Insh'allah*," Mamina had said, "God willing." Everyone wanted to believe these dreams. But Mamina and Nunu had their doubts, since they never went inside the Green Zone; for them this American world felt much less real. They saw what the rest of the country saw: unemployment, insecurity, and the rising influence of violent religious gangs like Muqtada al-Sadr's. Mamina wanted Zia to be happy, but she also wanted a resolution, quickly, for both daughters, who were already well within the age that they should be married. Two highly educated brothers, living abroad, was a dream offer. Nunu agreed. She reminded Zia about Aunt Huda, Mamina's oldest sister, who had refused several proposals when she was in her twenties. She had been in love with a Christian doctor, but he married another woman, and she never got over him. When she finally married at forty, it was too late to have children.

Nunu volunteered an idea: "I will marry this older brother, to save you for Keith," she said. "Then, if Keith doesn't marry you, you can marry the younger brother."

Zia liked this idea. But the plan soon fell apart. How could they explain to their aunt in London why Nunu would marry first? It was no use: their stubborn aunt had made it clear that the family wanted both of the sisters, or neither.

"Oh, Mama, I don't know what to do." Zia sighed, exhausted.

"Okay, *habibti,* go to sleep. I will delay your aunt."

Lying in bed, Zia felt torn between her love for Keith and her duty as a daughter. She knew her mother feared a big family fight. This aunt was a proud, forceful woman, who labeled herself a conservative Islamist, although Zia considered her a hypocrite. In London, she drove a fancy car and sent her children to good schools. She embraced conservative Islam only because she lived in a Western country, far from the reality of such extremism. From her life of luxury, she preached to everyone else about the dangers of romantic notions and about a woman's obligation to marry for duty. If she didn't get her way, her aunt invoked Islam to shame the entire family.

Should she discover Zia's relationship with Keith, she might convince the uncles to force Zia to marry this man. Perhaps they would conspire with the suitor's family to abduct Zia. Once Zia was in London, he would probably force himself on her on their wedding night, and then she'd have no choice but to be his wife. Zia shuddered at the thought. This had happened to other girls, and Zia was not sure Baba would stand in the way.

A FEW DAYS later, Nunu was home from university in time for lunch. She flipped on her battery-powered radio and sang along with one of her favorite Lebanese artists as she chopped some parsley, tomatoes, and onions. She ate quietly by herself, and left food for Baba and Mamina. After lunch, Nunu shuffled through the tiny hallway with the two doors leading to the bedrooms, flopped onto her bed, and pulled her pink notebook from the side table. She opened to a clean page, and her thoughts turned to her future husband. "I am going to get married!" she wrote. These last few weeks had been the most exciting of her life. She had completely ignored her university classes, giving herself over to fantasies of her new role as a wife and writing in her journal: "Soon I will be married and have a husband and a house before all my classmates. Oh, how they'll envy me! Will I go to London?"

She laughed at herself for being so vain, though she couldn't help but admit that this was what she truly wanted. She was scared to end up a spinster. Mamina always said, "All the women born in the 1960s are spinsters, and all the women born before then are widows." It is said that 100,000 Iraqis died in the Iran-Iraq war in the 1980s—most of them bachelors—and many more single men were killed in the Shia uprising in the early 1990s. After that, all the smart, successful men fled Saddam's regime. For this, many mothers hated Saddam: he killed the women's sons and made their daughters spinsters. She didn't have to look far for an example. Nunu had five uncles. All but one had fled Iraq.

Nunu felt her sister going in the opposite direction. *American women this and American women that . . .* Zia would go on. Nunu wished for her sister's happiness as much as her own. *May Zia reach the great destiny that she was denied during Saddam's time. If she loves Keith, may they marry and be given the greatest blessing of children.* But Nunu was secretly annoyed with Keith. Why had he not yet asked Baba's permission? Maybe he would wait a long time, in the unhappy American custom of "dating," and then change his mind. This was not acceptable in Iraq. Some Iraqi men asked women out on "dates" just to test their character. If the woman said yes, he considered her dirty and would never propose, but a no meant she had purity and deserved a proposal. Yet Zia had already been out on a date with Keith to a restaurant; they had even been alone together in his car. Nunu flushed at the thought. Although she knew her sister would not give in to temptation, she felt Zia was taking too many risks. If word spread of her relationship with Keith, she would never receive a marriage proposal from another Iraqi man, and neither would Nunu. The gossips believed that if one sister is dirty, the other one probably is too.

At the same time, though, she knew how precious it was to be in love, and couldn't believe her sister was wrong for chasing that dream. We are all weak in the face of love, Nunu felt. She had been in love once, with a young man at her university. When it went sour, the experience hurt Nunu like no physical pain she had felt before.

It all began one afternoon on campus shortly before the war, when she looked up and noticed a young man staring at her. He was movie-star handsome, with gelled short black hair and wide, soulful eyes. She had shyly averted her gaze. A few days later, she saw him staring at her again. They never spoke, but his attention had thrilled her. Each day, she rushed home to tell Zia everything.

Then, one morning, between classes, she saw him break away from his friends and walk toward her. Her heart galloped wildly. She felt her face turn red and her hands were trembling. When he reached her, all of Nunu's girlfriends fell silent.

"I want to propose to you," he said to Nunu. "If I do, will you agree?"

Nunu kept her gaze lowered. "Yes," she managed. He walked back to his friends.

All of her girlfriends had broken into feverish whispering as they congratulated Nunu. She had flown home on wings. That evening, she and Zia had sketched out designs for wedding dresses and imagined different bridal hairstyles. For weeks afterward, Nunu peered past the curtains to the courtyard, awaiting his arrival with his friends and relatives to see Baba.

But he never came.

When Nunu saw him at college after that, he looked once or twice at her, but then stopped looking. Nunu was shocked. She lay like a zombie on the bed at night. "Why didn't he ask Baba?" she wondered. She replayed in her mind the way she had said "Yes." Perhaps she had been too forward, and should have said "Maybe." She wondered if he had inquired in the neighborhood about her reputation, and learned something shameful that he didn't approve of. Impossible, Zia assured her: Nunu had nothing to hide.

Eventually, the shock was replaced by a deep depression. "I loved him," she moaned. "My heart is broken now."

Such memories saddened Nunu. At nineteen years of age, and having had no contact with men, she succumbed easily to romantic fantasies of destiny, fate, and pure love. She imagined Zia would feel the same if she lost Keith, and she couldn't wish that on her sister, no matter how much she wanted to marry the younger brother in London, whom she felt certain would be handsome, kind, and generous. If God wills me to marry him, then I will cook and clean for him, keep a garden with roses, and be a good wife, she vowed to herself. *Destiny will decide,* she thought. When she was done writing, she lifted herself off the bed and carried her journal into the kitchen. Nunu always burned her journal pages just after she finished writing them. She carefully ripped them out, turned on the gas, and lit them with a match. She held each of the pages as her curling script disappeared into black embers, and then dropped them into the sink before the flames singed her hand.

MAMINA HAD ALWAYS bent her will to the desires of her family in order to keep the peace, and she could do little to dissuade her bossy older sister. Eventually, her sister arranged for the suitor's family to arrive and propose to Zia. As the women raced around readying the house for the guests, Baba turned on the television and lit a cigarette, indicating his intention to be left out of his daughters' love lives until all the details had been sorted out and only his final approval was needed. The women disappeared into the bedroom and whispered furiously. Nunu wanted Zia to accept. Zia wanted to wreck the imminent proposal by turning off the suitor's family so they would rescind the offer; Mamina wanted the proposal to proceed to the point that Zia could use it as leverage with Keith.

Neither Zia, Mamina, nor Nunu knew for sure what would happen, but Zia was determined to scare them off if she could, even though she knew that would make things difficult for her mother, aunt, and sister. Before the guests arrived, Zia plucked a denim jacket out of the closet and slipped it on. She knew the suitor's family would recoil at the sight of her in Western clothing.

Mamina clucked her tongue in disapproval.

"Zia, think of your interests. This boy lives in London, and is getting his PhD."

But Zia kept the jacket and the tennis shoes on. She even smeared white powder all over her face so she looked pale and unhealthy. As she was looking at herself with satisfaction in the mirror, the doorbell rang.

A half dozen uncles, aunts, cousins, and close family friends crowded the small space of the living room, filling the hard-backed sofas lining the walls. Chairs were pulled in from the dining room, and nearly ten minutes of greetings, introductions, and blessings ensued. *"Salaam aleikum,"* they all said, kissing one another lightly on the cheek.

"This is the bride!" an uncle exclaimed, clasping Zia's hands as Mamina smiled. Zia admired her mother's composure, as she herself could barely hide her nerves.

Finally, everyone settled in, and Baba and the men lit cigarettes.

"Did you arrive here without any problems? Did the American soldiers stop you at any checkpoints? Were any roads closed?" Mamina asked.

Thanks to God, their travel was smooth, the family replied.

"This is good," Mamina said. "You know, the situation . . ."

"Yes, the situation . . ." the uncle said. No one spoke further, not wanting to introduce any biases or affiliations into the new relationship. On everyone's mind was Saddam, as he had just recently been captured in a spider hole after nine months in hiding. Zia's family had gathered around the television to rejoice in the images of the Americans inspecting Saddam's teeth and picking through his filthy hair. But the most obvious topic of conversation was the one most likely to be avoided. Sensitive political subjects such as Saddam, the Americans, and Sunni or Shia would be avoided for fear of disagreement.

Zia and Nunu disappeared into the kitchen to prepare coffee. As Nunu arranged a dozen tiny, gold-rimmed glass cups on a silver tray, Zia said to her sister, "You will serve coffee, Pepsi, and then bitter coffee." It was a loaded choice. If the meeting ends with coffee instead of juice, it is usually a sign of the bride's refusal. Once the coffee was poured, Zia pushed the tray at her sister.

"Zia, no!"

Serving the suitor's family was the first important indication of a potential daughter-in-law's temperament. Would she be eager, obedient, and hardworking, or a lazy princess? Sending Nunu out with the tray would send a strong message to the family that Zia was the latter.

Nunu stumbled out the kitchen door with Zia's hand on her back. As Nunu served the coffee and Zia settled comfortably onto a couch, the aunts exchanged looks. One swept her eyes over Zia's jeans and tennis shoes, and her face turned to stone.

"She doesn't really look like her photos," the woman remarked casually to everyone. "If she marries my nephew, she shouldn't expect to live the kind of life she has now, wearing tennis shoes and this *ajnabi* jacket."

Mamina cut in, explaining that Zia had returned to the house late because of "the situation." "She had no time to change," Mamina lied. Zia realized that mentioning her work was dangerous territory. If the suitor's family knew she worked with the Americans, not only would the proposal be promptly rescinded, but Zia's family would likely never receive another one for her, or for Nunu.

"Both girls studied at Baghdad University and are fluent in English," Mamina added, deftly changing the subject. Zia admired how her mother controlled the situation, all while sitting alongside Baba with deference.

The suitor's aunt had brought a camera to take pictures of Nunu and Zia, but she left it turned off on her lap. Instead, she pulled out some dog-eared photos of her nephew from her purse and passed them around.

"He is twenty-seven, and works in a corporation and supports many of the members of his family," an uncle said, describing the elder boy. "He has a master's degree in engineering, and is working toward his PhD."

When his remarks were met with silence, he continued.

"He will give her a house by herself."

Zia smiled at the uncle. She could see he was a genuine man, unlike his unpleasant wife, who was still glaring in her direction. For a moment, she vacillated. Maybe her suitor was a nice young man. She understood that few young Iraqi men could afford an entire house, especially in London. At best, most young men could only afford enough bedroom furniture to fill an empty room in their family's house.

But something inside Zia made her want to be rude to this family. Perhaps it was the arrogant assumption that Zia and Nunu would jump at the chance to get married just because the suitors were in London. Zia also felt a small sense of superiority over them because she worked with Americans. She knew that in America, it wasn't unusual for new couples to have their own houses.

She glanced at the photo of the suitor, which had been passed to her. He was okay. Not as tall as Keith and less handsome. He wore a tie and looked sophisticated. He wasn't so bad.

"Why doesn't she speak?" complained the aunt, who was still staring at her.

"I'm sorry," Zia said. "I'm tired from work."

"He will let you work!" the aunt said, as if she considered this a great favor. "And after so many years, if you wish to go back to school for a higher degree, he will consider it."

The silence returned. Nunu was not expected to say anything. As the conversation became more and more strained, the second aunt grew aggressive, referring to a pretty cousin that she had in mind who would be more suitable.

"They would already be married, but the boy says he refuses his cousin. So modern."

"She must make a decision quickly," the nice uncle said. The boy would come to Iraq in one month. A small wedding party would be held in Jordan, where most of the family had fled during the war. Six months later, she'd be in the UK, where his family would give her a big wedding party.

Zia had hoped her denim jacket and taciturn manner would change their minds, but the uncle clearly liked her. Finally, however, impatience got the better of him.

"Now, you see the man, you see the situation. What do you say?" he asked.

Mamina and Nunu looked at Zia. A million thoughts raced through her mind at once: rejecting the family outright would be a grave dishonor, and she knew this was a good offer. And it was an opportunity to get herself and Nunu out of Iraq and to the UK, where Mamina and Baba could visit. Maybe this suitor wouldn't fulfill her dreams, but he would offer a safe future for her sister and her parents. He was the sensible choice.

But Zia couldn't do it. She had lived a lifetime of forced choices. She loved Keith, and she willed herself to believe that the situation in Iraq would settle shortly, and she and Keith could carve out a life for each other in Baghdad.

She took a deep breath and said simply, "What is destined to happen will happen." The mood of the room seemed to deflate like a balloon losing air.

Nunu brought out the final round of acrid coffee, and the family left.

CHAPTER EIGHTEEN

BY THE TENTH month of the occupation, Manal and most other Iraqi women activists felt increasingly bitter. They were angry that the interim Iraqi government created in June had included only three women out of twenty-five members, only one female cabinet official, and no women on the committee selected to draft the nation's first constitution. The recommendations from Fern's "Heartland of Iraq" conference had been ignored. Its signature demand—for a quota of 30 percent women in government—was now being openly opposed by Bremer and the Bush administration, which, Manal was convinced, was allergic to the word *quota*. This was a far, far cry from the adminstration's prewar promises that women would play a signature role in the new Iraq.

Manal complained to Heather, but she herself was devastated by political turns of events. In late November 2003, the Bush administration decided to shorten the CPA's management of Iraq from two years to one year. Bremer, Heather, and the rest of the CPA had banked on running the country for two years, during which time they would transition the ministries slowly back to Iraqi control, assist them in writing their constitution, and oversee nationwide elections for a government.

However, they hadn't anticipated the opposition of Grand Ayatollah Ali Sistani, a powerful hermetic sheik holed up in Najaf, who refused even to meet the Americans. Sistani wouldn't stand for two years of U.S. control. He wanted elections to be held first, and demanded a shortened occupation—or he would call for a nationwide uprising. Under pressure, Bremer was forced in November to agree to cut the occupation to one year. The news demoralized the CPA. Everyone had been working on projects on the assumption they'd be around until June 2005. Now they'd be packing up their bags and leaving in June 2004—and all their work would be turned over to the Iraqi government, ready or not. No one thought it was ready.

For Heather and her women's centers, this was terrible, terrible news. After several months of almost finding the perfect building for a women's center and then losing it, she had thrown up her hands and decided to rent. She'd finally found a center to rent in the Mansour district, and they were spending $250,000 to renovate it. Now, come June 2004, it would fall into the hands of the Iraqi government, with no guarantee of being kept as a women's center. More likely, it would be given to a top official to live in.

To make matters worse, Manal and the other activists weren't sympathetic to the woes of the CPA. They had begun to point fingers and complain that women's lives were more confined than under Saddam. Heather agreed that things weren't going as planned, but she didn't believe it was because Bremer didn't want Iraqi women to have rights. Intelligence reports indicated that ex-members of Saddam's government were organizing raids with Al Qaeda, and suicide attacks across the country had increased in frequency. Muqtada al-Sadr's Shia militia was attacking police departments and army facilities, trying to undercut the basic foundations of security in the country. Most of the CPA employees were too terrified to leave the palace grounds anymore, and reconstruction had ground to a halt. Bremer was preoccupied trying to keep the country together, and women had been bumped down the priority list. Heather understood all this, but whether her aid-worker friends did or didn't, they weren't intending to sit silently on the sidelines.

INDEED, MANAL, FERN, and the Iraqi women's rights leaders decided to turn up the pressure. In early December, Fern led the charge. She and several other activists had circulated an open letter to Paul Bremer listing several facts that showed the absence of women in government.

"These facts demonstrate pervasive sex discrimination in the government structure established, appointed and supervised by CPA," the letter stated. "It would be a real tragedy if the Coalition were to leave Iraq with a government less intent on equal rights for women than the previous regime."

Rather than put her name on it, Fern had circulated it among Iraqi groups and gathered the signatures of twelve Iraqi women and men, including the heads of the country's human rights and women's rights groups. It also circulated among American women's groups and attracted the attention of the National Coalition of Women's Organizations (NCWO), which represents 180 American women's groups—collectively ten million women nationwide. The NCWO piggybacked with its own press release.

"This is a crucial time for women of Iraq, and the U.S. has an ironclad obligation to assure parity for women . . ." wrote Martha Burk, chair of the NCWO. "Clearly Iraqi women have been shortchanged, and the situation must be corrected immediately. President Bush has expressed strong support for equal rights for women in Iraq, and the U.S. government is obligated to make that a reality."

Yet, on December 27, 2003, things got even worse.

In a largely empty parliament chamber, the head of the radical Islamic political party SCIRI proposed legislation called Resolution 137, which would overturn Iraq's 1959 secular law, called the "Personal Status Law," that protected women's rights, and replace it with Islamic law, called sharia. Although less than half the chamber was in attendance, there had been enough for a vote, and the legislation had passed. Now all it needed was Paul Bremer's signature to be signed into law.

Manal and other activists received this news like a slap to the face. Already, the Islamists were quietly taking over top positions in the schools, universities, and ministries. Now they were throwing around their weight in government, too. Whether to have a justice system that followed Islamic law or secular law had always been one of the biggest debates among Arab-world feminists, with many saying that Islamic law was ultimately bad for women. Examples of oppression under Islam law were abundant, as Iran, Afghanistan, and Saudi Arabia all followed it, and women in those countries had few rights and suffered harsh punishments for transgressions. Some feminists, including Manal, argued that Muslim women were duty-bound to follow Islamic law. However, they called for a reinterpretation of the sections that dealt with women's issues.

Islamic law, also called Sharia law, refers to a body of laws derived from the Quran and the example set by the Prophet, as remembered and recorded by those who knew him. A country that follows Islamic law is still confined to the basic architecture of the seventh-century manuscript, but what, exactly, the Quran says and how it should be applied to modern-day life is open to wide interpretation by judges and scholars across the Muslim world. Over the centuries, they have interpreted the Quran's teachings in order to apply them to contemporary situations, similar to how the U.S. Supreme Court debates contemporary applications of the U.S. Constitution.

Like many Islamic feminists, Manal believed that sharia could be interpreted in a very progressive way for women. For example, Manal interpreted the Quran as protecting women from forced marriage. She felt it defended women's rights by stating that women could make any number of prenuptial stipulations—such as being allowed to work, or only having to bear a certain number of children—before entering into the marriage contract. In instances of divorce, the Quran defends a woman's right to keep her dowry, and allows her to remarry after three months. The Islamic societies in which women are denied rights are incorrectly following the teachings of the Quran, Manal believed. She had met many Islamic clerics who agreed with her and defended women's rights. One recent high-profile incident that Manal knew of involved an Iraqi woman who was refused a powerful position as a judge in Najaf. The ruling that rejected her said that women were "too soft and emotional" to be judges. She complained to Grand Ayatollah Sistani, who issued a fatwa, or judgment, in her favor. In his decision, Sistani wrote that "anyone with masculine characteristics" would be allowed to serve, hence opening up the job to women, as long as they could show they were as tough as men.

Manal saw this as evidence that women could progress under sharia, but she also recognized that Sistani was special; he was beloved for his wisdom and fairness, and he was a university-trained scholar of the Quran. Many Iraqi judges who would be confronted with cases involving divorce and child custody were not Islamic scholars; in fact, some in the countryside were semiliterate tribesmen. They didn't want women to have rights and twisted the Quran to justify their chauvinism. Manal knew enough about the highly conservative SCIRI party to fear that their kind of sharia would catapult women back hundreds of years and strip them of the rights they had been given under Saddam. The fact that SCIRI was proposing replacing secular law with Islamic law said plenty about the dark way in which it would be interpreted.

Iraqi women had long been proud of Iraq's 1959 Personal Status Law, and the current government's move to overturn it was shocking. It could be compared to the USA's 1964 Civil Rights Act, in the sense that it was overarching federal legislation that defended all individuals against discrimination. When women in Iraq brought forward any number of cases to the hundreds of Iraqi courts across the country, they could feel assured of the basic protection provided to them by the secular national law, despite any individual biases of the judge. *Imagine if the Civil Rights Act were overturned,* Manal thought. Some U.S. judges would still rule against discrimination, but others might not. This is exactly what she feared would happen without the Personal Status Law. Some judges would still interpret the Quran to defend women, but there would no longer be that guarantee. Furthermore, why seek to overturn it? What was SCIRI's intention?

Word spread quickly. This move went against the U.S. promises of democracy and freedom, but, when people turned to the American authorities for assistance, they were mostly rebuffed. In January, Manal even took a trip to D.C. to lobby U.S. lawmakers for help, but many dismissed her, reasoning, "The Iraqis must want this. The Iraqi government voted for it. We can't intervene." Manal even approached the offices of many of the fifteen female senators, urging them to pressure Iraqi lawmakers to overturn the resolution, hoping they could sympathize. She received mostly lukewarm responses. They didn't get it, she thought.

Back in Baghdad, Manal and several other female activists decided to approach Paul Bremer directly, seeing as his signature was required in order for any Iraqi legislation to pass. They had already met with Sir Jeremy Greenstock, the top UK representative in Iraq, and he had agreed to support the women publicly on all their issues, including overturning Resolution 137 and supporting the quota. His wife, Lady Anne Greenstock, met regularly with Iraqi women and had impressed Manal with her dedication. The UN representatives also offered their endorsement to the women's rights advocates.

But not Bremer.

In his office in the palace, Manal sat in disbelief as Bremer preached to her about "strong Iraqi women" who didn't need help. "You guys have probably worked across the world, but these are tough women," Manal recalls him saying. In other words, Iraqi women are fine. We don't need to do anything.

Just shoot me now, Manal thought. *This guy is out to lunch.* But she had persisted in trying to convince him. She made little headway. Bremer did promise the women he would not sign Resolution 137 when it reached his desk, but he didn't want to come out publicly and denounce the legislation, even though they argued that that would send a clear message to the government that women's rights were a U.S. priority. Instead, he encouraged the women to lobby the other members of the interim Iraqi government to overturn the legislation before it even reached his desk.

They left the meeting feeling unsupported and suspecting that Bremer feared upsetting the Islamic leaders with such a political hot potato as women's rights. He would stand up to them on some issues, but not that one. He wanted the women to go through the democratic process by lobbying and raising awareness enough that the Iraqi government would overturn the legislation. This idea had its merits, but the irony wasn't lost on the women. Bremer's office made dozens of national decisions every day, and no other group was told to "go out and lobby." Only when it came to women's issues did the Americans suddenly say, "That's an internal issue. That's for Iraqis to decide."

MANAL'S GROUP WAS not the only one lobbying Bremer. Another group of powerful Iraqi women had also gone to see him, including Zainab al-Suwaij; Nesreen Berwari; Ala Talabani, a civil engineer and women's rights leader; and Maysoon Damluji, an architect, whose father was the former head of Baghdad University's medical school and whose uncle was Iraq's former foreign minister. Damluji was currently the deputy minister of culture and head of the Iraqi Independent Women's

Group. They wanted Bremer's support both to overturn Resolution 137 and to implement a mandatory quota of women representatives in the new parliament. But this group received a similar brush-off to the one Bremer had given Manal, even after they explained that many other countries have similar quotas, including South Africa, Rwanda, and Sweden. Bremer nodded, but Damluji recalls him telling them, "I'm not going to support you, because I don't think quotas are the right thing. Go do whatever you want to do, go lobby, and do what you need to to get yourself in the government and in high positions, but we are not supporting quotas."

They left fuming, but undeterred. The women decided they would adopt Bremer's advice and take matters into their own hands. They launched a countrywide campaign of petitions to require a quota of female representatives in government, and protests to overturn efforts to implement sharia.

That month, an Iraqi committee was drafting the Transitional Administrative Law, which was to serve as Iraq's temporary constitution until a permanent one was drafted in 2005. Maysoon Damluji's cousin was a lawyer on the committee. She approached one of the more moderate members of the Governing Council, a secular Sunni named Adnan Pachachi, and asked him to add a line on quotas saying "women will make up no less than 40 percent of all future Iraqi governing bodies."

Pachachi laughed.

Damluji's cousin had drafted legal language. "Just put it in, and let's get laughed at. We'll see what happens," Damluji recalls telling him.

"I will put it in, but they will never accept it," Pachachi said.

Sure enough, when the mostly male parliament reviewed the document, and reached the line about 40 percent, laughter filled the chamber.

But the issue was on the table, as the Iraqi women activists had intended.

When the Governing Council tried to dismiss it, the women could negotiate. When the lawmakers took a break, Zainab al-Suwaij was waiting for them in the hallway, positioned strategically by the coffee machine. Many lawmakers knew her influential family.

"Zainab, my dear, what brings you here?" one greeted her.

"Well, I'm here for forty percent representation for women," she replied in Arabic.

He looked at her and said, "Zainab! That's too much to ask for. Even in Sweden they don't have forty percent."

"Well, okay, maybe, but look: we do so many things different from Sweden this year, so how about we do that too?"

He said he would think about it.

CHAPTER NINETEEN

ZIA OPENED HER laptop and saw an email from Keith marked "urgent."

"After work, we need to talk," it said. Her heart skipped a beat.

They hadn't seen each other in a week. Keith had been working in Mosul, and he had called her each night from his hotel room. Zia knew he was lonely. In Baghdad, he kept himself surrounded by his contractor family, that swaggering group of overpaid, divorced, middle-aged men who drank heavily and bragged endlessly—mostly about the last war, the current war, and the next war. Keith felt comfortable in that world; it was like anesthesia for reality.

But alone on his work trips, he couldn't escape feeling depressed, he admitted. They began to talk more openly and intimately. He had confessed that, in coming to Iraq, he was supposed to be escaping an already complicated life—a failed life, he sometimes thought. He hadn't expected he'd be allowed to even speak with the women. But he felt that, in Zia, he had found perhaps the closest female friend of his life.

Zia returned the sentiments and kept his spirits high. She told him the story of the London PhD and the botched proposal, and made him laugh. She stayed on the phone with him for hours and then went on her computer to write him email. Even she was surprised by the emotion that poured forth.

"I am no different than most Iraqis. I have always lived in the present, day to day," she wrote in one. "Life for women in Iraq means you try to make it through the day alive, without one of Saddam's sons taking you home and using you, or throwing you off a building. Life for 22 years had no future for me. I got up, went to work, and went home and whatever life was fortunate to give me was all I was going to get. There was no dreaming in Iraq. But now that I have met you, I have dreams. I feel like I have a future."

No sooner was Keith back in Baghdad than he wanted to see her. She was sitting in her office when he burst in. He closed the door. The sun was just beginning to set, and many of the workers had gone home already. "I had an epiphany in Mosul," he began. He missed her, he suddenly realized. A lot. He told her that he had spent New Year's Eve rereading her email in the airport. He confessed that while he had laughed with her about the marriage proposal from the London PhD, he'd been jealous and worried about losing her.

"It took me by surprise. The last thing I expected was to fall in love. But I have. And for the first time in my life, I am not falling in love with your body or the sex. We are friends. And I am falling in love with you as my friend, with your heart and your soul. This is a new experience for me. Zia, you are one of the toughest girls I've ever met. But underneath, you have this incredible warmth and innocence. I see all you've been through and yet you are so optimistic. Being with you makes me feel strong enough to face anything."

He got down on one knee. "I want to be with you, Zia. I will do whatever it takes for you," he said.

Zia was crying. This was the moment she had been waiting for. The excitement of the war, the liberation, the new job, her freedoms—all the momentum of the last eight months of her life roiled inside her. He leaned toward her. She didn't refuse him. Alone in the office in the warm air and pink light of dusk, she gave in to the swooning abandon of her first kiss.

THE CITY WAS too unsafe for Keith to venture into the busy, crowded souks to find a goldsmith, so Zia shopped for the rings. They had to ask Baba.

Zia had some doubts that he would approve, but Keith was all enthusiasm. He wanted to adhere to Iraqi traditions, and was sure he could win over Baba. Keith had many Iraqi friends inside the Green Zone who were eager to give him advice.

"What happens is you overwhelm the father by bringing along a co-hort of supporters," one man told him. The men must be passionate and speak so highly of the groom, the father would have no chance to refuse him. Traditionally, fathers, brothers, neighbors, and the local sheik are all present. Keith's group would include a few of his Iraqi friends, his brother, some South African mercenaries, and some contractors. Keith also found a sheik, and convinced him to come.

"If permission is granted he'll tell the mother to go and prepare some sweets," his friend Wisam said. "But if not approved you'll get bitter cof-fee. So if you see that coming, you basically have to keeping talking and talking, and he won't have a chance to say no. Before he knows it, he'll have said okay."

Keith was doing his best to understand the Iraqi rules, but he had al-ways been buddies with his past fathers-in-law. He knew about the time Baba had tried to hunt him down, but he was confident his charisma would win Baba over.

However, on the day set for him to go to Karrada, there was a secu-rity threat and no one could leave the Green Zone. The next time, he couldn't get in touch with the sheik. Soon, the crowd whittled down to just his brother and the South African mercenaries. At that point, Zia believed it would be better if Keith just came to their house on his own. Meanwhile, Mamina had mentioned to Baba that another suitor was in-terested, and had begun dropping vague hints that he was Western. From Baba's stone-faced reaction, she started to lose faith that he was going to agree. The Americans had lost much popular support over the first year of occupation, and Baba was susceptible to pressure from his friends, tribe, and family. "This is not going to happen," Mamina wor-ried. "Not now. It's more than likely he'll say no."

When Keith finally arrived, Baba looked grouchy. Keith realized he had seen Baba around IMN doing contract work, but hadn't realized that he was Zia's father. Nunu brought out drinks and a plate of fruit and nuts. All the women sat on one side of the room, and Keith and Baba sat on the other. Baba lit a cigarette and barely said anything. Keith, suddenly unsure of himself, tried to fill in the gaps. Baba did nothing but smoke and stare at Keith. Quickly, the conversation became awk-ward.

Searching for common ground, Keith asked Baba a question directly. "How do you feel about Americans in Iraq?"

A few weeks earlier, the U.S. State Department had issued a memo to CPA staff advising them to avoid conversations with Iraqis on three topics: religion, politics, and the future. That was all most CPA staffers talked about, but apparently the subjects were so controversial that talking about them had led to trouble. But Keith's style was upfront and honest.

After a few moments, Baba responded. "It is good that they came, but it's better that they leave soon," he said.

Keith nodded vigorously. "Hmm. You know, a girl in my office said to me yesterday, 'Everyone I know believes you're here for one thing: to steal our oil,'" Keith recounted. "Yeah, okay, I told her. We're spending eighteen billion dollars trying to reconstruct your country, and as fast as we can put it together, you're blowing it up. C'mon, don't you understand? This is tax dollars out of my pocket, to reconstruct your country. And we're not stealing your oil, we're buying your oil on the open market just like anybody else, and we're trying to fix your oil refineries and pipelines so you can get more oil sold."

Keith rambled on nervously.

"I've seen the maps. Practically this entire country sits on top of huge, huge amounts of oil. Everyone in this country should be living in a house of comfort with a nice car and parks. This is nuts, what's happening here. We're not trying to take it away, we're trying to make sure you have what you should have." He laughed.

Baba took a drag of his cigarette. His silence said it all. Zia knew he would refuse Keith.

After a few more painful moments, Zia ushered Keith out the door and quickly into the car. If the neighbors saw Keith outside their home, they would gossip.

"Gee, that went well," he tried to joke. He gave her a quizzical look, but Zia's face had gone ashen. She looked as though she was about to cry.

CHAPTER TWENTY

·

UNDER THE SUNNY, cloudless March skies, Manal hurried across the spacious pavilion, through the arched entryway, and into the sunny Mansour Women's Center. She couldn't believe that after six months of sweat and tears, opening day would finally arrive in less than a week. Once Manal had identified the Iraqi women who would be involved, and Heather had secured the property, the rest had gone fairly quickly and smoothly. Women for Women had done most of the work, subcontracting an Iraqi construction company to renovate the site, and working in teams to decide on a computer room, a meeting room, and the many different programs they would run from the center, including democracy training. The renovation still wasn't complete, but they wanted to open the center on March 8, International Women's Day.

The center would signify their biggest accomplishment thus far. Manal's staff bustled back and forth, hanging yarn artwork from Baghdad's Fine Arts Institute for Girls and arranging space for the Ishtar Iraqi Women's Ensemble to play their jangling music. Everything about the day was being designed to send the message that this was a center for Iraqis, even ensuring that the buffet included their favorite dish, *masgouf,* a fish caught in the Tigris and cooked over open coals. Manal expected one hundred guests, and had carefully selected local sheiks, business leaders, Iraqi media, and all of the many women's groups.

Despite the feeling of accomplishment at Women for Women, however, all was not well in the rest of Iraq as the first anniversary of the occupation approached. In Karbala, a Shia city in the south where Fern Holland had set up a women's center, suicide bombers had recently attacked a crowd of worshippers celebrating Ashura, a religious feast commemorating the death of the Prophet's grandson Hussein; hundreds of people were killed, mostly Shia. They left behind tens of thousands of grieving relatives and tribesmen, thirsty for revenge. Down south, tensions ran high. Traveling to cities such as Hilla and Karbala was now considered too dangerous for Westerners, which meant Manal could no longer safely visit Fern. In Baghdad over the past month, there had been several major suicide bomb attacks, including one outside the gates of the Green Zone that killed twenty-eight Iraqis. Manal felt that the danger was growing closer each week, like walls closing in. They were opening the center just in time.

Her phone chirped and she recognized Heather's number. The two of them talked several times a day. Six months had passed since Heather had estimated the nine centers would be an "instant thing," and instead they had just this one, which felt to both of them like a Herculean accomplishment. Manal had gotten used to Heather's reedy insistence, and for her part, she had toned down her reservations. They had become friends, despite talking about nothing but work.

Inside the Green Zone, Heather had been spreading the word of the center's opening in the international community, the Western media, and the various donor agencies that had given funding, such as USAID. She had received an overwhelmingly positive response. Victories and accomplishments were in short supply in the CPA, and even those people only tangentially involved in creating the Mansoor Women's Center wanted to be on hand to recognize its completion. Heather had spent most of the last few days arranging security convoys to shuttle dignitaries to the big event.

"How's it going?" Heather asked briskly.

"Pretty good," Manal said, filling her in on some last-minute details.

Then Heather paused, unsure of the reaction to her next sentence. "Bremer wants to come."

Manal stopped in the middle of the hallway. *Sure,* she thought bitterly. *Bremer wants to turn up for the Kodak moment.* But had he really stood by women when they most needed him?

"That's not a good idea," she quickly replied.

In Heather's world inside the Green Zone, Bremer's interest was a mark of recognition for the center, but in Iraq, Bremer was a lightning rod. As the most powerful symbol of the occupation, he was a moving target for the insurgency and his presence provoked suspicion among Iraqis and accusations that anyone working with his approval was a "collaborator." Manal suddenly envisioned Iraqi guests arriving to see Humvees parked down the block; robotic, machine-gun-toting security guards at the doors; and television cameras harassing the shy women.

"No, no, no. We need this opening to be an Iraqi event," she said.

In plenty of other places in the world, more experienced donors understood that the key to their success was keeping a low profile and letting the community take ownership. But the CPA was not experienced in aid work, Manal reminded herself, and cared as much about how the occupation played back in the States as it did on the ground. All her efforts to win over the locals would be destroyed if the CPA swished in to be thanked. Manal had spent months ingratiating herself into the neighborhood. The locals had been curious when they saw construction crews going in and out. Manal had immediately gone to meet the local sheik to assuage his concerns. She had had to quash a rumor that Women for Women was an Israeli front, which started because its offices closed on Saturday, the Jewish Sabbath, rather than on Friday, the Iraqis' day of rest. Manal was constantly fighting for credibility.

"We need an Iraqi face on this," she repeated to Heather.

Heather understood Manal's concerns, but this was a huge problem. She didn't care about personally receiving credit from Bremer for her work, but victories were in short supply around the palace. They had replaced the currency, opened the schools, and captured Saddam. Great, but that wasn't enough: the electricity supply was still at pre-Saddam levels, the police were more loyal to the militias, and the Iraqi soldiers were abandoning their posts in droves in fear of being seen as defending the Americans. Even reopening the factories, which would create thousands of jobs, had been delayed for months as the CPA tried to privatize them.

Therefore, Heather's tiny women's center was being seized on for publicity. She couldn't turn down the groups who had funded it, like the CPA and USAID, and top brass like Bremer. Plus, the deterioration of support for Americans was precisely because the Iraqis didn't hear about successful U.S. projects like the women's center, she believed. Plenty of Americans inside the Green Zone were working around the clock, but how would they convince the Iraqi public they were doing something for women if they couldn't take credit when they did?

"It's publicity and recognition for the center," Heather replied. "And we'll get more support to get the other centers done. The upside beats the downside."

A silence yawned between them. For the last six months, Heather and Manal had navigated cautiously toward a friendship. Despite their differences, they liked each other and shared a similar, wry sense of humor and a respect for each other's work ethic and commitment. But in moments like this one, they felt pulled toward their respective identities of soldier and aid worker. "The U.S. military is using the aid workers for its war propaganda" was what Manal heard from her friends. "The aid workers whine from their five-star hotels while we're getting shot at" was what Heather heard the soldiers say.

"I can't have a convoy of Humvees and tanks pulling up in front of the center, you know that," Manal said nicely. "The women won't like it."

"We're going to need to go to the CPA for funding for the rest of the centers," Heather pushed back. "We can hardly reject someone like Bremer and then ask for more money. And there's no way we can ask him to come without security."

Finally, they landed on a solution: get Bremer there first thing in the morning. Manal would make sure a few Iraqi women arrived early enough to sit next to him. He could have his photo opportunity, and then move on before any of the other Iraqi guests arrived and saw him. They could spin it as though they wanted Bremer to be "first" to "open" the center.

"This could work," Heather had said, relieved. "Let me talk to his staff."

Manal hung up and thought, *This is what happens when you make a pact with the devil.*

SINCE DECEMBER, IRAQI women had been lobbying for the quota in government and protesting against sharia law. They had collected tens of thousands of signatures. Zainab al-Suwaij worked the southern territories. The group Manal had trained and helped organize months earlier, the Iraqi Women's Network, held rallies and protests in Firdos Square, and painted signs and placed articles in the press. In their veils and pantsuits, with their purses and heels, they walked from door to door handing out leaflets.

Their actions thrust them into the spotlight, however, which was extremely dangerous. Aqila al-Hashimi's assassination was never far from the women's minds. In February, in the midst of the campaign, Yanar Mohammed, one of Iraq's most outspoken female activists, received an email with the subject line "Killing Yanar Mohammed Within a Few Days." The message demanded that she stop her activism on behalf of women's rights, described as "psychologically disturbed ideas about women's freedom," and promised to kill her if she didn't stop.

Some women did quit in fear, but she, and many others, refused to back down.

The women had none of the security of the Green Zone. Their houses didn't have concrete blast walls. They couldn't afford high-tech security companies like Blackwater USA, a private security company staffed mostly by ex–Navy SEALs, who Manal heard were paid about a thousand dollars a day. None wore bulletproof vests or drove armored cars. Many were volunteers, working without pay. Bremer's words echoed bitterly in Manal's ears. "This is good democracy training for you," he had said.

Yet, when it came to political propaganda, Iraqi women received plenty of attention from the Bush administration and the CPA. An op-ed article in *The Washington Post* by Deputy Secretary of Defense Paul Wolfowitz, whose hotel had been rocketed when he visited Iraq the previous fall, appeared on February 1, 2004. In it he wrote about visiting one of Fern Holland's women's centers in Hilla. It was entitled "Women in the New Iraq," and used the centers as evidence of U.S. progress.

"My second trip to Iraq since the liberation of Baghdad grabbed some headlines because of a rocket attack on our hotel," he wrote. "But a visit to a new women's center in the city of Hillah said more about Iraq's future than did the act of violence. . . . We should do everything we can to help them."

If women's rights is the CPA's biggest point of pride, we're in trouble here, Manal thought. There was no mention of the quota or sharia law, the two signature issues women were currently fighting hardest on. Wolf-owitz wasn't the only one to seize good publicity when he could, of course. In a speech First Lady Laura Bush gave in early March 2004, entitled "Progress in Global Women's Human Rights," she referred to photos of veiled women protesting against sharia in Firdos Square, ap-plauding their "freedom" to protest. She credited her husband for giving them this freedom.

"Earlier this week, during the signing of Iraq's interim constitution," she said in the East Room of the White House, "Iraqi women marched together and many spoke publicly after decades of oppression. In al-Fardous Square, more than two hundred women marched for greater rights, chanting, 'Yes for equality, yes for freedom.' They were supported and applauded by a group of Iraqi men. One man smiled and said that 'This is the first time women have demonstrated freely in Iraq.'"

There was applause. "We're making progress toward greater rights for women in the Middle East and around the world," Mrs. Bush said.

No, we're not, Manal thought. The first lady didn't seem to under-stand that Iraqi women were protesting the implementation of Islamic law—something they never had to worry about during Saddam's time but which had become a real possibility on George Bush's watch. They were fighting tooth and nail just to keep the few rights they had had under Saddam's government. The timing of the speech was like a slap in the faces of Iraqi women.

Nonetheless, the rhetoric from the Bush administration continued. When Fern opened another women's center in Karbala in the spring of 2004, Bremer arrived by helicopter at the opening.

"Your future is full of hope," he announced to the crowd. "We in the coalition are committed to supporting women's rights in Iraq."

Yet Manal suspected that Bremer's very presence at the center put it in great jeopardy. A self-congratulatory CPA press release was issued the same day. "During the former Regime, Iraqi women would never have dreamed of meeting to discuss their rights as individuals," it read. "Am-bassador Bremer provided encouragement to the women as they work for a democratic Iraq."

Despite the absence of practical support, the Iraqi women collec-tively gathered more than fifty thousand signatures supporting their quota. The pressure paid off. Soon enough, the discussion inside the committee drafting the interim constitution (the Transitional Administrative Law) revolved not around *if* there would be a quota, but around *how much*. Would the women agree to 10 percent? How about 20 percent? Each week women worked to bring another male member into their cause. With the signing of the Transitional Administrative Law, also on March 8, they got their victory. The government would have no less than 25 percent women. And that wasn't all: the Governing Council overturned Resolution 137. Iraqi women would not have to live under Islamic law, for now.

Both victories came just as Manal and Heather's center was opened. The women celebrated with huge parties. These were two battles they hadn't expected to fight, and there was so much left to do, but at least they had made some headway. For better or worse, the Iraqi women had done it largely themselves, with almost no support from the Bush administration. After that, Manal noticed a shift in attitude among the Iraqi women. When talk of the CPA arose their faces darkened and their tone became embittered.

THE MORNING OF opening day, Manal braced for Bremer's arrival. He would be the first guest and then, she hoped, leave. Negotiations with his staff had been bitter. Bremer's aides had wanted him to cut the ceremonial opening-day ribbon, but Manal had refused.

"Why are you making such a big deal out of this?" the aide complained. Bremer had cut the ribbon at all of Fern's centers. Fortunately, though, Manal had already been negotiating with the newly appointed minister of human rights, Abdul-Basit Turki, to cut the ribbon. Bremer's aides could bully a women's center, but wouldn't dare bully an Iraqi minister out of the spotlight. If they did, Manal threatened, she would contact *The New York Times* and embarrass the CPA. The aide backed down, and eventually agreed that Bremer would arrive at sunrise and stay briefly.

Shortly before his arrival, a low-flying helicopter passed overhead in a security sweep. Manal grimaced. Then a long motorcade pulled up. Manal watched from the gate as an entourage fit for a king parked in front of the neighbors' houses. No expense had been spared in protecting the viceroy. Several SUVs flanked his car, each with bulletproof tinted glass windows and armored doors. As the doors swung open, half a dozen beefy men emerged, each wielding an automatic rifle and displaying no ID. Bremer was guarded by Blackwater—not even the U.S. military was enough security for the CPA. Soldiers were bound by rules of engagement, but private security companies such as Blackwater were above the law in Iraq. Many Iraqis had told Manal stories of being run off the road or shot at by these men, but they had no recourse to justice. The men took up positions by the front gate as Bremer was hustled out of the car, past the flower beds, and into the center.

Despite her feelings of resentment, Manal was polite as he sat cross-legged in his pressed suit and tie, looking like the CEO of Occupation America, Inc., in the sitting room before a twenty-foot-long spread of platters filled with baklava and other sticky pastries. His translator sat by his side. Bremer's office had tried to orchestrate everything for the cameras, even sending Manal a list of Iraqi women whom they wanted Bremer to receive. The list included mostly women from the diaspora who had supported the invasion and who were professionals, eager to be appointed to the government, and were well versed in diplomatic protocol and photo opportunities.

Manal tossed the list.

This isn't some Potemkin village, she thought. Instead, she had hired a bus and brought in poor women from one of her programs—widows, war victims, and household breadwinners. They deserved a chance to meet the man running their country. Likewise, she wanted Bremer to hear what life was really like for the majority of Iraqi women.

Bremer made some remarks congratulating the women. He promised them that the center marked the dawn of a new day for women in Iraq.

"Where's the electricity?" one woman in a black abaya said between bites of food.

Unfazed, Bremer explained that the reconstruction process needed time. The conversation was conducted through a translator, making it awkward. Manal listened as some women made long speeches. Bremer's translator broke them down to a few simple lines.

"I still don't know who you are, but you're handsome, so I watch you on TV," said another old lady in black. "But you're *mabtinfani*," she added, waving her hand. Manal held her breath. *Mabtinfani* meant "useless to me" or "irrelevant." Bremer's translator looked furious. He fidgeted nervously. He hemmed and hawed and then softened the translation considerably.

Still, Bremer picked up on the hostile mood, Manal thought. "You can destroy a city in a day, but rebuilding it takes a while. And we need strong women like you. Your patience will help."

Photos were taken, and then he was ushered out. Within hours, the standard CPA press release from Bremer's staff was emailed to more than a hundred media outlets in Baghdad, from CNN to *The New York Times*. "The Mansour Women's Center represents another important step forward for democracy and freedom for all Iraqi women."

IN THE GREEN Zone, Heather was heading toward the dining hall, tea bag in hand. For the first time in her year in Iraq, she had had a long, hot morning shower, and was dressed in civilian clothes. *Almost like a normal life,* she thought, *except for the sandbags surrounding my trailer and the rockets whistling overhead.*

Her phone beeped. "Bremer just left," Manal said. "Everything went fine."

"Nice," said Heather. "I'm going to check to make sure we have priority on the convoys, and we'll be there by eleven."

The prior week she had left the château in which she had lived since the war began. She had been moved into one of the hundreds of trailers sitting in the shadows of the recently erected concrete blast walls that surrounded the Green Zone. The trailer felt thin enough to be blown away by a gust of wind. Heather shared it with her roommate, Leah, a female foreign service officer who was working on district councils for the CPA. Leah was out of town, and Jody Lautenschlager, Heather's friend from deployment, had moved in temporarily. As she tiptoed out of the trailer, carefully closing the swinging white door, Heather felt as though she was exiting a Porta-John. At least she'd had a shower.

Moving briskly past the rows of sandbags and trailers, she could see the balconies of Saddam's palace. She flashed her badge for the soldiers standing guard at the palace door, and flashed it again at the dining hall.

She rarely ate much before lunch, and on this day she was too nervous to consume more than hot tea. The palace breakfast counter of sugary cereals and ceramic bowls reminded her of a college dining hall.

From the cafeteria, Heather walked down a long hallway with dozens of offices on each side until she reached her own large office, which had been carved into individual workspaces for a dozen CPA staffers. Her desk was smothered in folders that represented dozens of projects undertaken in the past year—the hardest of her life. Yet she could count only two successes, both of which had come in the last month. The first was the ceremony marking the official transfer of authority over the food warehouses from the militias to the Ministry of Trade, which had happened in the summer of 2003.

The second was the Hindiya Club elections, just the prior week. The Hindiya Club was the Iraqi equivalent of America's Rotary Club. After the fall of Saddam, different Sunni and Shia groups battled to take control of the club and its coffers. A few members asked the CPA to get involved, and the task of overseeing an election for new leadership was handed to Heather. She had approached the archbishop of the Syrian Catholic Church to act as an impartial overseer. The elections were publicized, ballots were prepared, a plan was drafted to check the eligibility of members to vote, and a team was created to count the votes, with another team overseeing the count to prevent fraud. Iraqi police provided security on election day. Hundreds of members had arrived to vote and then actually watch the count take place. Heather had been thrilled to watch democracy in action, stepping back to snap photos of history in the making.

This was democracy. It occurred in towns, cities, school boards, and community groups across the USA every day, without much thought. But in Iraq, they were starting from scratch, and getting it right was a painstaking process that required dozens of different players working together in good faith. Sure, it would have been easier for the CPA to have just appointed new leadership, and Iraqis, in their impatience, often pushed Heather to take charge. But she always insisted that the slow wheel of democracy be allowed to turn in order to give the people a stake in the institutions that made decisions about their lives. The pressure could be intense. Had one person decided to bomb the club, or assassinate a candidate, the months of hard work would have been for nothing. Fortunately, no one did.

Watching democracy done correctly and its cautious acceptance by the Hindiya Club members gave her hope, for the first time since the invasion, that if this process was raised to a national level, Iraq had a chance to succeed, she thought. However rare these successes were, though, they pushed her on. These small steps convinced her that, despite the violence, most Iraqis did appreciate the Americans' presence. She knew that armchair critics back in D.C. called democracy in Iraq a "fantasy." Well, they could say what they liked, she thought bitterly. They didn't understand the stakes, or meet Iraqis whose lives depended on democracy's working out; Iraqis who shook her hand and thanked her for staying in the country to fight for peace and stability.

She was thrilled that they were finally opening the Mansour Women's Center. The center had taken six months to get up and running, which was not an unreasonably long time to open an entirely new establishment. But Heather had envisioned it would take a few weeks, and hence had felt disappointed. Everything in Iraq had to be done three times as fast, even as it seemed to take ten times as long, because they were racing against a brewing insurgency and a receding tide of goodwill. Perhaps it was due to the expectation, set by the Bush administration before the war, that the USA would arrive, deliver democracy, and be washed clean of the whole affair in a month or two. Whatever the reason, instant democracy was impossible. With all the struggles involved in erecting one center, it would be a miracle to get eight more up and running, as was the original plan. The CPA was dissolving in three months—many Green Zone staffers were looking online for D.C. apartments and sending out their résumés. Heather couldn't fathom packing her bags, shrugging her shoulders, and going home. No way. She had already put in requests to stay in Iraq beyond the dissolution of the CPA that summer. She had made promises, to herself and to the Iraqis she worked with, that this would work out. She wasn't ready to face what failure meant.

By 9:00 a.m., Heather was in the parking lot full of Humvees getting all the security organized, people in the right convoys, and a route mapped out. She was traveling with a senior-level CPA official and two public affairs officials, all women. Finally, after a couple of hours, everything was organized, and the convoy pulling out of the parking lot included nine soldiers, all with M16 rifles and 9mm pistols, and three Humvees, one with a grenade launcher and the other with a .50-caliber machine gun atop it—all just to escort four women to the opening of a women's center. *The expense! The waste of human energy!* Heather thought. *Oh, we could be doing so much, if not for the insurgency.*

Heather had directed the soldiers to drop them off in front of the center, and then park their Humvees in a vacant lot nearby. "Please don't come into the women's center," she said. They nodded, and Heather felt a twinge of injustice. These young guys would spend the next two hours standing outside in the hot sun, hoping not to get shot at. From their perspective, they were just trying to help, and it probably stung to be rebuffed by the locals. Heather saw both sides of the situation, and it was awkward.

She and the women headed inside the gates. Quickly she found Manal. They hugged.

"This is it!" Manal said. "This is what we worked so hard for!"

"Wow, you've really done it." Heather did a circle, amazed at the sun-washed building. "You've really made it happen."

Manal was feeling good about their friendship again, especially when she saw that Heather had the consideration to wear civilian clothes, knowing that Manal preferred not to have the military associated with the event. Her heart was in the right place, Manal thought. "Nice outfit!" she joked. They laughed and posed for a photo together. Manal showed Heather the photos she had snapped on her digital camera that morning, of Bremer sitting with the women. She left out the *mabtinfani* story, unsure of how Heather felt about Bremer.

"Oh, great. That'll be really helpful," Heather said, thinking of the publicity she could get to secure additional U.S. funding for more centers. "We have to use those."

As they walked around, Heather grew happier and happier. The American guests included many from the "donor community" such as USAID and the CPA. Young staffers milled around. Many Iraqis came, including women's rights activists, their husbands, and ministers and their staffs. Very few Western media came, but much of the Arabic and

Iraqi press was invited. She was upset when she saw a few female sol-diers standing around in their uniforms, but the Iraqi women didn't seem to mind. They vied to take photos with the soldiers.

The time arrived for the ceremonial planting of flowers around the center. Manal encouraged Heather to plant the first one. She tried to refuse but was quickly surrounded by a bevy of women in black abayas with trowels. They helped her pat in the dirt. Just as the plant settled into its new home, the women let out ululating screams that sounded to Heather like a battle cry.

"I thought that was for wars," she whispered nervously to Manal.

"No, we do that for good events too," Manal said, smiling.

Heather laughed. *"Mabrook!"* she said to all the Iraqi women, mean-ing "congratulations."

The rest of opening day went smoothly. *My third victory,* Heather thought. Her entire sense of success was riding on these small victories, even though, on some deeper level, she sensed the rising tide about to engulf her. She shook off such thoughts, wanting instead to just live in the moment. She was always criticizing her Iraqi staff for not planning for the future, but now she was beginning to understand the mentality. She thought about the hundreds of Iraqis killed at the religious festivals last week. Life was cheap and unpredictable in Iraq. Enjoy the rare vic-tory of today.

Who knew what would happen tomorrow?

CHAPTER TWENTY-ONE

THE MORNING AFTER the Mansour Women's Center opening in Baghdad, several of Manal's staff members drove down to Karbala to check up on the Women for Women programs running in Fern's center there. Manal was working on her laptop in her office when she got a call from Amjad, the driver in the group. She heard shouting and noise in the background. "We've been attacked," he said breathlessly. She could hear her female staff members crying loudly in the car.

Her heart skipped a beat. "What's happening?"

"I couldn't stop for them, Manal. They would have killed us," he sobbed.

"Get back here as quickly as possible," she told him.

A few months earlier the drive to Karbala would not have been considered dangerous, but things were heating up. Support for Muqtada al-Sadr had grown as the Shia in the south lost faith in the United States's promises of security and reconstruction. He fanned the flames of anti-Americanism with his newspaper, *Al Hawza,* which regularly published reports of abuse by U.S. soldiers. In recent months, truck drivers working for U.S. contractors had come under attack by members of Muqtada al-Sadr's militia. Alone on long stretches of empty highway, travelers were highly vulnerable targets, and choking off the Americans' supply route was a classic tactic of insurgent warfare. Those not attacked for political reasons were often carjacked or robbed for profit. Western journalists and aid workers were increasingly uncomfortable taking the road from Baghdad to Basra. Some female journalists occasionally traveled disguised in a black abaya, but most sent their Iraqi translators instead.

Manal had made the trip several times herself in the last year, but she had done so less frequently lately, fearing that she would be kidnapped.

Within thirty minutes, Amjad was back at the center. His face was ashen, his hair askew, and his shirt damp with sweat. When Manal saw the blood smeared on the hood of his car, she was mortified. "I couldn't stop, Manal," he kept saying. "People were reaching out for help, but they were chasing us and if I stopped, they would have killed us."

Amjad told her what happened as Manal called the police. On the way down to Karbala, he had been lost in thought on the long, straight highway and had begun to count the enormous potholes he had to slow down to pass over. The highway was divided by a deep ditch, and surrounded by vast, endless desert. Every few dozen miles, they passed a village, a shepherd and his flock, or a roadside vendor, but otherwise, there were very few other people around.

Suddenly, Amjad noticed a car whose occupants were wearing red-and-white-checkered headscarves wrapped around their faces. Trying not to alarm the women in the car, Amjad slowed down and pulled off the road as the car with the masked men slowly passed him, intending, he told Manal, to turn around and avoid whatever the men were planning to do. But he didn't have time. As he was turning around, the men opened fire on a cargo truck a few cars in front of him. Seconds after the gunshots, he saw the truck jackknife. The attackers swerved alongside the truck and blocked the road with their car. They fired recklessly into the cargo bed of the truck, and then began rampaging down the highway, shooting into the cars that were trying to reverse. Amjad was fortunate that he had a head start in turning around, but as he headed back up the highway, he felt his stomach drop—about twenty cars behind him, another vehicle with masked men had blocked the road. The men were working as a team. They had trapped the vehicles in between, and were walking up the line shooting into the cars. Amjad picked up speed before the shooters approached his car. Luckily, since he had been counting the potholes, he remembered where to slow down and skid out of the way. Other cars were trying to turn around as bullets flew. As he slowed to pass a pothole, a man with a bloodstained shirt stumbled toward Amjad's car and fell onto the hood.

"Please, let me in," he moaned.

Amjad had little time to react, but in a split-second decision he swerved and sped away, leaving the wounded man behind. The women in the car were crying and screaming.

"They were organized," Amjad recounted to Manal. "The front car must have been talking to the back car. This was a thought-out plan." He seemed unable to catch his breath. "Manal, we only escaped because I had been counting the potholes and I knew where they were and didn't need to slow down."

The police arrived. Whether it was a highway robbery or something even more nefarious—a targeted attack by Sunnis on those heading toward the Shia south—Amjad didn't know. It had all happened in seconds. Amjad kept reliving the moment, terrified, desperately insisting he couldn't have stopped for the people reaching out.

Manal spent the afternoon dealing with the crisis. It wasn't until much later that she suddenly thought of Fern. Amjad's car had not been far from Hilla, and it was on a road that Fern drove often, unguarded. Manal couldn't shake a feeling of dread. She walked to her computer and dashed off an email to Fern. She copied it to Salwa, Fern's Iraqi colleague.

"Guys, our staff was attacked en route to Hilla. Please be careful. I'll give you more details later."

Into the evening, Manal thought more and more about Fern, and patterns formed in her mind. She had been worried about Fern since she first met her, but in recent weeks something had changed. Although her and Fern's relationship revolved around women's rights work, Manal had spent enough time with her to feel she knew her well. In the frenzied activity of a typical day, Manal hadn't stopped to put herself in Fern's shoes, but she suddenly realized that Fern had a lot on her plate—too much. Her list of projects had grown incredibly quickly. She seemed to have as many as a dozen in the air; the funding was pouring in, and Fern complained she couldn't spend the money fast enough. The CPA in Baghdad had hundreds of millions of dollars and was under pressure to spend it, but struggled because so few workers were willing to leave the Green Zone to work on projects. Fern was someone in a position to get things done.

Manal knew Fern had received more than $1 million so far, in cash. Just two weeks earlier, Fern had received another $320,000. Without functioning banks, Manal imagined Fern must have been hiding it in suitcases under her bed, traveling between Hilla and Karbala with bricks of hundred-dollar bills in the trunk—it was the only way to move money. The CPA had tried to force Manal to take money for the women's center in this way.

"Come pick it up. Bring some duffel bags," the woman in the convention center had told her.

"No way," Manal had said. That was way too dangerous, and sloppy too. She wanted a paper trail, to protect herself. She had insisted that the money be transferred to Women for Women's D.C. bank account, and they brought the money in from Jordan, on an as-needed basis.

Rather than be thrilled at the excessive funding, Fern's recent emails to Manal had had a sense of increased urgency. Each project she got herself involved in seemed to carry with it complications and controversy. In addition to the programs at the women's centers, Fern wanted to take a team to Jordan for a democracy conference. She also helped individual cases: a small child who needed a medical operation, and an old woman who lost her land to a Ba'athist. Fern had pushed that particular case to a local court and won permission to bulldoze the man's house, despite her friends' objections that she was going too far. In typical Fern style, she wouldn't back down.

Fern had always taken on too much, though. What was new in her emails, Manal realized, was that she was also complaining about the Americans working in the CPA office in Hilla. Fern didn't trust the several businessmen and military officers in charge of subcontracting multi-million-dollar projects. The dollars were just disappearing, and she was making enemies by raising questions. None of the work was getting done, she complained.

Fern didn't have that many friends left inside the CPA. They called her naïve, even though Manal suspected their disapproval stemmed from their own defensiveness about staying inside the Green Zone. Manal defended her. Fern was smarter than people recognized. And the CPA certainly didn't disassociate itself from her when it came time to issue a press release on her CPA-funded women's centers. Manal had even heard that Fern was going to be fired for recklessness, and Fern seemed to be aware of that. Her latest email to Manal had been tinged with fatalism. "I've stepped on too many toes and I have made too many complaints. But you know, I am not going to back down."

THE MORNING AFTER the attack on her staff, Manal was back in her office. She still hadn't received a reply from Fern, which was odd. She was planning on holding a staff meeting about safety, when she received a call from an American friend in Hilla.

"Have you seen Fern?" she asked.

Manal felt her mouth go dry. This wasn't a casual question.

"No," she said. "What's up?"

"Three people went missing yesterday. I don't have any more information."

"Have you called the police in Hilla?" Manal asked. The friend hadn't, so Manal offered to. When she hung up, she found herself unable to pick up the phone again. For a moment, she bowed her head. She reminded herself that rumors abounded in Iraq.

Slowly, she punched in the number for the police chief in Hilla. Before she could even ask, he said, "Manal?"

"Yes."

"It's Fern."

"What? No, I don't think so," Manal replied. Mistakes were made all the time in the chaos and confusion of Iraq. False alarms occurred every day.

"Three people were gunned down on the highway," he said. "I'll drive over to the morgue to verify their identities."

Manal sat silently for what felt like an hour, staring into space. When someone entered her office to speak, she took a few seconds to look up, having not heard anything they had just said. She didn't dare share her suspicions, for fear of it being bad luck.

The police chief called back in less than an hour.

"Fern's dead. I saw the body," he said. In short, official sentences, he shared what he knew. Fern had been driving from Karbala to Hilla the prior day when gunmen opened fire. The car had swerved off the road and ended up in a ditch in a remote farming community called Abu

Gharaq. Her assistant, Salwa, was dead too. She had been hit in the car and afterward, it appeared, in the ditch at point-blank range. Another American was also in the car, and he was killed too.

Manal bowed her head. When she hung up the phone, she didn't know what to do. The first person she called was Heather. She was the only woman who would understand the gravity and meaning of what had just happened. This wasn't only about Fern's murder; this was the targeted assassination of a women's rights activist, done to send a message. When Heather chirped hello, Manal realized she had no easy way to break the news. "Fern's dead," she said. There was a long pause.

"Oh my God," said Heather. "Oh no. I'm so sorry, Manal. This is terrible."

"My staff was attacked right around the same time, also near Karbala," Manal said. Her pitch began to rise as fear flooded into her mind. "I have staff in Fern's centers. They need to be evacuated or protected."

"Absolutely." Heather was all efficiency, instantly prepared to fire off emails to military and political connections to get any necessary help.

"There are many, many Iraqi women who worked closely with Fern and loved her," Manal said, her voice straining. "They're going to be distraught. We have to get them counseling."

Each woman confronted her grief with a list of tasks to keep herself busy. She had to think of her staff, Manal told herself, and caring for others somehow felt easier than thinking about her own loss. However, every few minutes she would suddenly think, *Fern's dead,* and an image would flash into her mind of Fern laughing or talking about her projects. She had been so full of life—so vibrant and special. Now she was lying alone in a morgue in Hilla. It was too much to bear. Manal and Heather spent the rest of the day organizing a grief counselor for all the staffers who had worked with Fern and who loved her. Heather got the army counselors on board, and all the women were called to the convention center for a meeting. News flew through the CPA. *Fern Holland is dead.*

A MEDIA FRENZY ensued, as Fern was the first CPA worker killed in Iraq. Bremer called the FBI down to Hilla to investigate the deaths. A press conference inside the convention center was jammed with cameras and jostling reporters. Every major international news outlet carried the story. Back in D.C., memorial services were planned by women's rights activists who had worked with Fern.

Within two days of the murders, arrests had been made, but that only served to heighten fear. Of the six men arrested, four were members of the Iraqi police force, who had been issued proper documentation and wore police uniforms. Two of them belonged to the drugs division of the Karbala police, which had offices directly opposite the Karbala Women's Center.

"The slayings have shocked the Americans here, who now face the possibility that the men to whom they turn for cooperation in fighting the insurgency may include insurgent infiltrators or those paid to do their work," *The New York Times* reported on March 13, 2004. Another article quoted the local Iraqi police chief as saying that Fern had been targeted because of the controversial nature of her work.

"The killings raised questions about the American effort to promote values here that often conflict with local attitudes and traditions," another *New York Times* article, on March 12, 2004, said. "But senior American officials said that the effort to promote 'Western values' of sexual equality and other individual rights would not be curtailed."

Criticism rained in on the CPA: Why was Fern allowed to drive in a car without armor plating, and with no backup security? On this subject, CPA officials declined to comment. But inside the palace, criticism was directed at Fern for taking such risks. Many people said they weren't surprised to hear that she had been killed.

CHAPTER TWENTY-TWO

ZIA HEARD ABOUT Fern Holland's death—everyone in the Green Zone had. She suspected that Fern had not realized where she was or with whom she was working. "*Faithful* doesn't even begin to capture Hilla," Zia explained to Keith. "People there would die for their faith. Men and women down there don't eat together, the schools are segregated. If a woman works, her office must be all women—and even a thousand years won't change their mindset," she said sadly. Yet she was not surprised to think of a young American working to overturn a millennium of tradition. Zia had learned that Iraq attracted all sorts of unusual birds—wanderers and dreamers, idealists and go-it-alone adventurers. Just recently, she had gotten to know a young American man named Nicholas Berg. An engineer-in-training, he loped around IMN's campus, chatting with everyone and talking in airy, excited words about erecting communication towers to help Iraqis. What made this young guy, not much older than Zia, travel across the world to a dangerous place just to try and help? He wasn't simply after the money or the chance to play cowboy, Zia felt. He seemed sweeter, more naïve, and he had inspired Zia to keep her faith in the Americans.

But the terror of the murders, compounded by the fact that the CPA was set to disband in June, sucked any remaining life out of the agency. No one wanted to risk their life with such a short period to go. Anyone venturing out into the "Red Zone," as the rest of Iraq was dubbed, was considered a fool who would "end up like Fern." Around Saddam's pool, Fern was invoked as an example of an American "betrayed" by the locals she was trying to help. As the Americans withdrew into their shell, the Iraqis grew more frustrated and suspicious. At night, insurgents continued to shoot rockets from the outlying neighborhoods into the Green Zone. Paranoia set in.

Soon, Fern's death was eclipsed by even more dramatic events. In early April 2004 in Falluja, a Sunni city of about 300,000 people an hour west of Baghdad, four Blackwater security guards were attacked. Their SUVs were hit with rockets and gunfire, and they burned to death in their vehicles. Video taken by one of the attackers showed the blackened bodies being dragged through the streets and hung from a bridge. Rumor in the Green Zone was that some of Blackwater's Iraqi employees had set them up to be ambushed.

Many in Iraq hated the Fallujans, especially Shia families like Zia's, who considered them *khadaras,* or dirty people. They viewed Falluja as an insular, incestuous community whose loyalties lay with local tribes, not the national government. Fallujans were also tough and proud, famed for resisting the British occupation in the 1920s. Even Saddam had known not to challenge the sheiks of Falluja; he had given them jobs in his government to appease them. The Fallujans hated the Americans, just as they had hated the British. Back in April, soldiers had opened fire on a crowd in Falluja, killing scores of innocent people. Since then, the city had become a hideout for Ba'athists, Al Qaeda, and most other anti-American groups. Zia saw the steady reports of attacks on Americans there as insurgents planted Improvised Explosive Devices (IEDs), staged ambushes, and even downed several helicopters with rocket-propelled grenades. A U.S. effort to train the local police had ended when the police station was overrun and fourteen Iraqi officers were killed. The military had been threatening to attack Falluja, so after the Blackwater contractors were killed, the marines invaded.

Zia's family wanted the Americans to hit Falluja hard. But neither they nor the military anticipated the popular reaction. To their surprise, when the military bombed Falluja and sent in troops, many in the rest of the country reacted with outrage. Across Baghdad, Iraqis took to the streets to protest. They accused the Americans of being occupiers, not liberators, and chanted at rallies, "Sunnis, Shias, unite! Our brothers are being killed in Falluja by the infidels!"

Most reports coming from the Arab media fanned the flames by showing images of women and children bleeding and dying, buildings in ruin, and soldiers shooting indiscriminately. Some news outlets reported that innocent civilians were blocked by troops from fleeing the city or getting to hospitals. The Ministry of Health estimated that two hundred Iraqis had died, but the Arab media posted a much higher figure of more than a thousand. No firm number was ever agreed upon. Refugees who did get into Baghdad were given housing by Sunni families. Schools and stores closed down, some in solidarity and some under threat by militias. If there were many Iraqis who supported the Americans, they stayed silent out of fear. The country felt as reckless and chaotic as it had in the first few days after Saddam's statue fell, except this time, no one believed the Americans were in control anymore. The Green Zone went on lockdown, again, and no one was allowed in or out—not that anyone wanted out. The Americans, stunned by the countrywide uprisings, abruptly canceled the invasion after only three days of fighting.

At home, Baba thundered through the house. "The British were better. They would have destroyed Falluja," he said, echoing the sentiment of his circle of friends. Inside IMN, emotions ran high. The broadcasts were undeniably pro-American, but opinion was divided in the newsroom, as many Iraqi staff were publicly condemning the military aggression in Falluja, and some Americans agreed with them. On the other side were Zia and a handful of Iraqis saying the Fallujans deserved it for giving refuge to Ba'athists and foreign fighters who were attacking Americans and Shias. Meetings were tense, and friendships between Iraqis and Americans suddenly felt freighted with questions of loyalties and nationality.

Zia's male colleagues said the Americans were running and hiding like rats. "Look how the Americans are weak," they said.

"But just the other day you were accusing the Americans of brutality," she replied, annoyed.

They shook their heads. "The Americans ran from Falluja because they were scared," they insisted. "This is good. Next, we will force the Americans out of Iraq."

"And then what? Don't be an idiot! The Americans are the only ones keeping the peace. What will happen after they leave?"

Even Keith and Zia began to argue. Talk of their wedding was always at the back of Zia's mind but had not progressed, given Mamina's belief that Baba would say no if Keith formally asked. As the country plunged into a state of emergency, Baba's blessing seemed less likely and Zia was getting desperate. "The Americans should have done to Falluja what they did to Hiroshima," Zia said angrily over lunch.

Keith looked surprised. He tried to soothe her. "Hey. Relax," he said.

"Relax?" she shouted. She turned her irritation on him. "Everything with you is 'relax.'"

What, did he think democracy was going to solve this situation? "Keith, this is very bad." Her tears began to overwhelm her. "The Americans can't lose."

Zia didn't know how to begin explaining a situation in which she herself had only snatches of understanding. She didn't know half the insurgent groups running loose in Iraq now. Rumors were that Al Qaeda groups were in western cities such as Falluja, Iranian militias were in the south, and the radical Islamic Dawa Party was trying to take over the U.S.-installed government. In the north, Kurdish guerrillas were fighting to break away into an autonomous Kurdistan. Still, there were dozens more groups, in the neighborhoods and on college campuses, that no one had heard of before. In the absence of a brutal dictator like Saddam, Iraq regressed into all the tribal and religious identities that had reigned for hundreds of years until the British forced the country together in the 1920s. The country was fracturing, and the national government cobbled together by the Americans seemed weaker and weaker. The prospect of U.S. defeat in Iraq—which had seemed inconceivable only a few months ago—suddenly seemed a strong possibility. Iraqis who had stuck their necks out for the Americans were going to be at the top of the assassination lists when the Americans evacuated. If that happened, Zia and her family would be hunted down and killed, just as the Ba'athists had been hunted down and killed a year earlier. When the Americans had arrived last spring, she had thought Iraq's nightmare was over. But was the real nightmare only beginning?

Keith listened, and supported her, but she couldn't help but feel circumstances pulling them apart. He was an *ajnabi*. At any point, he and his friends could pack their bags and return to a peaceful country. But she was an Iraqi. This was her country, and she had nowhere else to go.

. . .

JUST AS THE marines were pulling out of Falluja, another, more portentous, front opened up.

In southern Iraq, Muqtada al-Sadr had used his widely circulated newspaper to call for all Shias to attack Americans. In response, the U.S. forces chained shut the newspaper offices and issued an arrest warrant. This provoked a huge outcry by the mullah's supporters, and uprisings spread throughout the Shia communities in Baghdad. In Sadr City, where he had most of his support, people rioted in the streets, and the U.S. patrols—sent to restore order—opened fire on scores of young men. Dead bodies left on the sidewalks evoked further anger toward the Americans. The soldiers had expected to face resistance from Sunni groups long loyal to Saddam, but now they were battling against Shia groups as well. Tensions ran high in the city.

At Nunu's university, Muqtada al-Sadr's black-clad militia tried to shut down the campus. On April 5, a demonstration kicked off near the college of architecture, and the protesters were setting fire to an Israeli flag. "No, no coalition forces," they chanted. "Sunni and Shia unite against the enemy."

Almost a year earlier many students had enthusiastically welcomed the U.S. troops, but now Nunu didn't know a single supporter who dared to speak up. The students were tired, suspicious, and felt disappointed by the CPA, or, like Nunu, were too fearful of retaliation to defend them. But that didn't mean they supported the militias.

Nunu decided the campus was unsafe and returned home. Later, she heard reports from friends. Although several thousand students milled around campus, only about three hundred had joined the demonstration. The rest of the students wanted nothing to do with the "radicals," and were just trying to get to class. As the protest drew to a close, men dressed in the uniform of Muqtada al-Sadr's followers—solid black with beards and headbands—brusquely herded the crowd into a line to march through campus. "We are a higher authority than the Iraqi police and the U.S. military," they said. "We don't recognize the Iraqi government or the CPA." A female demonstrator glared at the Iraqi women sitting silently on the benches in T-shirts and jeans and said loudly: "You girls who dress in a Western way think you are expressing freedom, but this is wrong. I'm not allowed to show my hair or body, and on Judgment Day, God will say 'you were good.' "

The protest had called for "Iraqi unity," but the rest of the campus looked intimidated as the militants passed. After that demonstration, many female students, like Nunu, began to fear attending classes at all without a veil. Students faced a bleak choice between U.S. occupation and religious fundamentalism. The majority of those in the middle had become too afraid to speak out.

THE VIOLENT UNREST in Falluja and Sadr City in March and April 2004 became known as the "Spring Uprising." The military said that 147 soldiers were killed in April alone, three times as many as in any of the prior months. An estimated 1,200 Iraqis were killed in the same period, twice as many as in each of the past months. Some reports gave a much higher Iraqi casualty rate.

The occupation would suffer yet another setback when, in late April, photos of prisoner abuse in Abu Ghraib surfaced. On her office computer, Zia shuffled through the images in dismay and disgust. They showed not only torture and abuse—which Iraqis expected in Abu Ghraib—but also sexual perversion. Images of female soldiers piling naked Iraqis on top of one another in pyramids, pointing at their penises and mimicking sexual acts, reinforced an already existing stereotype of depraved, sex-obsessed, godless America, a country that produced aggressive, whorish women. Zia was convinced that most Americans were good people, and only a few soldiers committed such atrocities, but in light of such images, her words fell on deaf ears.

One afternoon, her boss, Amar, walked into the office she shared with him.

"You remember the kid who was in here a few weeks ago, with the red baseball cap?"

"Yes," Zia said, thinking of Nick Berg.

"He's been captured by Al Qaeda. They killed him."

Zia's mouth dropped open. The last she had heard, Nick had been trying to pick up a contract erecting satellite towers across Iraq that could be used for IMN's broadcasts. She knew he walked from place to place with no guard, and traveled around the country. She looked at the black swivel chair where, just a few weeks or so earlier, Nick had been sitting, laughing with her and making jokes. He had worn dirty jeans, tennis shoes, and a T-shirt. He was biting his nails, which were filthy, and talking about how exciting it would be to work for IMN, which had been interested in hiring him because of his engineering skills. But the deal didn't go through because he didn't like the low pay or the Department of Defense's tight security regulations, which would have bound him to the office. She wasn't sure what had happened.

But now Nick was dead.

The next day, she heard the gory details. He had been beheaded, and the insurgents had recorded the act and sent a DVD to IMN. It was also being sold on the street in Baghdad for a dollar. All the news channels had the footage. They aired the edited version, which was chilling. Zia saw her friend Nick, awkwardly sitting on the floor in an orange jumpsuit with his hands and ankles bound. She recognized him, but he was cleaned up a little. He had lost weight and looked gaunt. His beard was a little bit longer. Five men stood behind him, swathed in black, their faces covered.

Amar had the DVD of the entire beheading, but Zia chose not to watch it. During the day, other employees came into her office to watch it. She turned away, and could hear them shouting, "Ahhh!!! Ohhh, man!" as though watching a sports event. She left the room, preferring to distance herself from something so brutal.

But after a few days, her curiosity got the better of her. "Okay, I want to see it now," she said to Amar.

Amar turned on the television. "I could tell this man would get in trouble because of the way he deals with the world," Amar said to himself. "He was the kind of kid who thought he could do anything. Nothing could stop him." As the video began to play, he added, "But I didn't expect it to be this kind of trouble."

As soon as the slaughter began, Zia regretted her decision to watch, but she couldn't look away. Nick had been sitting quietly on the floor of a white room for the first few minutes of the video, as men with faces wrapped in scarves stood behind him. But as two men took him by the arms, and a third brandished the knife, Zia felt like something inside

Nick snapped. He began to scream. Zia almost couldn't believe a human being could make such a sound. His scream was the earsplitting, terrified wail of someone who knows he's about to be slaughtered. With bound hands, he wrestled and struggled for his life. Zia watched the man slice into his neck. Beheading a human being is not easy, and the murderers needed several minutes to accomplish their grim task, as Nick's body twitched and resisted throughout. When they had finally finished, blood spilled across every inch of the shot. The murderer held up Nick's head by the hair, holding his knife in the other hand, and shouted, *"Allahu akbar,"* God is great. "This is what happens to the infidels and the Americans," he said. Zia felt she could still hear Nick wailing.

"Zia, are you okay?" Amar was shaking her. "Zia? Sit down."

She was crying and trembling.

"Why did you let me watch this?" she said.

She looked at the swivel chair where Nick had sat. Zia's head pounded as she sobbed. "I should have told him to go back to America. I should have warned him to be more careful."

"You should go home," Amar said. "Take the rest of the day off."

She went home, but in the silence of her bedroom, she still heard the wailing in her ears. She couldn't escape the grotesque image of her friend's severed head, and the calculated, measured movements of his murderers. She thought about Nick's parents, and she prayed for them. *What was his crime?* she wondered. He had traveled across the world to help, and they killed him without mercy. She lay in bed staring at the ceiling, trying to keep images from the video from flashing into her mind. Several times, she raced to the bathroom and vomited. Mamina tried to comfort her, but her headache would not go away. "Mama, the killers had no remorse. They had no more reaction to what they'd done than had they lifted and moved a chair across the room."

"*Habibti,* don't think of them. They are not Iraqis, they are foreign fighters. They are animals and not humans," she said. Neither woman wanted to acknowledge out loud an even deeper fear: somewhere, the killers were still out there, and they were calling on all Iraqi men to do the same thing to her if they could. They would kill Zia for working for the Americans, and they would kill Mamina for allowing her to.

"Mamina, if something happens to me, don't ever watch. Promise me," Zia said.

"Shhh," Mamina said, stroking her forehead. "Don't say such things."

When Baba came home, Mamina explained what had happened. He wiped his face with his palm and sat down. "These foreigners are sick in the mind. They are worse than Saddam. The Americans let them in. God help us if they don't drive them out."

ZIA RETURNED TO the office, and work continued, but she felt deflated. Now, when she sat alone, or in between conversations, her eyes took on a sad, worried look. When she spoke about the terrorists, angry sparks shot from her eyes. She was scared.

In the office, petty disagreements flared. Bloggers had been posting accusations that the Americans were involved in Berg's death; that they had created the video to distract people from the Abu Ghraib scandal. Others said he was killed for erecting satellite towers to spy on Iraq for Israel.

Zia ignored this talk, until she overheard one of her American supervisors agreeing.

"The Americans killed him just to make the terrorists look bad," she said. "It's propaganda."

Zia stared at her. "The Americans wouldn't kill their own," she said. "Why would they do that?"

"Look, Zia, I'm older and wiser and I know more about life than you," her supervisor said. "You saw the white plastic chairs? Those are the same chairs that are all over the palace. You see? Where did they get the orange jumpsuit from? That's from Abu Ghraib."

Zia walked away. Later, she thought about how, in life, the smallest of incidents can suddenly reveal the huge gulf between you and someone you thought you were close friends with. After a year of friendship with this woman, she now could never look at her the same. Every day Zia willed herself not to feel bitter about the easy life the Americans enjoyed in the Green Zone, and the often callous ways they referred to Iraqis, but she could not excuse her supervisor. The woman enjoyed the luxury of sitting in the palace thinking up crazy conspiracy theories and criticisms; she didn't have to live with the consequences. This woman was herself an immigrant to the United States from Colombia. The USA had given her everything. She had come to Iraq by choice, and had a fancy job with a rich American company, and was paid five times more than any Iraqi. At any time she could return home to the States, where she had rights and opportunity and freedom as a woman. But she never talked about any of that. She just ripped down her country.

"Stay away from her," Mamina advised. "If she's not grateful she's American, she probably isn't grateful for anything."

CHAPTER TWENTY-THREE

GRAVEL CRUNCHED UNDER the wheels of Heather's ten-speed bicycle as she leaned into the handlebars and pedaled harder. After more than a year living inside the Green Zone, she knew the streets as she knew her own neighborhood in Washington, D.C. Compared to the bus, her bike saved her about four minutes in travel time from the convention center to the palace.

Those four minutes really seemed to matter.

Since Fern had been killed, she had almost doubled her workload, but no matter how she occupied herself, she had to face facts: they had failed miserably. Sure, she and Manal were still trying to open two more women's centers. She had various democracy projects in the works. The elections and the vote on the constitution were still ahead. She could tell herself that they could *still make a difference*. But since the spring uprisings, the Americans had lost the widespread support of not only the Sunnis, but the Shias too. She felt a change in mood on the streets, and realized the Iraqis now saw them either as brutal aggressors or weak and irrelevant. The militias had gotten a foothold and were calling the shots. The window had closed.

Heather pedaled faster.

She was not a quitter, just as her mom had not been a quitter. When her mom had been told no by her high school guidance counselor, by her advisers at Cal Tech, by male students at Princeton, she had battled on and persevered. Heather would too.

For the first time in a year, she'd taken a vacation last month. She had spent Thanksgiving and Christmas 2003 in Baghdad, and after Fern died in March 2004 she felt she needed a rest more than ever. Her family had flown over to Spain to meet her halfway, and everyone had excitedly planned for the reunion.

But rather than relax, Heather was initially anxious, short-tempered, and distant. She didn't want to talk about Iraq, and stared off into space during dinner. Rather than go to the beach, she spent the day in a frenzied hunt to find computer stores to buy a new laptop that she couldn't buy in Baghdad. After thirty minutes in one computer store, customizing an order, the salesman apologized and told her they didn't have it in stock. She shouted at him and stormed out, and, much to the shock of her father, erupted into frustrated tears. She felt lost outside of Baghdad; she couldn't talk to her family about Fern, but she did share with them her misgivings and her hopes for the future. After several days of sleep, she felt herself relax and begin to reflect. But shortly thereafter, she got on a plane and headed straight back to Baghdad.

As the CPA began withdrawing in May and June of 2004, Heather made a decision to extend her time in Iraq again. Even as she felt all efforts were futile, she couldn't wrench herself away. She was in the bull's-eye of the biggest foreign-policy initiative of her generation, and the high stakes, the hope, the tragedy, and the fast pace were all part of the addiction. The work was exhausting, but it was also a natural outlet for her intensity and her desire to be involved in something larger than herself. The longer she stayed, the less she seemed willing to leave. Even if the ship was sinking she wouldn't throw up her hands and skip on to the next posting, as so many others had.

She had applied for the position of Iraq "Chief of Party" for the United States Institute of Peace, a D.C.-based think tank funded by Congress that produced research and programs to promote peace. She would take over the job from Sloan Mann, who was moving on to Afghanistan for USAID. Most important, her new job would be civilian, not military. She had been sickened by the photos that had surfaced in April of Iraqis being tortured by her fellow soldiers in Abu Ghraib prison, and she couldn't bear wearing the uniform any longer. But she also couldn't bear the thought of the USA losing the war. She didn't want to believe that the country she loved wasn't capable of pulling this off. She wanted to prove that intervening to topple Saddam had been the right thing to do. The alternative seemed unfathomable. Losing Iraq would be disastrous for the USA and its standing in the world. Worse still, what would happen to the Iraqis? She had befriended several over the last year, and they had begun begging and pleading with her not to leave. "Miss Coyne, the militias will take over," Thanaa said. "There will be civil war." She could see they were terrified. She couldn't fathom the thought of betraying them, and all the women's rights activists with whom she had worked, so profoundly. Staying seemed the only way to redeem her role, however trivial, in this colossal disaster.

Not everyone felt as she did. Many in the CPA were cheered by the thought of getting out. Most did not acknowledge the mess left in their wake, and if they did, they blamed it on Iraqi incompetence. They bragged about parlaying their "wartime experience" into jobs higher up the payroll at the State or Defense departments. Inside the palace, they snapped up souvenir T-shirts that read WHO'S YOUR BAGHDADDY? Others were busy planning a blowout barbecue at Saddam's palace, with fireworks for all of Baghdad to see, to celebrate the Fourth of July. Bremer, as a thank-you to his staff, was inviting different groups into his office for an official memorabilia photo. Although Heather didn't blame Bremer for all that had gone wrong, she couldn't grin alongside him, acting like some proud member of a successful team. When her office went in for a photo, she had stayed behind.

She thought about all of this as she pedaled faster, huffing and puffing as she approached the palace. Suddenly, a marine guard stepped into her path, almost causing her to lose control.

"Ma'am, no biking on the street. Only on the sidewalk."

Her heart was pounding. She was in a huge rush to get to the next meeting, and all she had to do raced through her head. There was no sidewalk. The road petered out into rubble and loose stone.

"The sidewalk is for pedestrians," she replied. "The street is where bicycles go."

"Sorry, ma'am," he said. "You can't proceed."

"That's absurd. I'm almost at the palace. Just let me through."

"I can't do that, ma'am."

Heather understood that marines just follow orders, but she lost her cool. This was exactly the kind of bureaucratic, illogical overreaction by the military that had screwed up dozens of almost-successful projects. Mounting stress and fatigue began to strain her normally tightly controlled public façade. Did he care that his "orders" made no sense?

"You know what? I don't have time for this," she said, and tried to pedal past him.

"*Stop!*" Several marines suddenly appeared. She found herself staring down the barrels of several rifles. Sweat poured down from under her helmet. Realizing that arguing would get her nowhere, she gave up. "Okay, fine, I'll turn around and be late for my meeting."

"Oh, no, sorry, ma'am. You can't turn around. You can't ride your bike up the street against traffic," he said.

"What? So I can't go forward. I can't stay here. I can't turn around." Heather threw up her hands.

An enormous stone-gray Jersey barrier ran between the two sides of the road. "You're going to have to cross the barrier and go back on the other side," he said.

Heather stood dumbstruck. He wasn't kidding. The marine watched awkwardly as Heather struggled to lift her bicycle to elbow height and wrestle it over the concrete barrier. It teetered and swayed, with the pedal catching on her shirt and the handlebars in her face. It suddenly flipped over, bounced, twisted, and clattered onto the asphalt. Books and papers she had in the carrier scattered everywhere.

Hot tears sprung to her eyes. Missing the meeting seemed unfathomable to her. But even more frustrating was the illogical reason, presented to her so innocently by a young soldier who was just following orders. She had confronted this kind of stupid military bureaucracy every single day since deployment and had fought in vain against it. The meeting—everything she was doing—seemed so senseless and futile. Before she could see it coming, the floodgates opened. She was sobbing. The marine shifted uncomfortably. Finally, she lifted herself and scrambled over the barrier. Irritation was compounded by the humiliation of crying in front of all these male soldiers.

Yet as she gathered herself, she caught a final glimpse of the marine's face. He looked apologetic, but she knew exactly what he was thinking, and it killed her: *I'm just doing my job.*

CHAPTER TWENTY-FOUR

ZIA KNEW SHE was in trouble, but she was convinced that the Americans would protect her. She had worked side by side with them for a year. They were her close friends. They trusted her. Or did they?

The mood in Baghdad changed after Fern was killed, then the Blackwater contractors in Falluja, then Nicholas Berg. Not only had Iraqis killed them, but rumors flew around that they had been betrayed by Iraqis posing as friends. Similar double agents had penetrated the Green Zone, people whispered. No one could be trusted. Iraqis working inside the U.S. compound found their bosses staring at them suspiciously, and their colleagues whispering when they were around. They were left out of meetings and email, and treated roughly by soldiers.

This poor treatment paled in comparison, however, to how Iraqi employees were treated outside the Green Zone. One afternoon, Zia opened an email with photos attached to it. They showed dozens of Iraqi women at American parties wearing lots of jewelry, with painted nails and big hair, holding drinks and dancing with American men. Some were simple photos of women in jeans carrying checklists, or in flak jackets talking to soldiers, or sitting at a lunch table in the Chinese restaurant with an American man. Others showed them in skimpy bathing suits sitting at Saddam's pool.

"I've seen these photos," Keith said. "They're on the palace's shared network."

"These are on the network?" she wondered. "What idiot did that? Didn't they realize how this will appear if it leaked out onto the street?" she said.

Within days, though, that's where they were, being sold as CD-

ROMs or posted on Islamic websites, where they appeared with the text, in Arabic: "This is a scandal. This is very demeaning and bad. You see, this is the liberty they brought us"; "All Iraqi women working with the infidels are whores"; "Look how the American men are here to steal Iraqi women."

These images confirmed the "brainwashing" that most Iraqi men had suspected. Once women were given a little freedom, they took a lot. Suddenly, the more extremist Islamic websites were calling for the women in these photos to be executed, made examples of for dishonoring all Muslim women. Soon after the CD, more photos appeared on the websites. These had not been taken by Americans. Zia could tell some images were shot from a cellphone, and the angle was crooked and taken from a distance by someone who clearly didn't want to be noticed. Zia realized that Iraqi men working inside the Green Zone were surreptitiously taking photos of women and providing them to insurgent groups.

Young women began to receive death threats. Handwritten notes were stuck under the windshield wipers of their cars: "Quit the coalition or you will have regrets." Others invoked Islam: "Those who deal with the atheists and the infidels on the soil of the Arab homeland deserve death and annihilation. We warn you to stay away from the Zionists and blasphemers, the followers of Satan." They were from a Sunni militia with ties to the openly violent gang Ansar al-Sunna, formed by ex-Ba'athists after the war.

In other cases, the women received threats via text messages on their phones. This raised the disturbing question of how the insurgents knew the women's phone numbers. In one case, a list was tacked onto the wall of the Green Zone Café naming all the Iraqi women marked for death. Zia had somehow avoided being named, but most of her friends were on the list, and its accuracy confirmed a deeper fear—that those making the threats were not only groundskeepers or uneducated radicals. They had to include the women's young, educated male colleagues who also worked for the Americans. In other words, these messages did not come from a tiny, extremist minority. The threats were endorsed by the urbane, English-speaking Iraqi men who shared their office space.

Suddenly, everyone became a suspect. Women became paranoid.

Cellphone cameras made it impossible to know who was being pho-tographed. Women who were targeted threw away their cellphones so as not to receive the threats and stopped eating lunch in public places. Zia disguised the names in her cellphone. If she was kidnapped, someone might scroll through her contacts list and target her friends. She took different routes to work.

Many women suspected that the tea seller in the parking lot was an informant. He was a mustached middle-aged man who smoked most of the day. Zia speculated that he was a former employee of the Ba'ath Party, or maybe an Islamic fundamentalist. Or maybe he was just a poor man who needed money so desperately he would work for the insur-gents. Either way, each morning, he arrived by donkey at the lot outside the Green Zone and set up his tea stand. The cart had two metal rods propping up a strip of canvas, which shielded him from the sun. At his feet was a plastic gallon of kerosene. A stand alongside him held dozens of small glass cups and saucers, tiny silver spoons, a plastic pitcher of water, and an enormous bowl of sugar cubes. He worked over two small boilers and always included two cubes of sugar in each cup.

Alongside his mobile tea shop sat several plastic chairs, open invita-tions for idle Iraqi men to keep him company with conversation. When Zia left the Green Zone at the end of the day, she would often see these men stare at her, dishdashas bunched between their knees, a cup of tea in one hand, prayer beads in the other, and hatred in their eyes. Other young women noticed the same thing. The tea seller was watching them, noting when they arrived and left, perhaps what they were wear-ing, and writing down the license numbers of their cars.

This practice of spying and recording people's every move had been commonplace during Saddam's time. The Ba'ath Party kept copious files on everyone. When the regime fell, an Iraqi scholar found five million documents in the Ba'ath Party headquarters, many of them filled with mundane details of life, even recording people's trips to the toilet. After so many years of twisted spying, men like that couldn't imagine a differ-ent kind of life.

Zia asked the Americans to make him leave, but they wouldn't. They claimed to take her concerns seriously, but each day she saw he was still out there. She kept pushing them to do something, but she also sensed that they didn't want to be bothered, or to hear the stories of how bad it had gotten. They didn't want to believe that a campaign of assassination had begun against their Iraqi employees. And besides, although Zia was on the same contract as Keith and the other Americans, her security fell on her own shoulders, because she was Iraqi. They didn't want to have to worry about her.

So she bought a gun, a small silver Beretta that fit into her purse. When the beefy American security contractors saw it, they thought it was funny. "You think you're one of Charlie's Angels," they said, laughing. She laughed too. She wanted to feel that they were all still on the same team.

ONE AFTERNOON, ZIA was sitting in her offices at IMN when an Iraqi security guard entered, his green eyes filled with fear. Zia knew him only vaguely, from when she had given him money at the end of Ramadan. He had thanked her warmly. Now, though, he looked around sheepishly and spoke with a low whisper.

"Miss Zia, I must tell you something," he said. "There is a plot to kidnap you, in three days."

Zia's heart skipped a beat. She felt that she was finally receiving the bad news she had expected for a long time.

"Muqtada's army came to my house. They wanted to kill me for working here," he said. "Instead, they asked me if Americans ever leave the compound. They asked about you—they knew your name."

The militia gave him a choice: they would kill him, or he could work as a double agent, and report on the movements of other, more important individuals, whom they could kidnap and hold for ransom. "Everyone knows you have relations with Mister Keith, and that he will pay a high price for you," he said.

Zia called Keith immediately, and he jumped into his white SUV and drove the five minutes from the palace into the Salhiya compound to be by her side. He insisted on getting IMN security involved.

Soon, the room was filled with people. Zia's heart sank as she discovered that the militia had gathered an alarming level of detail about her life: her street address, her route to work, her time of departure. The guard said the gang members drove a dark blue BMW. They planned to kidnap her, take her to a safe house, and send the ransom demand to Keith.

"They wanted," he added, hesitatingly, "to do forbidden things to you. I have a daughter your age. God would not allow me to let this happen."

Zia's eyes widened and filled with fear at the thought. She and Keith met with Reed Security, which had the contract to provide security to all IMN employees. They wouldn't give her the particulars of their coverage, but that was fine, Zia was accustomed to security details operating confidentially. "We've got your back," they told her.

Days passed and Zia was too nervous to eat or drive even a few seconds without glancing at her rearview mirror. But nothing happened, and she tried to remind herself that the Americans were keeping her safe. She continued to commute between her house and the IMN offices.

One evening at the end of the week, there was a knock at her door. Zia had told her family about the kidnapping threat, but reassured them that the Americans were protecting her. Still, the knock made everyone jump. Baba checked through the curtains, then opened the door. It was the owner of a small grocery store on their street. He sat heavily on the sofa.

"I want you to know there's a man lingering around in front of your house. He is shabbily dressed and pretends he is drunk," he says. "Every day he stands in front of your house looking at my store."

The grocer assumed that the man was intending to rob his store. "I confronted him today. I said, 'You're acting drunk, but you're not. Get out of here,'" he recounted. He said the man had pulled out a cellphone. A few minutes later, a car showed up and he climbed in. It was a dark blue BMW. Zia swallowed hard. "Could you please keep an eye out for this man, and alert me if you see him?" the grocer said. The family promised to keep a watchful eye, not wanting to reveal that Zia was the more likely target.

The next day, when she arrived at work, she called the men from Reed Security into her office and related the story. "I thought you were protecting me."

They told her not to worry, that "it's been taken care of."

When she pressed them for specifics, they were vague, until finally one admitted, "We did what we could, but U.S. policy is not to get involved when it's 'Iraqi on Iraqi.'"

Zia felt the blood rush to her head in terror. "What are you talking about?" she said, trying to remain calm.

"We don't guarantee security for locals. That's not our call—that's corporate's decision."

"But you told me you were protecting me," she said.

"We handed it over to IP. They said they would deal with it," one said. "They said they assigned a detective to cover you."

"IP? Iraqi police?" Zia sputtered. "Are you crazy?" Now the Iraqi police knew she worked for the Americans—that was truly dangerous. Everyone knew the police had been infiltrated by Muqtada al-Sadr's army. Not only would they not protect her, they might organize her kidnapping themselves.

A horrible feeling sank in as she realized the depths of the betrayal. "I thought you guys were my friends," she said softly.

She called Keith, who once again rushed to her defense. He discussed the situation with the Reed security guards, and one man came back with the group's recommendation for her.

"Go home. Don't come into the Green Zone. Keep your gun with you. Stay in the house and keep your family inside and stagger their leaving, if they must leave at all."

"How can I stay in the house? I work here. I have my job!" she said. They just shrugged. She felt her face burning with humiliation, and realized she was going to have to solve this problem on her own.

And what about the loss of money—who would take care of her family? When she asked if she would receive compensation during her time in hiding, the Americans shook their heads. Zia knew her house and her neighborhood were very dangerous for her now, but they would not help her with relocation costs either. Even though Zia and Keith were both classified as contractors for the same Florida company, which had been given $165 million to run IMN for the year, Keith not only had a salary that was five times higher than Zia's, he was compensated for moving costs, housing, security, meals, vacation time, and travel. But Zia was Iraqi. When she tried to apply to move into one of the thousands of trailers erected inside the Green Zone, her request was denied.

Standing around the office several days later with several sympathetic colleagues, Zia fumed. "They are basically saying: So what. It's your choice. If you don't want to take the risk, go home. Quit."

"God, that sucks," someone said. Silence followed. Zia could see that her colleagues didn't want to hear the details. Her danger was just one more failure for which they didn't want to take responsibility.

Only two people took real action in standing up for her: Keith and Amar. Amar drove her home each day, both of them in the front seats with their guns at hand. As he dropped her off, he said, "If you have problems, call me and I will be here in five minutes. If there is no place safe for you to go, Zia, I will get out of my bed and sleep on my doorstep and you can sleep in my bed."

"Amar, you are the only person to really act. You are a real man," she said, gratefully but wearily.

Zia knew a secure hiding place existed—Keith's trailer. She could move in with him and lie to Baba, but she refused, and Mamina wouldn't even consider the idea. Meanwhile, Keith worked his female contacts inside the Green Zone. He talked to every friend he had, and eventually found a woman with space in her trailer. He convinced her to take in Zia, like a refugee in her own country.

SO ZIA MOVED to the Green Zone, into a flimsy trailer no bigger than one of the palace bathrooms. She shared it with Camille Elhassani, an IMN employee who was raised in the States but had an Iraqi father. She was a pretty thirty-year-old who had worked at ABC Television news in New York before coming to Iraq. They had a skinny bed each, just a few feet from each other. Zia would wake up earlier, but wait for Camille to use the bathroom first, since she was a guest. Camille let Zia stay out of kindness, and Zia wanted to be a thoughtful roommate. They made up small rules (no combat boots in the trailer) and each hung her CPA badge on the door when she came in. As Zia was in the Green Zone unofficially, she had no right to come and go. If she left the grounds, she couldn't be guaranteed she'd be allowed back in. When she bade farewell to her family and drove over the Tigris, she was going less than a mile away but couldn't be sure when she would see them again. Mamina and Nunu had cried in saying goodbye, but Mamina expressed relief that her daughter would be safe and close to Keith. Baba reacted coldly, in the same unemotional way as when she, Mamina, and Nunu had left for Hit. During the spring uprisings he had cursed at the television, frustrated by both the Iraqis and the Americans. Since then, his anger had given way to hopelessness and resignation. He seemed tired and older. Perhaps he was cursing himself for relenting to allow his daughter to work with the Americans. But if he felt this way, he didn't say so openly to Zia.

Life in the Green Zone was safer but still not safe. Before moving into her hiding place in the trailer, she had floated a story around IMN that she was leaving Iraq, but now any one of the hundreds of Iraqi staff—groundskeepers, cleaning ladies, translators, technicians, or engineers—might recognize her. If they caught her, word would spread that not only was she still in Baghdad, but she was "really important" because she was being given housing by the Americans. Potential kidnappers could go after Nunu and use her for ransom. Whenever Zia saw an Iraqi who knew her from the office, she'd have to race back to Camille's trailer and hide. It was a bizarre life, and yet one that had become increasingly normalized in the war zone of Iraq.

She had only one friend whom she trusted. But this girl was preoccupied with her own problems. She had recently become engaged to a young man who was head of the guards at IMN. Zia had considered this man to be too uneducated for her friend but stayed quiet because she knew her friend was in her late twenties and under tremendous pressure from her family to marry. Shortly after Zia moved into the Green Zone, the girl approached her. Her cheeks were tearstained.

"My friend, I need a favor."

She wanted to borrow seven thousand dollars. She said that her fiancé was insisting that they put on a splashy wedding for the public, and that he give her a big dowry of gold and set up a furnished household—except he had no money with which to do this. He wanted his fiancée to secretly give him the money. In exchange, he promised, he would let her continue to work after they were married.

"He has paid for nothing. I paid for this and that and now he wants seven thousand dollars to furnish the house. He told me, 'If you don't get the money, I will break up with you and make a big scandal so no other man proposes.'"

Zia felt frustrated for her friend and lent her fifteen hundred dollars. The episode bothered her tremendously. "Successful Iraqi women cannot marry their equals," she said to Mamina on the phone one evening. "Most Iraqi men now are alike—thinking they are bosses of their wives." Zia would have struggled with a husband like this before the war. She had changed and grown so much in her job with the Americans, she couldn't bear to do so now. This situation only reinforced Zia's appreciation of Keith, and yet made her feel uncomfortably desperate at the thought of losing him.

AFTER ZIA'S FRIEND married, she paid back Zia, and they tried to keep up a friendship. But Zia felt that her friend was becoming more quiet and subservient, adapting as she must to keep the peace in her marriage. The changes were obvious to both, and the friendship grew strained. Her friend didn't want to think about the path she had chosen, nor Zia of the consequences of not following the same path. For the first time since the war, it crossed Zia's mind that women were facing fewer choices now, not more. These thoughts only added to her anxiety over her own future, and she preferred to distract herself rather than to dwell on it.

Life inside the Green Zone itself wasn't as easy as it had once been, either. After the first checkpoint, people were able to roam freely. But fears abounded lately that Iraqis were smuggling in bomb-making materials piece by piece to construct bombs inside the Green Zone. Security checkpoints had gone up across the compound. One rumor suggested that $35,000 was being offered to any Iraqi who kidnapped an American woman, and female soldiers were being strongly advised not to jog, ride their bikes, or walk back to their trailers alone.

The ubiquitous checkpoints were a huge hassle for Zia, as her badge still had the red rim around it marking her as a "local." Since she wasn't technically supposed to be there, she could be arrested and evicted from the Green Zone by an unsympathetic checkpoint soldier. The simplest tasks became difficult, even just eating. Her trailer with Camille had no kitchen, so she couldn't cook for herself. "Locals" couldn't get into the palace cafeteria, where all the Americans ate. So she had to eat at the Green Zone Café or the Chinese restaurant. Yet, if she had to go through a checkpoint to get there, she needed to be escorted by someone with authorization, which meant phoning around looking for an American to interrupt his or her busy workday and take a "local" to lunch. If not for Keith, she would have starved. She tried to keep up her job, working on her laptop and occasionally attending morning meetings in the Red Room, the ambassador's room, which had a red carpet, couches, and a wall of mirrors. But the real work was being done back at Salhiya, and she couldn't be there. She found herself hanging around the tiny trailer, feeling increasingly unwanted.

She was not the only Iraqi seeking refuge inside the Green Zone. It was June 2004, and the CPA had officially dissolved. The ministries were returned to Iraqi control. As the U.S. teams had packed their bags, their Iraqi staff scrambled to secure their futures. Under a death threat, and tainted by their ties to the Americans, they were applying for scholarships, visas, or jobs with any Americans who would stay on in Iraq or in the future U.S. embassy. Many, like Zia, feared for their lives and tried to move into protective custody, but the only ones with any luck were those with good connections—usually romantic entanglements. Rumors flew around Baghdad that Iraqi women were hiding in American men's trailers inside the Green Zone. One newspaper, *Al-Mashriq,* reported that six Iraqi women were being kept inside the Green Zone because they were pregnant by American soldiers.

Zia found herself clinging to the small asides Keith made in regards to their future. His contract ended in six months. They spoke about leaving Iraq, getting married, and moving to the Gulf, maybe Dubai, where jobs were plentiful for Americans. Zia dreamed of this day and prayed for patience. Once she got settled somewhere safe, she imagined, her family would join them.

· · ·

BUT EVEN THINGS with Keith weren't problem-free. In the Salhiya office of IMN, Zia and Keith had been around only a few of Keith's American friends, and they had hidden their new relationship as best they could. But once Zia moved into the Green Zone, they came clean and socialized nightly together with dozens of his friends, including his brother Loren.

One day, Loren pulled Zia aside, and the awkwardness she always felt around him became clear. "I don't know how to tell you this, Z," he said. "But Keith's still married."

Zia felt her stomach drop.

"He's separated from Cathy, but they aren't divorced."

Zia felt a pang of jealousy run through her at the woman's name, and how Loren said it with such familiarity. She rushed to Keith to confront him. "You said you were divorced!"

He assuaged her. "We've been separated for years. We're in the process of getting a divorce. It takes a long time because of California law. I thought it would go through by now, but it hasn't."

After months of the tension of living under death threats and fearing for her family, Zia finally cracked. In an environment where Zia felt she could trust no one, her relationship with Keith—they were *soul mates*—had been the only source of security. She broke down. He insisted she could trust him, but her suspicions ate at her. One afternoon, Zia went on to Keith's computer and checked his email. As she scrolled through months and months of communication, she paled as the same name appeared again and again: *Cathy,* often several times a day. The emails were perfunctory, involving bills for their daughter or tax issues. There were no romantic exchanges or emotional missives, but neither was there any mention of Zia. She felt blindsided. Cathy clearly played a big role in his life, and yet, eight months into a relationship in which he and Zia spent hours together each day, this woman's name had never once come up.

A HUMAN BEING can do without many things in life, and under Saddam, Zia learned to live without a comfortable home, meat and vegetables, soaps or schoolbooks. Mamina was a master at making do. The abundance of love with which Mamina showered her girls only increased as the shortages had grown worse. What she could never give them, though, was choices or control over their destiny. This was what the Americans offered that Zia had been so drawn to. Yet she now found herself feeling more desperate than she ever had under Saddam.

Her pride made her want more than anything to storm away from Keith, but she literally couldn't move more than a few hundred meters without encountering a military checkpoint that she needed Keith and his security clearance to accompany her through.

She went three more weeks living in her trailer. By July, she felt she couldn't take it anymore. She felt outside herself and couldn't think straight. She couldn't sleep for nights on end and then would sleep fourteen hours straight. Meanwhile, there was chatter among the security guards that "Zia had to go." More Americans were arriving to help with the reconstruction, even though most work was being done inside the Green Zone. "We need the space and she's got to move out of here."

Zia tried to obtain a visa to Kuwait so she could relocate her job to the company's Kuwait office. But the Kuwaiti government refused her a visa because she didn't have a Department of Defense badge. She turned to her supervisor for help, but their relationship had chilled since Zia had challenged her over the rumors surrounding Nicholas Berg's murder. Many of the American friends she had made—people who had always been so kind and supportive of her—seemed to be at a loss as to how to help her. The answer always came back the same: "It's not our decision" or "No way."

At one point, she had lunch with an Iraqi friend who had a similar story of abandonment. "They are just trying to get us off their shoulders now," she said.

Zia nodded bitterly. "They don't care how many Iraqis die. Would they have to pay for me? No, I don't have insurance. Would they have to pay for my family? No. If I were to die, they'd miss me as a friend, but formally? No one at IMN would care."

The only person who stood by her, and didn't make excuses, was Keith. He knew Zia felt betrayed and angry, and he vacillated between apologizing and defending himself. They argued, and the relationship became tense, aggravated by the fear they both felt for her life. He pushed their employer, the Harris Corporation, which in 2004 was given the contract to run IMN, to write a letter to the U.S. government appealing for its help in relocating their Iraqi staff. He lobbied hard to keep her in the trailer. But it wasn't working. Finally, Zia decided she'd had enough, and she knew she'd soon be forced out anyway. She called Mamina.

"I can't stand this anymore, Mama," she said. "I have to get out of here."

CHAPTER TWENTY-FIVE

FOR THE FIRST month after Fern's death, Manal wore only black—black abaya, black pants, black shirt. She wore no makeup. Although she had changed back into regular clothes, she still felt a black cloud around her, and she had lost her energy. In the months after Fern was killed, one bad event had followed another—the marines invaded Falluja, Muqtada's militia had risen up in the south and in Baghdad's Sadr City, and then the photos from Abu Ghraib were released. As the chaos worsened, her staff had begun arguing. Some were appalled by the photos from Abu Ghraib, but others, including Ahmed, were convinced the photos were a hoax, orchestrated by Saudi Arabia to further embarrass the Americans and undermine support for them in the Arab world. Allegiances often broke down into Sunni versus Shia, and Manal struggled to keep everyone united.

Yet she, too, was losing heart. *It's over,* she thought. *The window's closed. We've lost.* She wanted to go home.

Three months after the pomp and circumstance of opening day, darkness fell over the Mansour Women's Center. During the spring uprisings, a bomb had been placed outside the building. It never detonated, but shortly thereafter, gunmen drove past at night and opened fire, pockmarking the courtyard walls with bullets. In southern Iraq, someone bombed the Karbala Women's Center, which Fern had been coming from when she was gunned down. A guard was killed. After that, Manal withdrew her programs from Fern's centers. She felt guilty about abandoning the projects that Fern had died to build, but she couldn't put her employees in any more danger. Plus, stories of corruption were rife after Fern's death. Manal heard reports that the Iraqi staff was charging women for the classes. The Iraqis who took over after Fern died were hungry only for U.S. contracts and used the women's centers as cash cows. Manal's instinct was to charge down to the center and confront the bullies. But she thought of her family, and her promises to them to be careful; and of her staff. By now, she had met all of their families, shared meals, spent hours exchanging stories. Ahmed, who once treated her with condescension, had become her closest confidant. They discussed most decisions beforehand, and Manal openly expressed that she'd never forgive herself if something happened to her staff.

Even so, Manal's staff begged her not to close down the center. "Manal, this is the only job we have. We have worked so hard." So she kept the Mansour Women's Center open throughout the spring and summer to keep them on the payroll, even though little happened inside. To protect the center, she and Heather contracted to have a ten-foot-high security wall built around the perimeter, to absorb the shock if someone placed a bomb outside the building, as was increasingly common. Sympathetic to complaints that a concrete wall would destroy the gentle atmosphere of the center, Manal and Heather made plans to plant flowers all around it, but they never had the chance. Before it was even finished, the wall collapsed due to shoddy construction. Manal had gone through the Americans to hire the contractor, but he refused to fix it. With no rule of law, Manal had little recourse. When she shouted at him, he threatened her and the center with violence. Manal sighed—paying a man to protect them had created only another threat. The wall stayed crumbled.

More than anyone else, Ahmed grew concerned about Manal's safety. Bigger aid organizations, with more security than Women for Women could afford, had already packed up their bags. "Sooner or later you will be noticed and they will come for you," he said worriedly. But Manal was adamant about not abandoning her staff and the women she worked with. Still, as the attacks on Westerners increased, Women for Women required Manal not to leave the house where she lived and worked at night, and on some days she was told not to leave at all.

Ahmed openly cursed their decision to work with the Americans on the center. "All of our problems at Women for Women began with this center. It brought us bad luck."

Manal had not wanted to admit to herself her growing misgivings about teaming up with Heather. "Everything started going wrong in March," she replied wearily. "Not just for women."

ANY MOVEMENT ON behalf of Iraqi women's rights had to come from Iraqis now. The CPA was gone, and most aid workers had fled the country, unable to afford security and terrified they'd be kidnapped or killed. In spring 2004, Secretary of State Colin Powell had announced a $10 million contract to promote women's rights in Iraq, the first such financial contract aimed specifically at Iraqi women, but much of it went to the Independent Women's Forum (IWF), the Republican group started by Lynne Cheney, and to the America Islamic Congress, which had backed the invasion. The IWF didn't even have an office in the country, Manal thought bitterly; it was just a political payout.

The Iraqi government wasn't doing anything for women, since it was preoccupied with trying to stop the constant terrorist attacks, both across the country and on its own members. Of the three Iraqi women in the government, in particular, the attacks were relentless. The conservative member Salama al-Khafaji, who had replaced Aqila al-Hashimi, had risen to national stature on the back of her defense of the veil and her accusations against Western women. Yet, in May 2004, she was attacked in exactly the same manner as Fern had been killed. Gunmen pulled up alongside her convoy of cars and opened fire. She survived, but her bodyguard and her teenage son were killed. Still, al-Khafaji refused to quit, saying, "I am not the only woman in Iraq who has lost her son. We must go on."

Every month, a different government member was attacked, whether Sunni or Shia, pro- or anti-American. Manal felt the country slip into anarchy. Iraqi women's rights activists were terrified that their association with Women for Women would be discovered, that they would be attacked for "collaborating" with Western infidels. The gangs were now thriving in Baghdad, and kidnapping a foreigner was the fastest way to bring in tens of thousands of dollars in ransom.

"I am making little difference, and putting myself in danger," Manal worried.

She began to think of leaving Iraq. Her office was a prison. She couldn't leave without an armored car, couldn't meet openly with women or visit their homes, couldn't be seen going in and out of the convention center, couldn't hand out literature with non-Arabic text. But still, leaving felt cowardly. She couldn't abandon these women after leading them into the protests and activism that now threatened their lives.

She gazed out the window of her office, across the balcony overlooking the Tigris. The old house had been built by Zainab Salbi's grandfather in the first half of the twentieth century, during the British mandate. It was a beautiful piece of Islamic architecture—a symbol of what Baghdad had once been and the beauty it had created.

As she sat there, women leaving her twice-monthly "rights awareness classes" passed by. The door to Manal's office was open and they stuck their heads in.

"How are you doing?" one asked, concerned. Manal managed a smile. "Every night I pray to Mohammed and Allah to protect you," the woman added.

The next day, more women came by. They were from one of Manal's skills training classes.

Sitting on the pillows in the corner of her office, they smiled. "Manal, everywhere I go I tell women about the classes and how they are affecting our lives, and the lives of so many women."

Each day, more and more women visited her to share a smile or give an encouraging word. Soon she realized what was going on. The women saw she was grieving. Word had spread that she was giving up hope.

"My daughter took your class on the importance of education, and she learned that women have a right to education. Now she is enrolled in school," said one.

"Your trainer helped me find the medicine I needed for my husband," said another.

Manal was in Iraq to help them, and she felt the support Women for Women provided circling back to lift her up in her time of need. More than anything else, the women thanked her for the skills training. Some had started their own businesses. One old woman told Manal she had opened her own fruit stand. Before, she had been a beggar who survived from handouts at the mosque, but after enrolling in a skills training class, she learned the basics of business, gained confidence from the support of other women, and started selling fruit herself. To show her appreciation, the woman had brought into class a watermelon to share. "If not for the center, I never would have done this," she said. "Before I begged for watermelon, and now I can provide it to others."

Manal felt humbled, and pushed to go on. She could barely handle one year of the life these women had suffered through for decades. She realized that gains came in small, invisible ways, through personal contact—not the erection of a glossy women's center. They were small moments of victory—they didn't make the news or merit a CPA press release, but they mattered.

She sat her staff down.

"Thank you for all you have done for me in the past few weeks. Your support has kept me going," she said. She took a deep breath. "But I want to give you the option of putting the programs on hold. As much as we try to do, working with the programs puts you in direct danger. We can't create a force field around us."

A cry arose from her staff.

"Manal, how could you possibly crush the very hope we have spent so many months building?" They pointed to the six hundred women their program had helped. "We are making a difference, Manal. We work with these women every day—we cannot abandon them."

Even Ahmed piped up. "These women had nothing and we've taught them women's rights, how to stand up for themselves, how to have confidence, and to care about the elections. The center has been a place for them to get out of the house, sit and network and meet."

"Even the money has helped them, Manal," he said, smiling.

Manal smiled too. The prior year, she had decided to give the women who attended her workshops a stipend of fifteen dollars a month. Ahmed had resisted this, arguing it was too little to matter. "I saw how it helped the women," he conceded.

Ahmed's support meant the world to Manal. He was now her constant companion, keeping her spirits high by bringing her sandwiches and playing board games with her during the long evenings under curfew. And when Ahmed stayed late, so did his two coworkers, Mustafa and Fawaz, so Manal never felt uncomfortable in being alone with him.

Manal realized that just as there were human beings committed to wanton violence—both Americans and Iraqis—there was a majority in both groups who were dedicated to the humanitarian effort. She had to help that majority find a voice. She had to encourage their small hopes, not let them be extinguished. *Yes,* she thought, *we will stay in Iraq.* She would stay as long as she could.

CHAPTER TWENTY-SIX

THE BLUE, GREEN, and gold lights of the bustling downtown twinkled at night. Students in headscarves milled outside McDonald's and Burger King, and the skyline was ablaze with the well-lit names of five-star hotels like the Four Seasons and the Hyatt.

Feeling her time had run out in the Green Zone, Zia made a bold move. She booked a plane ticket to the neighboring country of Jordan. Zia had decided she would start over. Rather than dwell on feelings of betrayal, she forced herself to think optimistically: *Maybe the Americans didn't come through, but at least they opened the door for me to make a new life for myself instead of slowly suffocating under Saddam.* She had twenty thousand dollars saved up from her IMN job and a vague plan. Jordan was a Muslim country, but afforded many freedoms to women, especially in the capital city, Amman. She would move into a small hotel until she found an apartment. She would look for temporary work and apply to universities in the USA and the UK. She might have to cut corners and do without, but, after years of hardship and prejudice in Iraq, she would finally have her pride, dignity, and freedom. This was going to be her new life. Every inch of her told her she'd made the right choice. Leaving Keith had been difficult, but it had become a matter of pride. She loved him and believed his relationship with his wife was, emotionally, over. But when he couldn't say for certain when his divorce would be finalized, she felt ashamed of their relationship. She wouldn't be the "other woman," and she wouldn't let herself become desperate. A woman had to be in control of her destiny and create choices for herself, Mamina had said in supporting her decision to go to Jordan. She was going to have a big career, and a new life of freedom in this new country.

. . .

THE FIRST FEW weeks of living in Jordan were like a dream. Walking around the city freely without the fear of kidnappings or bombs was a pleasure in itself. Baba took a bus with Nunu and Mamina from Baghdad to join Zia in her two-bedroom apartment in the quiet University of Jordan neighborhood, Jubaiha. Baba returned immediately, but Mamina planned to stay for a month and then go back to teaching and to take care of Baba, while Nunu—who was on break from her university—would stay with Zia until classes resumed in October. Baba was happy to have the family in Jordan for a while. Although the man acting drunk had not returned, since Zia left they had been living in fear that the house would be bombed or Nunu would be kidnapped. Zia's absence in the neighborhood was gossiped about, and Mamina and Baba had agreed to say she had accepted a job in Kuwait. But Zia's employment inside the Green Zone had become a well-known secret, and gossip abounded that she was hiding or even dead. Mamina let such rumors spread—better the insurgents think her daughter was dead than try to come after her. Nunu, however, couldn't bear the pressure of lying. At the university, she tried to avoid the militias on campus but couldn't escape the prying questions into Zia's whereabouts by girls whose older siblings had known her. Nunu felt herself a terrible liar, and preferred to duck her head and race from class to class. Without her sister to confide in in the evenings, she increasingly felt isolated and alone.

In Amman, Nunu's high spirits returned. Maybe things would improve by the time they returned, she wondered aloud to Mamina. *Insh'allah,* Mamina said.

While she was in Jordan, Keith called Zia several times a day. In August, he came to see her. They took a day trip to Aqaba, a picturesque seaside town in southern Jordan, that felt like a honeymoon—that was how Zia liked to imagine it. But it was merely a respite from the realities of their troubled romance. When he was back in Baghdad, every time she pushed him about their wedding, he pushed back. "Divorce takes time in California," he said. "Sometimes years." Keith's brother Walter, backed him up, telling Zia that his own divorce in California had taken several years. After a while, she let the subject drop. She was too proud to ask him to marry her. She didn't want to even risk the possibility that Keith or anyone else thought she was just "trying to marry a passport." She didn't want to believe she needed Keith. She had her family, after all. She told herself she could stand on her own feet and be an independent woman.

The only problem with this plan, though, was that as weeks went by Zia was finding Jordan to be a difficult place to be an independent woman. Her plan started with a hunt for a temporary job to earn some cash, but almost all of the jobs listed in the local newspapers said "Jordanians only." A few people she called hung up on her when they found out she was Iraqi. Other job offerings were suspect. One position was described only as "Admin. asst." for a private company. The man behind the desk told her, "Your job is to drum up business and please clients." When he told her the hours were 9:00 p.m. to 11:00 p.m., she left immediately. Another job offered only $150 a month, a pittance that wouldn't cover half the rent. Another was for a secretary in a dimly lit basement office, a job she felt was depressing and beneath her. One potential employer tried to argue with her about IMN. "Saddam was a great man," he said. "Why would you betray your country by working with the foreigners?" Zia picked up her purse and left.

Meanwhile, her plans to leapfrog over to university in America had also ground to a halt. She was shocked to discover tuition costs of between $15,000 and $35,000 a year, and she hadn't realized master's programs in business administration required two years in the USA, unlike the single year in the UK and Iraq. That was an extra year of tuition and housing before she could graduate and apply for jobs. Zia had come to Jordan with a vague plan to work, save money, and then move to Britain or the States until the situation improved in Iraq. She wasn't particular about where she went, but she wanted to get her master's degree and keep moving her life forward professionally. But each way she turned, the doors seemed closed.

Each passing day left her feeling more deflated. Occasionally, she and Nunu saw other Iraqi women in Amman at Internet cafés, employment offices, or at the embassy. She knew they were Iraqi by their accent. When she chatted with them, she realized they had sadder stories than hers: "My father was killed; my brother has no job and we have no money." Others were even more desperate. In the food court of Amman's Mecca Mall, she saw Iraqi women wearing lipstick, dressed in tight pants and high heels, strutting past the Kentucky Fried Chicken looking for clients. Whenever she felt sorry for herself, she remembered these women and prayed for them. While Zia was looking for a job, Nunu stayed inside the apartment watching Egyptian soap operas and episodes of *Oprah,* cooking, and cleaning. She didn't like to venture outside by herself, as taxi drivers often made nasty comments to her. She had few places to go, anyway.

Many American companies contracted to work in Iraq were moving their offices, conferences, and meetings to Jordan because of the terrorism in Iraq, so Amman was thriving financially, which made it even more frustrating for Zia that she couldn't find a job. An enormous billboard was erected on the highway from the airport promoting the country as a place for those with Iraq contracts to live and work: "Jordan: established rule of law; thriving private sector; competent labor force; gateway to the Middle East."

Yeah, that used to be Iraq's dream, Zia thought sadly, *only a year ago.*

After five weeks of rejections, in her last and final attempt at a job, Zia enrolled in a stewardess-training class advertised in the newspaper. Stewardess was not the career she had dreamed for herself, exactly, but she had always loved clouds and the thought of flying felt freeing. The class was full of young, pretty women from Chechnya and Moldova with big dreams and vague personal histories. Some shared apartments in Jordan. The teacher was an unkempt Jordanian man who said he had worked for Royal Jordanian Airlines, and would teach them to hostess for airlines. She and the other women each paid him one hundred dollars. He taught them the flight-safety message and they went over emergency exit procedures. By the fifth class, however, the teacher became crude. He cursed and talked about his relationship with his Mexican wife.

At the end of the six classes, the teacher said they were ready to take an exam, but there would be an additional fee of one hundred dollars for their certificate. This fee could be waived if the young women signed a contract to work for his company for a year. When Zia learned the details of his company, she quickly realized the whole thing was most likely a scam. He flew charter flights for pilgrims going to Mecca in Saudi Arabia. Pilgrims were often religious radicals, and, she knew, the stewardesses were often prostitutes. Once in Saudi Arabia—or wherever the plane landed—any unaccompanied young women on board could be kidnapped or trafficked. A single woman in Saudi Arabia has few rights. If she was raped, the government could punish her, even kill her, for the crime of traveling without a male relative, which they believed was forbidden in the Quran. Although many of the other girls signed up anyway, Zia decided the class was no longer for her and didn't take the test.

Still, she thought she had the training to become a stewardess, so she took her receipt and set up an interview with human resources at Royal Jordanian. The minute she stepped into the office and opened her mouth, the woman snapped at her, "You're not Jordanian. Only locals can apply."

Zia knew that Royal Jordanian hired stewardesses from around the world, but the woman just shook her head and repeated herself. Furious that they were rejecting her for being Iraqi, Zia wanted to scream at the horrible woman that this job was beneath her anyway, and she had worked with the U.S. government, as a *transmissions site manager*, with people from the *White House*. How dare she treat her like this? Before the tears could rush to her eyes, she swiveled on her heels and stormed out the door.

BY ZIA'S THIRD month there, Amman started to feel dirty, congested, and noisy. She fell into a deep depression and spent nights crying in her bed. Nunu tried to comfort her, but she had little understanding of Zia's ambitions or professional disappointments. "If God wills it, you will be with Keith" was all she could think of to say. Zia missed Keith, but she also really missed her old job. When she remembered the early days at IMN she broke into tears. *Good dreams don't last long,* she thought. She had worked for a year, trying to prove herself and get promoted, but it had all been for nothing. Occasionally, someone would email her, needing something, and she'd reply instantly with the item's exact location. She could walk into that office blindfolded and find anything. That was *her* office. *It's not mine anymore,* she reminded herself. *It's theirs now.*

Instead of her being part of the team, now all the people who had talked about helping her either weren't returning her emails or had disappointing news. Even her former supervisor wouldn't help. There was a branch of her company in Amman, and Zia wanted to apply there. But instead the supervisor wanted to talk to Zia about her relationship with Keith, of which she disapproved. When Zia defended it, the emails stopped.

What was she fighting for now? she wondered. She had left behind her country, her job, and her real love, thinking she would find something better and be able to move up and out on her own. But Jordan didn't want her, no one would hire her, and things with Keith were only making everything worse, on all fronts. In late September, Mamina and Baba came to fetch Nunu, and brought Zia a new package from a matchmaker. Inside was a long letter and a passport photo. A Jordanian man in his forties, who ran his own business and lived most of the time in the States, was looking for a young bride who would be willing to stay in Jordan and manage the domestic end of his business. Had it come to this? Zia stared at the photo stapled to the letter. He wore a cheap white button-down shirt and a sports jacket. He was pale and balding. Nunu laughed. "You will become a Catholic nun before you marry this man."

But Zia felt much more serious about all of this now than she had just a few months ago. What if this were her last offer? Soon, Zia would be twenty-three. Her aunt in London wouldn't send another prospect after the debacle with the London PhD, and no Iraqi man would marry her without first snooping around her neighborhood asking about her reputation. By now, all the neighbors knew she worked for the Americans, and it was possible they also knew about Keith. Once a suitor uncovered that news, he would certainly withdraw the offer.

And yet she knew she could never be happy in a marriage that began like this. Since the Americans had come, her expectations were higher. She wanted to marry in the Western way, where the couple become friends first and fall in love. She knew what she was telling herself. Really, she wanted to marry Keith. She loved him. But what if Keith never divorced? What if her supervisor had been right, that he was using her? More than a broken heart was at stake. She would end up a spinster, or married to an old, penniless widower. She wondered which fate was worse, to be a spinster or a slave?

She looked again at the photo of the balding Jordanian, and sighed to her sister. "Why not? Maybe I should marry him. He will take care of me. I will have my problems solved."

"No way," Nunu said, horrified. She hugged her sister. "I will never let you marry this man." Zia had to smile. "Come on," Nunu said. "Come with us back to Baghdad."

Nunu was right. Zia didn't want to stay in Amman alone, where she had no friends, no family, no memories, no job. She packed her bags, and emailed the same friend she had emailed so excitedly in her first week:

> Sometimes you move vertically and sometimes horizontally. This time in Jordan turned out to be a horizontal move. I learned something and I got some knowledge of life. But it's time to go back. I'd rather die once in Iraq than every day here.

BUT BEING BACK in the cramped apartment in Karrada brought Zia no sense of returning to the comforts of home, though it had been four months since she'd last lived there. The apartment was a perverse prison, she decided, where the innocent people were locked inside and the criminals roamed the neighborhoods freely. Zia felt incredibly alone. On the streets, Zia noticed almost no young women walking around. Those who did were veiled. The rest were taking shelter in the refuge of their bedrooms, a life that, no matter how depressing, was, ironically, their only chance for survival in the "new Iraq." Zia knew she couldn't live for long like this.

Within a few days she arranged to meet up with the bureau chief at the American channel NBC, who she'd heard was hiring reporters. As she walked past the concrete blast walls and up the white marble steps, she passed dozens of unemployed Iraqi men who waited outside in the hopes a Westerner would emerge looking for a driver or translator. Even though they, too, were vying to work with the Americans, the men hissed at her as she went in, calling her a whore. She snapped back at them, although she knew she could no longer count on the safety of the Green Zone and it was reckless to make enemies.

The NBC producer turned out to be a rude Australian who thought too highly of himself. After the interview, he offered her $250 a month, less than $10 a day.

"I don't work for less than five hundred dollars a month," she replied. It wasn't just the money; the producer and his staff rented several floors in Baghdad's nicest hotel. They had fancy equipment, a fleet of SUVs, bodyguards, and all the nicest imported foods and liquor—she saw it as she walked in. Yet he offered her a slave's wage and acted as though he were doing her a favor, even though it was she who would be risking her life driving to and from the office and going out on stories.

The more desperate Iraqis became, the more prideful Zia felt. Mamina's words were her wings. She told her, "Don't work for nothing. We have survived worse than this before and we will do it again. But don't lose your dignity." The producer upped his offer to $300 a month, and when Zia refused, he showed her the door. She went home and lay down. She didn't sleep or talk, she just lay there. Three weeks passed.

All the while, Keith called and called. She hadn't seen him since their Aqaba trip.

Finally, Zia couldn't stand another day locked in the bedroom. "I want my old job back," she told Keith.

Keith told her about a vacancy in the Project Contracting Office in the Green Zone.

They talked to some people. There were plenty of jobs available for Iraqis, but they couldn't offer her safe housing, any security escorts, or anything other than her salary. Zia took it, even if it meant making the dangerous daily commute from her home to the Green Zone each day.

"I will die before I lose this job again," she said.

CHAPTER TWENTY-SEVEN

POP, POP. GUNSHOTS rang out in the cool night air of the Green Zone.

Standing with their drinks on the patio of the U.S. Institute of Peace headquarters, not far from Saddam's palace, Heather Coyne and her friend Clarke exchanged an alarmed look. They both recognized the sound from their military training. "A nine millimeter?" Clarke said.

She nodded. "That was a little too close for comfort."

"Could have been a negligent discharge?" he asked hopefully.

He and Heather were the only two soldiers at the party. Around them, the other party guests—embassy officials, State Department officials, and consultants to the United Nations—noticed their alarm. It was late October 2004, and over the prior months more and more houses in the Green Zone had been handed back to Iraqis as the CPA had moved out, and no one was quite sure anymore who was living nearby, and where a threat might come from.

"You think an insurgent slipped through?" someone whispered.

Whatever it was, it stopped the party. Heather had started throwing these weekly networking events after she joined USIP in September 2004. This new gig was, at last, the nation-building job she had dreamed about as a twenty-something in the Office of Management and Budget. Free of the crippling bureaucracy of the U.S. military, Lieutenant A. Heather Coyne was now just Heather, and she dressed in plain-clothes and no longer carried a weapon. She viewed her job as part of a loyal, determined effort to bring the country back from the brink of civil war. Either that, or she was just unable to wrench her eyes away from the train wreck she had helped create. She had to admit to herself that, at thirty-two, she wasn't trying to get back to the States and get on with some other more traditional life. Her career was her life, and, after eighteen months, Saddam's palace compound had become her dysfunctional home. Her prewar existence felt like a distant memory. As bad as things had gotten, Heather told herself that the situation could be turned around. She found reason to hope in the upcoming elections, and in the drafting of the constitution. She still wanted to believe that she could make a difference.

Since the dissolution of the CPA on June 28, Iraqis seemed to be on tenterhooks wondering what would happen next. Signs were bad. For most of July and August, relations between the military and the Shia militias worsened as they battled in southern Iraq for control of the city of Najaf. Meanwhile, in western Iraq, Sunni insurgents had moved back into Falluja. Attacks against Western civilians were down, mostly due to the fact that most had left the country or were staying inside the fortified walls of the Green Zone or their hotels. But soldiers patrolling neighborhoods were constantly under attack. By September, the death toll of U.S. soldiers had reached one thousand.

Even more worrying for Iraq's prospects of long-term stability, Heather thought, were the reports of increasing sectarian violence. Immediately after the spring uprisings, Sunnis and Shias had united in their opposition against the Americans, but lately they were turning against each other. Many believed that Al Qaeda was provoking tension by attacking Shias, while others accused the Americans of secretely trying to spark a civil war to weaken the country and prolong their occupation. The embattled Iraqi government launched a campaign, "Sunnis and Shias Unite," but random acts against Sunni tribal leaders or Shia shrines continued across the country.

From her limited reach inside the Green Zone, Heather's hope was to, at least, get the structures in place for a civil society that could function once the anarchy abated. She had some reason to hope. Most of the ineffective Republican Party loyalists had left in June, and many of the new arrivals were trained Arabists from the State Department, seasoned diplomats and experts in constitutional law and postwar reconstruction—although they gravitated to office work over getting out and meeting with Iraqis. She felt confident in the Iraqi employees on her team. The first nationwide elections for parliament were scheduled for January 2005, and she was running training sessions in campaigning and governance for Iraqi leaders. She was working with Manal to recruit female candidates and prepare them for lawmaking. The elections would be followed by a yearlong effort to write and finalize the national constitution, and Heather was doing her best to advocate for inclusion of a 25 percent quota of female representation in government.

Yet, as hard as they worked, and as monumental as were their tasks, Heather had to acknowledge the possibility that no one was paying any attention; that the Iraqis were on course for a civil war; and that the Americans were just a bunch of bureaucrats writing a constitution that no one would read and forming a government that no one would respect. They were tired, stressed, and lived in constant fear of attack. That month, a suicide bomber had snuck into the Green Zone and blown himself up inside the Green Zone Café, killing one and wounding five others, including Heather's good friend Kristi, who had been sitting near the bomber and was hit with shrapnel and hospitalized. She had spent the hours after the attack recuperating in bloody bandages on Heather's couch. Heather knew they had to get the right structures in place before the rising tide of violence consumed them all.

Guests started pulling out their cellphones to report the shots. When they determined there was no widespread attack, they broke off into groups to investigate the sounds. As she wandered around the artificial pond behind the bungalow, Heather could hear Clarke shouting *taha khuli* for Samson, the friendly one-year-old border collie he had adopted as a puppy from the streets. Clarke didn't go anywhere without him; he was the Green Zone's beloved neighborhood dog. After a few minutes of wandering, Heather came out onto the empty street, where a dog was barking agitatedly, but it wasn't Samson. When she turned around she saw Clarke a few yards away, bent over under a fluorescent streetlight, strangely concentrating on a pile of leaves. Then she realized; it was Samson.

Clarke was trying to scoop the dog up, but as he rose to stand he wobbled. "I feel dizzy."

Horrified, Heather leaned in. "How is he?" she asked, knowing the answer.

"He's dead. As soon as I picked him up I felt the heat and the blood," he said weakly. He patted Samson's stomach. "Here's the entry wound."

Party guests gathered behind them, silhouetted by the lone street-light. "Oh my God."

"Someone shot Samson?"

"Why?"

Heather knew how much Clarke loved that dog. "Oh, Clarke, I'm so sorry." She laid a hand on his shoulder. She searched up and down the long, empty asphalt for a clue or a motive, but there were only the usual gray Jersey barriers lined with barbed wire. "There's no reason for this. Why the hell would someone hurt an innocent dog?"

As the crowd thickened, paranoia set in. Was this a wanton act of cruelty, people wondered, or an orchestrated attack on Clarke's boss, like a warning? Was this a veiled threat against the Americans, or a revenge killing? Had the gunman fled, or was he watching them right now, from the bushes or even standing among them? Heather overheard someone calling for security on their cellphone. The crowd huddled together for safety and a few guests fought back tears. Heather didn't feel like crying, she just felt tired.

Then a voice broke through the din of the crowd. "Hey, man, it's just a dog." The accent was Iraqi. His words cut through the group.

Heather swiveled around to see who had said such a thing. It was her friend and translator, Firas. "It's not *just a dog*."

Glaring back at her, Firas walked over to Clarke. "I'm sorry, man," he said, putting his hand on Clarke's shoulder as he leaned over Samson. "But there's all kinds of crazy shit going on here. I've got cousins who have died. There are worse things."

Clarke looked up, embarrassed. "Yeah, I know. It's okay."

But Heather felt he was missing the point. "Don't make an excuse for this. It's just violence, an innocent death for no reason," she continued, her voice rising. "What, whatever whim you have, you indulge it with your weapon and who cares about the consequences?" It was clear they were no longer just talking about the dog. In Heather's mind, this was yet another example of a well-intentioned effort crushed by reckless violence.

Another Iraqi emerged from the group, one who also wanted to seize the moment to make a broader point. "I'm sorry, but people are getting killed all the time out there," he said. "There's a lot of pain. It's a luxury that your loss is just a pet, and not a brother or sister."

Clarke tried to placate the group. The conversation was interrupted by the arrival of several Humvees with troops, responding to the shots. Someone suggested burying Samson, and ran off to fetch an ATO mailbag with which to contain him.

Guests began to wander back to the house, to get their belongings and leave. When Heather returned to the château, she saw Samson's red leash hanging by the door. Maybe he was just a dog, but such a random act of cruelty against an innocent animal stung. Heather knew exactly how Clarke felt. He had poured his attentions and affections into the one thing that he could control. He thought he could make a difference, even if it was just to a dog. Now that promise was destroyed as well.

CHAPTER TWENTY-EIGHT

ZIA RETURNED TO work for the Americans, but it was not the same.

By the late fall of 2004, the CPA felt like a distant memory. It had left behind an interim Iraqi government headed by Ayad Allawi, a doctor who had led efforts to overthrow Saddam for thirty years. He would run the government, officially, until elections the following January. But the country felt adrift. Kidnappings, abductions, and public assassinations occurred weekly. Suicide bombers struck every few days, explosions rumbling for miles, sending thick clouds of smoke into the air, filling up the morgues. The militias publicly refused to recognize Allawi's government. Iraqi police hung around, but they were poorly trained and increasingly loyal to local militias such as Muqtada al-Sadr's. The feeling around Baghdad was that no one was in charge, and uncertainty hung in the air as Iraqis waited to see who would fill the power vacuum before they aligned themselves publicly. Women, for the most part, stayed indoors unless accompanied by a male relative or husband.

Feeling shut down and embittered, Zia now socialized with no one but Keith. She drove each day to and from the Green Zone, despite the growing risks. Sometimes Baba drove her and sometimes she drove herself, but she always kept her hand close to the gun in her purse. Neither Nunu nor Baba challenged her about it; it would have been useless. Each morning as she walked out of her house to her car, she put on a false face of confidence for her sister even while she silently hoped she wasn't saying goodbye for the last time. "What is destined to happen will happen," she would say to Nunu, hoping to comfort them both.

Outside the Green Zone, she watched in horror as Islamists stood at

the gates of schools and universities, and at checkpoints in neighborhoods, threatening terrified women to veil. Zia refused. She would prefer to die than live like a caged bird. All around her, women's rights
activists had been killed for speaking up for their rights, professors were
murdered for supporting secular laws, and Iraqi lawyers, judges, and
journalists were being assassinated. Soon enough, she felt sure, they
would come for her as well.

AT THE END of one brisk winter's day, a few days after she returned to
working inside the Green Zone, Keith drove Zia to the edge of the zone,
according to their new routine. Before them was a maze of concrete
blast walls and heavily guarded security sites. Perched in a tower above
were American and Iraqi snipers. The border between the Green Zone
and downtown Baghdad was as fortified as if it separated two countries
at war, which, in a way, it did. Since cellphones were banned near the
checkpoint, she called Baba from the car to confirm he was waiting for
her at their regular meeting spot, beyond the barbed wire, parked close
to Zia's exit. Keith quickly squeezed her hand goodbye and they exchanged intimate glances, the most public display of affection they
could risk. She got out and crossed the 14th of July Bridge, named for
the day the Iraqi army overthrew the British-installed king in 1958. As
beautiful as the view of the city was beyond the sparkling waters of the
Tigris, this passage felt to Zia like walking a plank.

Though she'd done this before, Zia could not stop her heart from
pounding as she exited the checkpoint, stepping out onto the crumbling
pavement of downtown Baghdad. The city throbbed before her; cars
whizzing past, vendors crowding the sidewalks, groups of unemployed
men gathered under the shade of a tree. Was everyone staring at her?
Every face felt hostile. She checked the nearby rooftops for snipers, but
saw none. With all the radicals crawling around the city, feeling empow-
ered by Muqtada al-Sadr, fewer and fewer unveiled women could be
seen. Zia wore a veil and dark glasses and a bullet-proof vest under her
coat. She had had to leave her gun at home, because the Americans
wouldn't authorize her to be armed inside the Green Zone. She remembered the taxi driver from the goldsmith's, shuddered, and hurried to her
father's car.

"Hi, Baba," she said breathlessly, sliding into the passenger seat. He drove off immediately in silence. As they drove Zia repeatedly checked the side mirror, purely from force of habit. She wondered how many times she would have to make this trip before she'd be able to relax—if ever. Though nothing had happened so far, each time it gave her the same panicky desperation.

Today, however, not even a few blocks had passed before she noticed something that made her heart sink.

"Baba, make this turn," she said quietly, hoping against hope.

He turned, and then turned again.

Both times, a man driving a blue Toyota turned and followed behind them. His license plate indicated that he was from Samarra, a city north of Baghdad, where attacks against Americans were common.

Minutes ticked by, but Baba drove calmly, steadily through the streets.

"How many in the car?" he asked.

Zia took a deep breath. "Just one."

Without turning around, she sized up the man in the side mirror. He was in his early thirties, with a mustache and an open-neck shirt. He had no distinguishable features but a maniacal, focused look on his face. Zia's entire body stiffened, thinking that at any minute he might shoot into their car.

Baba deftly navigated through side streets, then turned back onto the busy main road. Zia didn't know which was safer. Whatever happened, they had to avoid stopping. A side street might be blocked off by a makeshift checkpoint, but on the main road they could hit a traffic jam. Baba straddled the middle of the road, attempting to prevent the car from pulling alongside them. Zia tried to focus on the practicalities, but her imagination went wild. *What does he want?* Were these the kidnappers with the dark blue BMW? Or was this someone with a wholly different intention? She remembered the story of the two sisters, working as army translators, who had been gunned down on the street. Now she understood the horror of the last few minutes of those girls' lives. This was the moment she had dreaded for months. She felt stupid for putting herself in this position. *What if he kills Baba too?* There was no honor in any of this—what had she been thinking? "I'm sorry, Baba," she said, tears clouding her vision.

But Baba was calm. "No one is going to die at the hands of this idiot," he assured her. But her panic continued to swell. Not knowing what else to do, she called Keith.

KEITH HAD SAT in the car for a long time, as he almost always did, watching Zia walk away from him in the evening sun, her gorgeous hair hidden under a veil. Dropping her off like that was never easy. He worried about her constantly. As he finally made a U-turn, Zia's number appeared on his phone. His stomach sank. She would never call him in front of her father, unless there was trouble.

When he answered, her voice was panicked. "There's a man and he's following us."

"Jesus Christ, where are you?"

Zia named a cross street, but he had no idea where that was. Keith swerved his car around and sped toward the bridge. *Where am I going?* he thought. He hadn't been in downtown Baghdad in almost a year, and the complicated maze of city streets was impossible to navigate anyway. To leave the Green Zone could be a death sentence for an American; it meant risking kidnapping and possibly a beheading, not to mention automatic termination by his company. But he wouldn't leave Zia out there on her own.

The phone cut off. They both redialed and Keith got through. Zia was switching languages rapidly, cursing in English and saying, "Baba, turn. Turn here!" and then falling into Arabic again.

"Can you find the police or a convoy?" Keith asked.

"We're trying. He's right behind us now. He's really close."

Driving as they talked, Keith neared the bridge and almost flipped his car crossing a speed bump. Suddenly he hit the brakes. *Am I nuts?* he thought. Racing his car toward a checkpoint of nervous soldiers was the surest way of getting himself shot in the head. These checkpoints came under regular attack from suicide bombers, who often tied their hands to the wheel to avoid a change of heart. Only a few months earlier, a bomber had rammed into the main checkpoint of the Green Zone a mile away, nicknamed Assassins' Gate, killing about thirty Iraqis and wounding dozens more.

Keith stopped momentarily, trying to figure out what to do. Should he really exit the Green Zone? Zia could be a stone's throw away, or she could be deep into one of the neighborhoods. Keith didn't even know what kind of car her father drove. He managed to get hold of her one more time, to tell her to come back to the bridge, that he'd warn the soldiers what was happening, but by now she was so hysterical he couldn't understand where she was or what she was saying. She was crying and gasping for air and speaking rapidly in Arabic to her father. The last thing she said before the phone cut out again was, "Oh God, I don't want to die."

ZIA AND BABA were trying frantically to return to the Green Zone gate, but turning around in Baghdad's ancient street system was not easy.

An intense silence returned as they tried to figure out the safest route back to the Green Zone. Suddenly Zia's hysteria left her, and she felt incredibly focused on surviving, navigating the streets with a power of concentration she didn't know she possessed. Baghdad seemed so quiet, all of a sudden. Zia felt they were gliding nearly invisibly. She stared almost calmly out the side window, taking in the sidewalk scene as if in slow motion: women in black abayas balancing six-packs of bottled water on their shoulders; couples sitting at tables eating dinner. People were going on with their daily life. Her nightmare didn't affect them at all. Baba passed a car and her eyes met those of a woman in the passenger seat. Three small children were in the back. The woman's eyes locked for a moment, but then she looked away. Just as suddenly as the calm had come, it receded. Zia felt like screaming to the woman, begging her family's help, but the car moved on.

Finally she recognized, ahead of them, the entrance to the 14th of July Bridge, but her heart stopped as she saw a huge line of traffic. She started crying uncontrollably, wracked by terror.

Baba screeched to the side. "Get out and run," he shouted.

Zia jumped out of the car like a wild woman. Out of the corner of her eye, she noticed the Toyota swerve alongside her. The man leaped out. He was fat and sweating. "Hey, you bitch," he said, pulling a curved knife, a *harba,* out of his jacket as he chased her. He was waving the knife and gaining ground, now less than ten feet from her. "So you work for the Americans? You will see," he said. Zia stumbled over the sidewalk and raced blindly toward the checkpoint. Her voice—"Help! Help!"— sounded feeble and hoarse. "Please, I work for Harris Corporation. This man is going to kill me!"

BY THE TIME Keith convinced a marine guard to walk him outside the perimeter, it was over. The Iraqi attacker was sitting with a bag over his head, under guard, and Zia was sitting on the wall in a daze, surrounded by concerned soldiers. Nearby, her father was staring off into the distance, smoking. Keith rushed toward them. Zia was numbly relieved to see him, but she didn't move. She couldn't. She kept losing consciousness, and when she came to, she shook all over. With Baba there and all the people milling around, Keith knew he had to stop himself from embracing her.

"Are you okay?" he asked, looking into her eyes. She was crying.

"Can I get them into the Green Zone?" he said to the marine guard.

"Sorry, sir, he doesn't have the proper ID," the soldier said, nodding in Baba's direction.

Some discussion ensued. The crowd of Iraqis gathering around them swelled and the soldiers were getting nervous.

Keith had on a wedding band that Zia had given him. Frustrated, he blurted out, "Look, this is my wife and my father-in-law. I'm going to escort them in."

Zia's eyes widened—nothing had ever been made official with Baba. But her father didn't react, and Zia wished she could hug him. Finally, the guards relented.

Baba and Zia headed back to get the car to drive into the Green Zone, where they would be safe, for the moment.

NUNU AND MAMINA were very worried. They kept calling and calling but no one answered. Zia and Baba were always home by eight o'clock, but at eleven there was still no sign of them. When they finally did arrive, around midnight, Zia was pale and trembling, with red-rimmed eyes.

Nunu was alarmed. "What happened?"

Mamina looked at Baba, but he just collapsed on the sofa. "Don't ask me any questions. Just let me sit. I feel very tired."

Iraqi guards had come back with them, and stood politely by as Mamina and Nunu learned an abbreviated version of the day's events. Zia spent that night in the house, but it was for the last time. The next day she packed a bag and left her family's home for good.

Once again, Zia moved inside the Green Zone, but this time it was legal, albeit temporary. She was put under protective custody. This didn't make it any easier than when she'd been hiding in Camille's trailer, however, since she was forbidden to leave, and didn't have the authorization to bring her family in.

She and Keith never again talked about that day. Baba parked the car far from the house and sold it four days later. The U.S. Army said they had found in the pockets of her attacker photos of him with Saddam, and surmised he was a disgruntled Ba'athist. In his confession, the man admitted that he was intending to follow Zia and Baba to their house and kill the entire family as an example. But because Zia had seen him, he changed his plan and just tried to kill her immediately. Zia never saw him again, and never knew if he was sent to jail, or released, or what.

But it hardly mattered. At night she lay on her cot staring at the ceiling. There were thousands of others like him, waiting for the day when the Americans either kicked her out of the Green Zone again, or left Iraq themselves. Then they would come after her.

She needed a plan.

CHAPTER TWENTY-NINE

 ONE AFTERNOON, A representative of the neighborhood sheik knocked on Manal's office door. He had once sworn on his honor to protect her.

"I am here to tell you that we cannot honor our promise to protect you. There are too many outsiders in the neighborhood now. We don't know them, and we can't predict what they will do."

Manal thanked him, but fear flooded over her as she closed the door. She knew this was happening in neighborhoods across Baghdad: traditional leaders were being overtaken by insurgents and foreign fighters. Some even said that Muqtada al-Sadr had lost control of his army.

The security situation everywhere had steadily deteriorated since the spring uprisings, and Manal's neighborhood was widely considered a battleground between the troops and the insurgency. Her Shawaka office was located on Haifa Street, also the location of IMN. It ran directly up to Assassins' Gate, the main entrance to the Green Zone. At the edge of the neighborhood was a bridge leading across the Tigris to a Sunni area. Sometime after the spring uprisings, insurgents had begun using Manal's neighborhood as a launching pad to shoot rockets into the Green Zone. The Americans ran missions regularly into the neighborhood, and Manal could almost always hear gun battles raging in the distance.

Manal knew her office meetings would have sounded insane to an outsider. "Look, I don't want to be paraded in front of the camera like Nick Berg," she announced once. "I would prefer to be shot dead instantly than kidnapped." But her days were relatively normal, made up of mundane tasks such as fixing the photocopier or filling out paperwork. The more intense her fear became, the more she, and others like her, normalized and adapted. Not even Ahmed's presence could calm her, as he was nervous himself and increasingly haranguing her to leave. "The extremists are taking over," he worried. She was so enmeshed in the situation that she seldom stepped back to think about the danger she was in, or that the obvious choice was to leave. *It won't happen to me,* she thought, even as it was happening to those all around her. She had stayed after the UN bombing. She had stayed after Fern's death. When some Red Cross workers were kidnapped that fall, she stayed after that, as well. Fear was like a strange, disorienting drug, and Manal was losing her ability to judge her own safety.

Manal knew of at least fourteen women who'd been murdered during the eighteen months she'd been in Iraq. There were high-profile murders like those of Fern and her coworker Salwa, and the lawmaker Aqila al-Hashimi. Unreported were so many more deaths of women whom Manal had come in contact with in her work. There was Dina, a reporter for the U.S.-funded Al Hurra TV, who was shot while waiting for a taxi to go to work. Enaas, a translator for U.S. officials, had talked to Manal about her fears a few days before her death. "People keep threatening me, saying I should stop working for the Americans, but I have no other way. I have a son." Soon thereafter, insurgents broke into her home and shot and killed her and her brother in their living room.

There was Zeena, a pharmacist and businesswoman, who had received death threats for refusing to veil. She had been an old friend of Zainab Salbi, Manal's boss and the head of Women for Women International. Zeena was kidnapped, murdered, and dumped on the highway, with a traditional headscarf wrapped around her hair. There was Wijdan al-Khuzai, an activist and parliamentary candidate for the first national elections, who had attended many of Manal's women's meetings. She had been tortured and shot in the face, her body found on the side of the road by a U.S. patrol. The list could go on and on. Manal imagined there were hundreds more victims across the country that she didn't hear about. Such deaths rarely made the news, and only a few people sensed that these crimes were not random. They formed a pattern: women were being executed for standing up and speaking out, for working and refusing to veil.

For so long, she felt unable to abandon her efforts. After so much time in a place, the rest of the world seemed to slip away. She had forgotten life was possible outside Iraq. She stayed throughout the summer of 2004 and into the fall. Even when she had spoken with her staff about shutting down all her programs, she had still intended to stay in Iraq, privately doing what she could.

But then her friend Margaret Hassan was killed.

An Iraqi citizen born in Ireland, Margaret was the fifty-nine-year-old head of CARE International in Iraq. She had lived in the country for more than thirty years, and was married to an Iraqi. Kidnappers ambushed her car on her way to the CARE offices, and she had been heard of only once since, in a videotape released by her kidnappers in which she pleaded for her life. Manal had become friendly with Margaret over the last year as their paths occasionally crossed, and she admired her as a determined, gentle woman whose commitment to Iraqis predated the war and the media attention. She spoke Arabic and, during her many years of living in Iraq, she had helped children by organizing deliveries of medicine and food. She was utterly beloved by the people. After she was kidnapped, two hundred Iraqis protested for her release outside the CARE offices in Baghdad. Manal allowed herself to hope that the force of Iraqi public opinion would save Margaret.

But she wasn't released. A month after she was taken, a videotape surfaced showing her brutal execution by handgun. It was a senseless killing, of a woman who had done so much for her adopted country, and everyone in Manal's office had mourned—and worried. And then, on the heels of Margaret's murder in November 2004, Amal Malachi, an adviser at the Ministry of Municipalities and Public Affairs and the co-founder of the advisory committee for women's affairs, was killed. Her cellphone was taken, and the women listed on it, including Manal, were terrified they would be next.

Iraqis who once pleaded with her to stay had changed their minds. "Manal, you should leave now," said one woman visiting the center. "This is not a good situation."

And so she had.

Her departure had been sudden, and felt as dramatic as the embassy workers clinging to the last helicopter in Saigon. She could tell no one she was leaving for fear that a leak would give kidnappers time to ambush her car. She couldn't say goodbye, although the women she worked with would understand why. Her work would continue from Jordan, she promised her staff. She would set up the office and oversee the Iraqi staff and programs from Amman.

She had lain across the backseat as Ahmed, Mustafa, and Fawaz had driven furiously to the airport. Flights out of Iraq were always targets for rocket fire, so the plane ascended at an angle that felt almost vertical and spiraled rapidly, making her feel dizzy and disoriented. As she looked back down on the country she was fleeing, Manal's eyes welled up with tears.

BY JANUARY 2005, Manal had permanently moved the headquarters of Women for Women to Amman, and had begun a campaign to register Iraqis living in Jordan to vote in the national elections. Five Iraqi staff had come with her, and Ahmed traveled back and forth. Free from the intensity of Baghdad, and the close scrutiny of the society, Manal felt suddenly aware of how much attention Ahmed paid to her. He had always kept his friends at hand, so as not to make her feel uncomfortable. He had even introduced her to his family at the same time that Mustafa and Fawaz introduced her to their families—so as not to make the introductions feel too freighted with intention. Manal had always thought, *What good guys,* but as her head cleared in Jordan, she suddenly realized that this had been Ahmed's smooth way of making her more comfortable with him; of flirting, Arab style.

On a visit to Jordan for a training session, he proposed marriage. Manal was confused. In the frenzy of Iraq, she hadn't had time to think about romance. She had never intended to remarry—never believed she would receive another offer—but Ahmed knew about her divorce and had accepted it. She realized that she trusted him completely and felt safe around him. He had become her closest friend. She introduced him to her parents, who had recently retired and bought a house in Jordan to be closer to their Palestinian family. They agreed to be married later that year.

As Iraq prepared for the first national elections, Manal's staff were monitoring the few voting booths set up in Amman for expats. In Iraq,

Manal had put a couple of Iraqis in charge of the programs, and she intended to continue running them from Amman.

It was much safer in Jordan, and she was glad to be able to continue her work for Iraq, but she felt lost and distant from her previous life. She hated working by remote control. She felt even worse when, three weeks later, the election returns came in. It was a disaster for women's rights.

Everything always turned out to be harder than the Bush administration claimed, and she was kicking herself for ever forgetting that. After the CPA disbanded in June 2004, the Americans had tried to prepare Iraq to hold national elections in January 2005, but many people didn't think Iraq was stable enough yet to do so. It would have made more sense to get the factories running, secure the borders, and normalize day-to-day life, and only afterward have the elections take place, in an atmosphere in which people could feel safe and rational.

But the problem was Ali Sistani, the white-bearded grand ayatollah who refused to allow the constitution to be written until an elected body of Iraqis was in parliament to oversee the process. The Americans didn't want to leave until security and a newly elected government were in place, but too many Iraqis were swearing there would not be security until after the Americans left. In the end, the Iraqis had won.

Manal knew the Americans' departure, and the election, didn't guarantee peace; she knew she wouldn't be able to walk back into her Baghdad office any time soon. She also knew all too well that one national election didn't mean the country was democratic. She could see that this wasn't an election so much as a census. No one had voted on issues. In fact, throughout the campaign not a single party had even mentioned where it stood on the critical questions facing the country: Now that the CPA was gone, should the U.S. military also leave? Should the Iraqi legal system be based on Islamic or secular law? Should the country remain united or divide into three regions based on Sunni, Shia, and Kurdish identity? The victors of this election would oversee the drafting of the constitution in 2005—yet no party ever discussed its vision for the constitution.

Instead, the parties campaigned for the elections on one issue: Are you a Shia, Sunni, or Kurd? Since most of the country was Shia, they dominated the election returns. Manal felt defeated. Rather than unite the nation, the election had only deepened the divisions between the ethnic groups.

The Shia United Iraqi Alliance won 48 percent of the vote, earning 140 out of 275 parliamentary seats. Top Shia clerics had encouraged Iraq's many Shia parties to unite under one block that would sweep the elections and ensure their dominance in the new Iraq. They did so. The Kurdish parties did the same and came in second. Their group, the Democratic Patriotic Alliance of Kurdistan, received 26 percent of the vote. The secular party, the Iraq List, led by the interim ruler, Ayad Allawi, came in third with 14 percent. George Bush, who had recently defeated John Kerry for a second term, heralded the elections as a great victory for democracy in the Middle East; but Manal felt like choking.

"Great—American-style democracy has just installed an Islamic theocracy!" she said to Ahmed, who was equally glum.

"Iraqis are voting for security," he pointed out. "That's it."

Yet the election results promised only more violence. The real losers were the Sunnis. Although they made up one third of the country's population, their party received only 5 percent of the vote because, at the last minute, Sunni leaders called for a boycott of the elections. Anticipating a Shia victory, they had hoped to scuttle the entire process. In some Sunni areas, turnout was negligible on election day and many were threatened against going to the polls.

But their plan had backfired.

The election had gone forward, and was largely considered legitimate, and now the Sunnis found themselves with few seats. They would have almost no political power in a government that would run all the country's ministries, and oversee the drafting and writing of the constitution. Sunni leaders soon regretted this boycott, and the Americans went to great lengths to bring them back into the power process, but the whole government was so chaotic it was difficult to control or direct.

The other group that suffered, ironically, was the women.

They had won more than their required quota of representation: about eighty-seven members of the new government would be women and there would be six female ministers. Women were allowed to join the army and the police. A "women's ministry" had been added to the cabinet. On paper, Manal saw, women had done well. Percentage-wise, they now had higher representation in the government elected by Iraqis than in the one imposed by the Americans.

But when Manal looked at the women in office, she was very concerned. They were all on the ticket of the conservative Shia parties. She was furious and frustrated. *Well, we got our representation of 25 percent women in government,* she thought, *and guess what: they're all covered in black from head to foot and even more conservative than some of the men.*

So much for the hope that the quota would mean *snap—women's rights! It's harder than that,* Manal thought angrily. Of course it is. Although they had risked their lives to campaign and were educated professionals—dentists, scientists, and professors—these women all supported Islamic law, which would forbid almost all freedoms for the women they governed. Nasty gossip abounded that they were merely puppets for the male party leaders and would do whatever they were told.

As for the women's ministry, it wasn't even given a budget.

In only a few months, this new government would begin to draft Iraq's first constitution. Would these women fight for the rights of their Iraqi sisters, or would they rubber-stamp whatever the male leaders decided? If they pushed for women's rights, what kind of rights would they be? For certain they would vote for Islamic law, but would they favor a progressive interpretation of that law on family matters? Would they defend women on issues such as divorce, child custody, polygamy, and inheritance? Would any of it even matter if the violence persisted?

CHAPTER THIRTY

ZIA DECIDED AGAIN that she would have to leave Iraq. She knew her plan might take months, maybe even years, to execute, but after she made up her mind to get out, she was determined to make it happen. Even if she had to go alone.

Keith, for his part, showed no signs of wanting to leave. In the spring of 2005, he signed another yearlong contract with the Project Contracting Office, this time to wire up the new U.S. embassy and adjacent buildings. Zia was devastated. He assured her he loved her, and that he wanted to finalize his divorce and marry her—but he just couldn't leave. Keith felt he had to stay because the pay was incredible for the work he was doing, and his expenses were minimal. He needed the money, he explained, since his daughter would be going to college soon, and his ex-wife was always emailing him about child-support payments and bills. There were other reasons Zia suspected: she knew that, to him, the rockets overhead, the long hours, and the lack of modern conveniences were easier to handle than the responsibilities and stresses of life back home. Like so many others, he had become sucked in and lost perspective. Keith had become addicted to an experience that gave his life meaning. He felt a moral obligation to the Iraqis not to abandon them. The United States had to finish what it had started. It was an ironic reversal from the days when she dreamed that they'd both find work with the new government and build a life together in Baghdad. They argued.

One evening, Zia saw Keith staring at his computer screen with a distant look in his eye. Someone had sent him images from a suicide bombing: mangled intestines, arms stuck in trees, legs severed and scattered alongside empty water bottles and plastic bags. "Jesus," he muttered.

The contractor who had forwarded the photos was complaining about how the media ignored the mass casualties of the suicide bombers to focus on the acts of a few soldiers in Abu Ghraib, that no one understood what it was like to be living there, in fear of this kind of thing all the time.

"Hey," she said, her hand on his shoulder. "C'mon. Don't look at these."

"This is what you and your family see every day," he said. "I'm here. I have to see it too."

"It's a privilege not to see this. Don't punish yourself."

Zia finally began to understand that, for whatever reason, Keith couldn't tear himself away from Iraq. If she wanted to start a new life somewhere else, she would have to leave without him.

But how? She knew she couldn't move back to Jordan again; last summer had been a disaster. And European countries were all denying visas to Iraqis. She could simply roll the dice and apply for a tourist visa or a student visa to the States, but that was complicated and success was unlikely. Although the largest U.S. embassy in the world was in Baghdad, just steps from her, the State Department refused to accept visa applications. In hopes of thwarting the many legitimate claims for asylum flowing from Iraq—and all the bad press this would engender—the State Department had made applying for visas as difficult as possible. Iraqis wishing to visit the United States had to fly to Amman, usually twice, to submit their paperwork and have an interview. The cost of a round-trip flight was twelve hundred dollars, beyond the budget of most. She couldn't imagine going through all that only to be turned down. Furthermore, denied applicants got a red DENIED stamped on their passports, making it almost impossible for them ever to be considered in the future. Plus, other countries looked suspiciously upon applicants rejected by the United States.

Months passed, and Zia refused to give up. Everyone told her, "You've got to know someone." She gathered letters of recommendation from everyone she'd ever worked with, expounding on her loyalty, her dedication, her natural leadership style. She photocopied images of her badges and security clearances, evidence of the two years she had worked for U.S. companies in Iraq. She had bank statements showing more than ten thousand dollars in savings. She had documented the attempt on her life, and that it had happened because she worked for the Americans. In any other time or country, such a background would have been more than enough to award her instant asylum, but the Bush administration didn't want the political disaster of thousands of Iraqis leaving the country for the States. America was supposed to be winning the war. Sorry, they told her—the State Department is rejecting everyone.

Summer 2005 approached. Zia's second stint in the Green Zone had lasted six months, and U.S. officials were making noises again about her leaving. Her old friends the IMN security contractors Pappy and Pat were gone. Their replacements distrusted Iraqis, and had no sense of trust or sympathy toward her. There wasn't space for Iraqis, they said. "No locals on embassy property," they said. They were going to kick her out again. Her only alternative was to move in with Keith, and share the one small bed in his trailer. Other Iraqi women had taken that route, out of desperation. She wouldn't do it. Zia felt the walls closing in on her.

She desperately started emailing every American friend she had: "Please, can you help me?"

A REPORTER WHO received Zia's email had recently met a senator's aide at the March 2005 funeral of the aid worker Marla Ruzicka, who had been killed, along with her Iraqi colleague, Faiz al-Salaam, by a suicide bomber on the Baghdad airport road. Marla had been a popular figure in Baghdad, and she had started an organization, the Campaign for Innocent Victims in Conflict (CIVIC), to aid innocent Iraqis who were accidentally harmed by U.S. military action. Although Marla was only twenty-eight, she had successfully lobbied for more than $10 million in funding for her cause. Her car had been on the highway when a suicide bomber slammed into a convoy of diplomats. Unable to afford the kind of armored car that diplomats drove, Marla and Faiz both died from the blast. Zia herself had been on the airport road after the explosion, and had seen the plumes of smoke and charred, carcass-like remains of the vehicles.

After hearing of Zia's desperate situation in the Green Zone, and that it was due to her two years' working for the Americans, U.S. senator Patrick Leahy agreed to write a letter on Zia's behalf to the U.S. embassy in Jordan.

After several months of emails and paperwork, Zia formally applied for a visa to the United States and flew to Amman for her interview. A tourist visa would give her only three to six months in the country, but a temporary solution felt better than nothing. She was taking a chance in applying, and she knew it. But it was her only chance.

The U.S. embassy in Amman was a sorrowful scene. Hundreds of Iraqi refugees crowded into chairs and stood along the walls. Embassy officials, through thick glass, were shaking their heads. Finally, Zia's turn came. She approached the counter and spent ten minutes answering the questions of a young man with sandy hair who couldn't have been much older than she was. He sat comfortably under the U.S. flag, safely behind bulletproof glass. The senator's letter lay in front of him. Zia knew she was just one of millions across the world who dreamed of going to America, but she tried to make him see that to reject her was to issue a death sentence to someone who had fought for and believed, more strongly than anyone, in the values of freedom and justice that the United States was supposed to stand for. She just couldn't let him deny her.

Finally, the official started nodding his head. She watched in awe as he stamped her passport APPROVED. She wanted to sing and dance. Her relief was so great that she leapt into the air. "Thank you," she said to him, almost in a whisper.

He smiled. "Ma'am, we appreciate all the work you've done for us in Iraq."

It was the first time she had ever heard those words.

·   ·   ·

NUNU ANSWERED THE phone.

"Nunu, they accepted me!" Zia was practically yelling for joy. She would return to her trailer in the Green Zone until her tourist visa went into effect two months later, in September 2005. She didn't have a long-term plan, necessarily, but she was sure something would happen.

Mamina and Nunu were thrilled to hear the happiness in her voice, though it was all happening so quickly. Nunu envied her sister: at least her life was moving. She, on the other hand, was stuck in this tiny house with Baba. He, for his part, opposed the idea of Zia's move: "You don't leave your country" was all he said.

Zia explained to Nunu that Keith, too, was upset, and didn't want her to leave him. "Good," Mamina said. "When he sees he is losing you, this will force him to make a decision." Privately, in recent months, Mamina and Nunu had grown irritated with Keith's inaction and spoke disparagingly about the American custom of "dating" that Nunu had learned about on television. If an Iraqi man desired to spend so much time with a woman, he had to marry her and provide a furnished home. Yet Keith wanted to enjoy the best of both worlds: a first wife in the States and a younger "second wife" in Iraq. From Mamina's viewpoint, a man had no incentive to marry a woman with whom he was already sexually active. So her daughter's only advantage was her virginity, and the hope that Keith had fallen so in love that he couldn't live without her. But as the months passed and Keith made no move to leave Iraq with Zia, Mamina and Nunu had begun to doubt that he truly loved her. Knowing the depths of Zia's feelings for Keith, neither she nor Nunu dared share their concerns.

Zia was also frustrated with Keith. But she felt sadness mixed with pride that she had made her own destiny, without his help. Nunu admired that about her big sister—she wasn't sure she'd ever be able to do such a thing.

Zia flew back to Jordan in September, and Mamina and Nunu flew in to meet her with clothes, makeup, and jewelry for the trip. Almost a year had passed since the family had all seen one another. When they arrived, Zia had been napping. She opened the door half-lidded and in rumpled work clothes, and the three women hugged with happiness. They spent two days rushing around preparing for Zia's voyage. At night, the mood was bittersweet. Who knew when they would see one another again? Mamina thought of all the relatives she had said goodbye to over the years. Her family had been torn apart and scattered across the world. Now she was losing her daughter as well.

"Mamina, sleep with me," Zia called out from her bed. "I want to be close to you. I will miss you."

Mamina felt that her entire body was being twisted. She swallowed her tears. "Don't be sad. The way was closed for you, and at the last moment, God opened up this passage, like a crack in the door, and the light is coming through. This is the way intended for you. Go through the door."

It broke Zia's heart to leave her family, but returning home would only put them in danger. She took Nunu's T-shirt to sleep in, for comfort. As she drifted off, Nunu tried to picture what the future might hold for her sister, but it was impossible to imagine. She had never left her family, or taken such a journey in her life. Iraqi women were not expected to leave their homes unaccompanied, and here she was getting on an airplane by herself and flying halfway across the world. All Nunu could do was shake her head and say, "It takes guts to do what you are doing. I would never have the bravery." They were worried for Zia; it never occurred to them to worry for themselves.

They didn't know when their family would be together again. She didn't intend to stay in the United States illegally, but as Zia lay in bed with Mamina and Nunu, they all knew, silently, that she didn't plan on returning to Iraq.

The following morning, they decided to say goodbye in the apartment, not at the airport, to avoid drawing attention with tearful scenes. The morning of Zia's departure, she spoke with Baba. He seemed sad. Zia suspected he wanted to say more, but he was trapped in the mentality of an old Arab man; he had to be tough and show no emotions. Upon leaving, all he said was "I am happy that you are getting what you want out of life. Maybe I'll visit you in America, but I'll never leave

Iraq." Nunu figured that was the closest he'd ever come to giving his blessing.

Nunu barely remembered the goodbye. Had she not steeled herself against her emotions, she would not have been able to let her sister leave. She watched through her tears as Zia softly closed the door behind her and left the Middle East for good.

CHAPTER THIRTY-ONE

ALTHOUGH SO MANY of the people she had known and worked with over the past two and a half years were leaving or had already left, Heather was determined to stay in Iraq. When she had arrived, she had been filled with such a deep hope to help turn Iraq into the Arab world's first true democracy. She now knew that was impossible, but her new dream, however unlikely it might be, was to see the country rescued from complete disintegration and brutal civil war.

Such a goal was getting harder and harder to achieve. The tension she felt between the Westerners and their Iraqi staff on the night Samson died had only grown worse as more and more Iraqis were retaliated against due to their jobs. Heather had hoped the January 2005 elections would move the country toward peace, but it had only marginalized the Sunnis and deepened the divisions. Every day brought new, extremely worrisome signs of division between Sunnis and Shias. A letter had been intercepted by the U.S. military from the Jordanian terrorist Abu Musab al-Zarqawi, who had ties to Al Qaeda, calling for Sunnis to attack Shias as a battle strategy to regain Sunni dominance in Iraq. Shia shrines, mosques, and neighborhoods were coming under attack. In retaliation, the new Shia-led government was systematically purging government ministries of any Sunni employees. Iraq's Interior Ministry, which was running the police force, was accused of arresting and torturing Sunnis. Sunnis were planning attacks on Shia neighborhoods, and vice versa.

Heather saw the upcoming constitutional vote in October 2005 as the only way left to save Iraq. The drafting of the constitution was being called the most important event in the country's steps toward self-governance. If one believed the U.S. rhetoric, the constitution would be the nation's messiah, rescuing it from the fires of civil war and leading it to a peaceful future. Heather hoped, however naïvely, that the process of getting Shias, Sunnis, Kurds, and other ethnic groups to the table to talk about the issues could bring about the reconciliation needed to stop the street attacks. Around the U.S. headquarters, workers compared their efforts to America's constitutional process in the late 1700s. They felt sure this historical document would serve as the supreme law of Iraq. Do this right and Iraq could still be saved. Do it wrong, and it would all be over.

But Iraq was a country long accustomed to a one-leader-one-decision style of rule. Debate and consensus didn't exist under Saddam. Hence, it took months for the 275 members of the parliament to stop arguing over who would take which government positions, and who would be on the drafting committee for the constitution. After the Shias finally agreed on their government, the Americans tried to drag the Sunni leaders into the process, even though they held only a few seats, having boycotted the election. Instead of solidifying the nation, the drafting process dragged on for months as the politicians shouted at one another; assassination attempts occurred weekly and most politicians had to move their families to Jordan. Heather brought in experts on constitutional law from the United Nations and briefed women's rights groups on the drafting process to keep them involved. She led the effort to have Iraqi groups do their own analysis and develop strategies, and felt that Manal would be proud of the way she was supporting local groups to solve problems rather than implement her agenda. Yet she knew it might be too late. She worked tirelessly and collapsed into bed at night feeling hopeless. *One day this will matter,* she thought, not quite believing it.

By the time the government had formed, the team had only six weeks to write the constitution in order to make the Bush adminstration's target deadline of October. Little time was left for a proper consideration of each article. At the end, many said it was vague and rushed. The negotiations had been antagonistic and brutal, crystallizing differences among the groups rather than bringing them together. The Sunnis and Shias would not agree. Even after four deadline extensions due to lack of agreement, none of the fifteen Sunni members of the drafting committee signed the final document.

By the fall of 2005, the constitution was finalized and presented to the public for a referendum. It described Iraq as a "republican, federal, democratic, pluralistic system . . ." It opened:

> In the name of God, the Most merciful, the Most compassionate. We have honored the sons of Adam. We, the people of Mesopotamia, the homeland of the apostles and prophets, resting place of the virtuous imams, cradle of civilization, crafters of writing, and home of numeration. Upon our land the first law made by man was passed, and the oldest pact of just governance was inscribed, and upon our soil the saints and companions of the Prophet prayed, philosophers and scientists theorized, and writers and poets excelled.

What followed were 144 articles, laying out the separation of powers, rights and freedoms, and the role of justice. It passed the referendum, and the Bush administration heralded it as a victory. But women's rights activists from both sides were outraged by it.

The so-called secular women made it very clear: they wanted no reference whatsoever to Islam in the constitution. Invoking Islam as a source of law would "take us back to the Dark Ages," as one women's rights activist said, and be interpreted as allowing public floggings and the stoning of adulterers. But conservative religious women insisted that Islam be enshrined as "the fundamental source of legislation" in Iraq. They represented the majority in government, and seemed determined to press forward.

The U.S. officials consulting on the process came down strongly that Islam be considered "*a* fundamental source," not "*the* fundamental source." In order to please both sides and get the constitution signed, compromises were forced. As a result, the language was intentionally vague. By the end, many women considered it a weak document that lacked consensus, and that could be interpreted in wildly contradictory ways.

The women managed to pressure the lawmakers into including a line that the articles forbid "discrimination based on gender." But the constitution clearly states, "Islam is the official religion of the State and is a foundation source of legislation." Elsewhere it says, "No law may be enacted that contradicts the established provisions of Islam." Furthermore, it requires that the federal supreme court be made up of "experts in Islamic jurisprudence." Women's rights activists understood this to mean that supreme court judges would all be clerics.

Unless the constitution made perfectly clear, in specific language, the rights of women, then it would almost certainly be interpreted otherwise by the judges appointed under Shia leadership. The progressive women felt that this vagueness left them in an even weaker position than they had been in under Saddam.

"The liberation of Iraq has unleashed the darkest forces in the country," said Yanar Mohammed, one of Iraq's best-known women's rights activists. "We will be losing the basic protections as women and public citizens."

And Heather knew that not only progressive women felt cheated. Over the past several months, Heather had been working closely on the constitution with Salama al-Khafaji, the leading female conservative Shia assembly member, who had once so controversially told a reporter that Iraqis wouldn't accept "Western-minded women who came with the occupation, carrying weird ideas and wanting to teach young Iraqis that it's their right to have premarital sex."

Heather worked with her because Salama had, much to the surprise of many of the expat Iraqi women and international workers, become the most popular female politician in Iraq. As a Shia woman who had never left Iraq, she had suffered under Saddam, the same way most of her countrywomen had. A year earlier, she had lost her son—as so many Shia women had in Saddam's wars over the years. She was neither an unveiled Kurdish woman who worked with the Americans nor a fancy expat who was most comfortable with the international press corps. Salama was one of the people, and they loved her for it. Opinion polls called her the most popular woman in Baghdad.

As the top female representative for the majority Shia party in government, Salama was also a leading voice for women as she and her colleagues drafted the constitution. In her capacity as a member of parliament she had begun to work with Heather, and they had become very close. Manal had also since met with Salama and had come to believe that she was opinionated and smart and no one's puppet.

Though Heather didn't instinctively agree with Salama's conservativism, she cared mainly that the political processes were in place to give Iraqi women an equal voice—and if they saw Salama as their spokeswoman, and agreed with her conservative beliefs, then Heather would not interfere. She came to respect Salama as dynamic, intelligent, and aggressive, and she understood that while Salama was a conservative Muslim, she did not want a theocracy. She had faith that although Salama would support Islamic law, she would insist on an interpretation of it modest enough not to allow violence against or oppression of women. As a former dentist and current politician, she was, after all, a working mother.

However, as the constitutional process moved along in 2005, Heather watched in horror as even Salama was edged out of the inner power circle by the male leadership. A constitutional committee was formed of fifty-five members, including ten women. However, a series of closed-door sessions began, with only the heads of the main political blocs. They were nicknamed the "kitchen cabinet." No women were included in these meetings. Informally, they made all the big decisions. When full parliamentary sessions were called, Salama and the other Shia women were instructed by the leadership to stay quiet and vote with the party. Should Salama protest, she would be forced out. This was all done in the name of moving negotiations along more quickly.

CHAPTER THIRTY-TWO

EACH MONTH AFTER Zia left was bloodier than the one before it. In September 2005, more than 140 died when a suicide bomber detonated himself in the Khadamiya neighborhood, home to the goldsmith Zia and Mamina had visited a year earlier. In November 2005, several suicide bombers killed 60 people in one day. In January 2006, another 150 people were killed in several attacks in Karbala and Ramadi.

News of horrifying violence filled the television screen at night, along with a report that the Sunni insurgent Abu Musab al-Zarqawi, who was linked to Al Qaeda, had declared on his website an "all-out war" against Iraqi Shia. Then, in February 2006, a bomb destroyed the famous gold-domed Shia mosque in Samarra. *The Sunnis did it,* everyone said. Suddenly, whisperings of a civil war turned into open declarations of it.

In the wake of the escalation in violence, Mamina and Baba spent days scouring the apartment for any evidence of Zia's time with the Americans, including photos, IMN documents, or souvenirs available only inside the Green Zone. The photo of George Bush was taken out of the closet and burned along with all documentation from the CPA. The family couldn't let on that Zia was in the States. Word would spread instantly—to the brothers of friends, to neighbors, to other students at the university—and someone might come after her family. They might kill them as traitors, or kidnap Nunu, assuming that a family with relatives in America could afford a rich ransom.

They continued to allow a rumor to spread that Zia had been killed by the militias. For close relatives and friends, they would say she was in Kuwait, a country few Iraqis ever visited. Nunu was surprised, but

Mamina even lied to her own sisters, because she didn't trust their spouses—like Uncle Jalal, the Sunni from Hit. It was strange to think back on those early days of the war; a trip to Hit now would be a death sentence.

Nunu felt sadder each day about her sister's departure. She was relieved that she was finally safe, and loved hearing stories about her new life in Washington, D.C. But now Nunu felt empty inside, and very alone. Even though for the last year Zia had lived like a refugee in the Green Zone, at least she was still close by. Now she was across the world, somewhere distant and foreign to Nunu.

In her emails, Zia described her wondrous new life, and Nunu tried to live vicariously through her. She was staying in Washington, D.C., with an American friend whom she'd met in Iraq, and she talked of riding a bicycle through the tree-lined streets with no one watching or criticizing. She said everything was massive in the States; even the men were tall. There was a sneaker store so large, she couldn't see the back of it. The bookstores had escalators inside them; the food markets were all indoors and called Giant and Super. "Everything is at your fingertips when you need it," she wrote. Houses had laundry machines, dishwashers, microwaves, irons, and blow-dryers. Every home had endless supplies of water and gas, and people left water boiling on the stove or ran the air-conditioning around the clock. In Baghdad, Nunu still had to wake up in the middle of the night to shower because there might not be enough electricity during the day for the water pump. But Zia's roommates stood under showers for twenty minutes at a time.

Zia sent Nunu pictures of herself in front of all the D.C. monuments they had seen together in movies. She described the thrill of walking outside without the fear of being shot, and of the evenings that felt so silent without Baghdad's nightly orchestra of booms, rockets, and gunfire. She heard only an occasional police siren or dog barking. She also described American money, which had coins, unlike Iraq. Everything cost extra in Washington, she said—not just because prices were higher but because there was also something called sales tax. Often Zia would wake up in the middle of the night and forget where she was. She called Nunu just to hear her voice, and they chatted until Zia felt sleepy again. Nunu tried to imagine her sister's new world, but she couldn't.

. . .

AFTER ZIA LEFT, Mamina and Nunu made a pact not to burden her with any worrisome news about Iraq. Even as the violence and bloodshed increased in Baghdad, Nunu never mentioned it. She understood that the renewed attacks had something to do with the Sunnis being left out of the government, but none of it made sense to her. All she saw were neighbors turning on neighbors. Every night she wanted to scream at the TV, "Stop this. For God's sake. Sunni and Shia are brothers, not enemies!" Each day ushered in so much fresh carnage, the news channels couldn't keep up. Nunu squeezed her eyes shut every morning, wishing the sun would not rise, that they would all be spared from having to endure another day. She wished the Americans would just drop a bomb and destroy everything.

Even the drafting of the constitution—an issue that commanded the nightly news for months—seemed like pure theater; it had nothing to do with Iraqis' actual lives. Nunu and her family went back to the polls to vote in support of the constitution, but the act held none of the energy or hope of the last election. When the constitution finally passed, it seemed insignificant. None of the Sunni members had signed it, and its promises of unity and equality seemed like the advertisements on television that promised silky hair or sparkling countertops. These were politicians' promises, and no one believed they would make a difference in their lives—especially the talk of enshrining women's rights. *Stop killing the men,* Nunu thought bitterly. *That is the best way to help women. We need peace and husbands. The rest will come later.*

The fear of suicide bombers kept Nunu in the apartment most days, except when Baba agreed to accompany her outside. But the two of them rarely wanted to do the same thing. Baba wanted to sit with his friends, and Nunu wanted to shop or go to the Internet café to check for email from Zia.

"At your age, you should be going to the cinema and to the markets with your friends," he said. "If we were in the 1970s, I would let you go out because no one would hurt you; but I can't let you go alone now and I am too old to take you everywhere."

Nunu felt sad for her father. Sometimes, when he went out alone to run an errand while Mamina was at school, and the silence of the apartment overwhelmed Nunu, she sneaked out by herself. Relying on Baba made her feel like a child.

One day, she washed and blow-dried her hair, put on jeans, a long-sleeve top, and her gold jewelry, and headed to the Internet café a few blocks from her house. As she walked out the door, she felt brave, like Zia. She was escaping the prisonlike apartment, and standing up to the *irhabeen*, the terrorists, in her own small way. It was a risk, but her neighborhood was safer than the outskirts of the city, where the militias thrived. Shias, Sunnis, Christians, and even Jews lived in Karrada. Baba and his friends were proud of this diversity and had managed to defend it. The other day, a young man on the corner had cursed at a passing convoy of troops. "Hey, you," Abu Hassan called out. "Don't give them problems. They are people of the book." The young man looked ashamed and apologized.

Nunu enjoyed being outside. Over these months of virtual house arrest, she had missed the small moments of human connection—waving to her neighbors, jostling through crowded sidewalks, exchanging pleasantries with the shop owners she'd known most of her life. *Letting boys see me,* she added, smiling to herself. Nunu was now twenty years old, and she was beautiful. She'd lost some baby fat around her face, highlighting her prominent cheekbones. Whenever she sauntered down the road or across the Baghdad University campus, she felt the thrill of male eyes on her. She had learned to flick her eyes up at young men as they passed, smile, and then lower her gaze. From a safe distance, she and her girlfriends would then peek over their shoulders to see if the young men were still watching. They always were. Many tried to throw scraps of paper, with their cellphone numbers, onto her armful of books, but Nunu just gasped and brushed the notes away. Shock was the expected reaction of a "good girl," so that's what she gave them. But she couldn't deny that she enjoyed the attention.

Baba lamented her beauty as a mixed blessing. "You are beautiful, educated, and well mannered. We will never find you your equal." Nunu wanted only to be free, to enjoy life, and she longed for the day she would feel the thrill of her first kiss. Each passing day, her childhood bedroom felt smaller and smaller.

· · ·

THE NEIGHBORHOOD INTERNET center was in a shopping complex, up a dingy flight of stairs. The room might have once been an apartment, but now cubicles were arranged around ten computers, and a loud fan blew cigarette smoke out the window. The café was packed with young men, most of whom whiled away the afternoon trying to send instant messages to girls. On a keyboard sticky with spilled tea, Nunu logged on to see if she had any email. There was a joke forwarded by a relative, and an email from Zia, with several attachments. She opened it to see pictures of three different types of curtain, all lace, with different panels and trim, for Zia's bedroom in Washington. The cost, almost thirty dollars, was exorbitant to Nunu. *What do you think?* Zia had written. *Show Mamina.* Zia explained that she had devoted days to visiting the different stores and comparing prices and styles, but that her American friends didn't understand her fascination. They bought and spent as they pleased. Nunu couldn't imagine that.

She emailed back that she liked the red curtain because it was cheerful. She saved the images on her memory card, so she and Mamina could go over them tonight on her laptop with Zia on the phone—as they did almost every night. Zia had a long-distance phone card, and they often talked for an hour or two, connecting through the small, familiar details of life; the same sorts of things they had talked about in Baghdad. But now all of Zia's stories were filled with joy and plenty. Nunu loved hearing about America; it really was just like in the movies. The people were rich and had everything they needed. Even as Nunu missed her, she was excited at her sister's adventure.

Nunu paid for her time on the computer and left. She was disappointed she hadn't gotten any email from friends. She had been distant lately, she knew that, and she had to keep her distance because of Zia. The other week, Nunu had been accosted by a group of female classmates. "Oh, hello, Nunu," they said sweetly. "How is your sister? We haven't seen her lately. We will be looking for jobs and we're curious where she is working."

The classmates knew Zia had worked for the Americans—by now everyone did—and they surrounded her like dogs sniping for scraps of gossip, not caring about Nunu's obvious discomfort. Nunu hated lying and saying her sister was in Kuwait, because that led to so many other questions. *Why Kuwait? Did she get a job? How did she get a visa?* Nunu was a terrible liar, and she knew that attention to detail was important. She had seen girls' lives endangered due to small slips. At the university she had overheard a female security guard conducting a routine search of a student's purse. "What is this?" the guard said, fingering a small manila business card. "Why do you have a card with an *ajnabi* name on it?" She spoke in a loud voice in front of all the other guards. "Do you work for the Americans?" The terrified young student pleaded ignorance, and they eventually let her pass. But Nunu had no doubt the woman had dropped out of college by now.

When she did summon the courage to attend classes, she avoided the student center. In class, she sat in the back. What was the point of socializing, anyway? She couldn't talk openly about her situation to anyone. And no Iraqi man would propose to a girl with a fallen sister.

NUNU FELT EXHAUSTED from even the short walk back from the Internet café to the apartment. She never got any exercise anymore. The family used to spend Fridays at the park or driving to the countryside. Mamina used to take them to the pool on women-only afternoons once a week to swim. But such small pleasures were impossible now. Baghdad hotels with pools were targeted by terrorists because they housed foreigners. Crowded public places were dangerous. Shia families had to think twice before leaving the city if the route took them through a Sunni neighborhood, and vice versa.

Suddenly, she noticed a young man following her. Her heart froze. He was closing in on her quickly, and his eyes looked at her hungrily. Nunu didn't know what to do. As she was contemplating trying to make a run for home, he was already upon her. "Whore," he said, leering grotesquely in her face. He grabbed her by the hair. Panic rose in Nunu's throat as she gasped for air.

"These are the jeans of a dirty, naughty girl." As Nunu struggled, he reached around and grabbed her crotch. Nunu gasped in revulsion and began to sob. She kicked and punched as hard as she could. She tried to claw his face with her hands as he fondled her. Finally, he released her and walked off laughing. Nunu crumpled to the sidewalk, her hair tangled and her face blotchy and tearstained. Her shirt hung unevenly. She was sobbing so hard she could barely stand, and she had no idea what to do.

The sun beat down on her. As soon as she realized he was gone, and she was not hurt, she brushed herself off and stood up, wheezing as she tried to regain her composure. She looked around. The weather was cool, and it was a bright afternoon. Many people were on the street, and her screaming had attracted their attention. She knew they saw her, and saw what that man had done to her. They hadn't moved to help, nor did they come to her now.

She walked unsteadily home.

When Mamina saw her, she rushed forward. Nunu explained the attack.

"He attacked me because I was wearing jeans. No one defended me, Mama. Maybe they were scared, but he didn't have a gun!"

"They are cowards, Nunu," Mamina said.

"He was Sunni, I know it. They think I am just a Shia and because I have no veil I'm worthless. They think it's their right to rape and kill me."

"Don't talk like that, Nunu."

She sobbed. "Only God the Merciful will stop this."

There was no question of calling the police—it was too trivial an incident; better to try and keep it quiet.

Mamina and Nunu didn't tell Baba, but he found out about the attack from a neighbor anyway and was furious; not at the neighbors for just standing by, but at Nunu for being outside, for wearing jeans. She wouldn't leave the house again, he declared. Mamina argued with him, but she agreed that it wasn't safe for Nunu to be alone outside. She had escaped lightly this time.

It hardly mattered. Nunu didn't want to go anywhere anymore. She had constant nightmares in which she was not only molested, but kidnapped and raped. She refused to leave the house. She stopped getting out of bed. "I'm so tired, Mama," she would say when Mamina fretted over her.

Baba said it was too dangerous for her to drive to the clinic, and all the doctors were fleeing Iraq anyway. "If she's tired, she can sleep," he said.

MONTHS PASSED AND the violence spiraled. By late spring, Nunu was struggling to finish her final year at the university. All that mattered to her anymore was obtaining her degree. Everywhere, militias roamed, bombs detonated, and more and more women quit their jobs, donned the hijab, and feared for their lives. *If only I can graduate,* Nunu thought, *at least I will always have my college degree.*

News reports estimated that at least four thousand professors had left Iraq since the beginning of the war; at least three hundred more had been murdered. Many, it was rumored, were killed by an Al Qaeda–led campaign to eradicate Iraq's professional class. Lawyers, doctors, and English teachers had also been targeted at random. But no one knew for sure. Entire departments, running on a skeleton staff, had been shut down. Some of Mamina's colleagues had been murdered, too, and some had escaped to Germany. Most of Nunu's classmates weren't at graduation when the day finally came. Nunu estimated that at least half of her freshman class had disappeared. Of those still remaining, few felt they could stay much longer. They feared being targeted as professionals, and despised the prospect of living under radical Islamic law. The medical students, the engineers, the teachers, the scientists—they all wanted to go elsewhere. Lately, Zia had been bringing up the idea of Mamina and Nunu leaving. Baba would never go for it, Nunu knew, but Zia said they should leave without him. But how? And where would they go?

Still, it was something to consider. Nunu herself had received two threats in the last few months. The first came while she was sitting in her living room with Aunt Ilham and Mamina. Her cellphone rang. "Can I speak to Nariman?" asked a male voice. Nariman was Nunu's full name.

"This is she," she answered, wondering who the strange voice belonged to. Since cellphones had become popular in the past couple of years, boys had developed the habit of randomly dialing numbers in the hope that a girl would answer. But this man's voice was older, and he had used her name. "Yes," she repeated into the silence on the other end. "This is Nariman. Who is talking?"

"This is your last year in college. Do you want to be just like your sister?"

His voice was casual, as though they were friends. She was too shocked to answer.

"Take care," he said, and hung up.

When she told Mamina and Baba, they debated what the caller had meant by "just like your sister." Was he warning her not to work for the Americans, as Zia had? Or was he warning her to veil or she'd end up dead, as many believed Zia was? How did he know her phone number? Many girls had received similar threatening calls, and Nunu didn't know if this was a serious threat or just one of her friends' brothers, a kid who just liked to hear himself sound dangerous. There was no way to know.

Then, after classes one day in the early spring of 2006, Nunu was standing outside the gates, waiting for her father. Many students mingled outside in a crowd. A car passed, and someone threw something out that hit her on the shoulder.

"Nariman, this is for you," he yelled.

She looked down and saw an envelope at her feet. She hadn't had time to recognize the car or any of the passengers. She picked up the envelope. She knew there was something bad in it. It was a single handwritten page, a quote from the Quran followed by a threat.

"Don't dress or put on makeup like the ignorant people from the past. Guard your modesty and cover yourself or we will kill you." It wasn't signed.

Baba arrived and read the letter. As they drove away, Nunu could see that Baba was nervous that they were being followed. "These are not men," Baba muttered. "If their mothers had raised them better, they'd be men."

They took the note to court, and the judge read it and documented it, but he could do nothing else. "My advice would be for her not to go to college every day" was all he said.

Nunu was depressed. She had only a few months left in a college experience that had been a struggle from the beginning, and now it would be even worse. After the letter, she went only when she had an exam, sometimes a few days a week and sometimes not for a few weeks. Her professors understood. This time, she veiled. She would go to collect the lectures, then read them at home. When Baba picked her up, she waited inside the college until he called her and said, "I'm here now in front of the gate." Nunu would hurry out into the car, her veiled head bent down, indistinguishable from the dozens of other women around her.

CHAPTER THIRTY-THREE

ZIA'S EMAILS AND phone calls continued to be cheerful, but not everything was perfect, even in the States. The immigration officer had granted her a six-month tourist visa, but after the first heady month she confided to Nunu that, as time went by, she was constantly worried about her next step. Where would she go and what would she do? Plus, she said, she was lonely. She really missed Nunu and Mamina.

At first she had made friends quickly, since people her age were fascinated to hear she was from a country they had seen so much about on the news. But young people in D.C. were antiwar and they hated George Bush, she discovered. Although they knew little about the reality on the ground, they couldn't handle her casual mention of suicide bombers, assassinations, beheadings, and rocket attacks—and her wish that the troops would stay in Iraq was met with awkward silence. "I make people uncomfortable, Mama," she said in her nightly calls home. She said she had stopped talking about Iraq at all, but it didn't mean she could forget about what was happening in her homeland. She talked to Keith for hours each day, transporting herself back to the Green Zone from her bedroom in Washington. Though Nunu and Mamina decided not to tell her about the attack on Nunu, she still heard grisly stories about the world she was trying to escape. She called crying one night after Keith told her that Enaas, the young woman who had replaced Zia in her job at IMN, had been attacked. "They got her as she was leaving her house. Shot her nine times right on her street." Amazingly, she was still alive. But Zia knew that could have been her.

Eventually, things started to stabilize. She had some friends from Iraq who had worked at IMN. Soon she found an internship at the offices of the Independent Women's Forum, which described itself as a Republican women's organization, a characterization that meant little to Zia. Unlike most Washingtonians, the women at IWF could listen to her praise George Bush all day. They reminded her of the White House people in the CPA. Even though it was unpaid, the job got her out of the house and gave her much needed distraction from thoughts of home.

I am starting over, she told herself. She researched applications for university scholarships and State Department programs that could keep her in the USA. Best of all, no one knew her past, or could define her future. This was her new beginning. As such, she was determined to be independent and not lean on anyone. As a part of that new philosophy, she decided it was time to break off her relationship with Keith for good. Nunu and Mamina agreed that, if he was never going to leave Iraq, she had to move on without him, and make a new life. As much as it pained her, Zia slowly took fewer of his calls and responded less often to his email.

ONE AFTERNOON, ZIA'S Iraqi colleague from IMN came to the house with a letter for Mamina. When she opened it, she saw it was from Keith.

"Dear Mamina," it began. "I'm stupid and I hope you will forgive me. I have been in love with your daughter since the first day I met her. It took me a long time to realize this."

He explained to Mamina how he had first understood how much he loved Zia when he was stuck at the airport in Mosul during Christmas 2003. He told her he had kept all of Zia's emails, and that he had loved her ever since.

Mamina cried over the letter. She thanked God for making Keith see the light.

She called Zia immediately. The next day, Nunu pleaded with Baba to accompany her to the Internet center, where she secretly scanned the letter into the computer and sent it to Zia. Mamina had worried night and day that Keith had not been serious about Zia, but the letter convinced Mamina that he truly loved Zia. "He will act now, Zuzu," Mamina assured her. "Tell him he must come to America to be with you."

Nunu downloaded a song about two lovers from different countries and sang it for Zia. "Who gives you the right to come across the ocean and to my country and steal my heart?" They all laughed.

That evening, Zia received an email from Keith. "I'm coming to America, and I'm going to marry you."

IN KEITH'S RENTAL car, they drove down to the waterfront in Georgetown, one of Zia's favorite places. The sunlight glinted off the Potomac River as they strolled along the dock. This kind of casual time together in public was a new experience for them. Their two-and-a-half-year courtship had occurred entirely behind barbed wire, under rocket attack, in one of the most heavily guarded fortresses in the world. The last six months of their relationship had been conducted by cellphone and email. Now there were no belligerent security guards, no Iraqi grounds-keepers snapping cellphone photos to post on Islamic websites, no checkpoints to remind them that he was an "occupier" and she was a "local." It was Keith and Zia holding hands, as unremarkable as any other American couple.

Zia cried, finally releasing months of tension. Keith cried too. Away from Iraq for the first time in years, he felt like someone had splashed cold water on his face. He was in shock, feeling as out of place as he had initially in Baghdad. He had forgotten about the rest of the world.

He told her about his colleague Mike, who had fallen in love with an Iraqi poet. After their relationship was revealed she'd had to flee the country for Jordan. She'd waited for him for a year, but Mike refused to leave Iraq. So she gave him up.

"Mike is heartbroken," Keith recounted. "And I just saw that happening to me."

He got down on his knee and properly proposed. Then they walked to a jewelry store and bought rings.

ZIA SPOKE WITH Mamina and Nunu every three or four days, telling them about the proposal, about all the paperwork that Keith was getting to finalize his divorce, about her own meetings with immigration lawyers, in which she had decided to apply for asylum. She told them that she and Keith were moving to California, where his family was.

"California!" Nunu gasped with excitement. Zia's life really was just like the movies.

They knew she'd have to be married before she and Keith moved in together, but it was still a shock when she finally broke the news one night on the phone. "I'm getting married in a few days."

Mamina went quiet and began to cry. She passed the phone to Nunu, who didn't know what to say. She had never imagined that the sisters wouldn't be together on their wedding days. Zia explained that Keith said this would just be a civil ceremony, and that they would have a big wedding later, when Nunu and Mamina could be there. But Nunu knew it wouldn't be the same. After a few minutes, Mamina took the phone back. "It's okay," she said to Zia. "Don't think about us or miss us."

Nunu heard Zia begin to cry. "I'm sorry, Mama."

"No no no, Zuzu. You must be tough and hold in any tears," Mamina said. "Think about your future with Keith and be grateful for it."

Then, for two hours, she talked to Zia about the wedding night. Mamina explained in graphic detail everything that would happen. For some portions of the conversation, Nunu was allowed to listen in. But for most of it, Nunu excused herself to go into the other room. She didn't want to hear it yet, but she also couldn't help thinking about the box in the bedroom closet where Mamina had been collecting pieces of racy lingerie for her daughter since Zia had turned eighteen. Nunu remembered shyly watching her big sister examine the lingerie with fascination, trying on the lace thongs, scarlet red teddies, and peekaboo nighties, and deciding which styles best flattered her figure. Mamina believed that titillating lingerie—and a bride's savvy know-how in pleasing her man—signaled that the mother was educated and reflected well on the entire family. A woman's sex appeal could also afford her incredible power to influence her husband both in the bedroom and outside it, but only if she knew how to wield it.

But, Nunu thought sadly, how could they give these slips to her now, all the way in California? What if something went wrong—who would Zia go to? In the other room, she could hear Mamina finish explaining what would physically happen on the wedding night. The Quran encouraged pleasurable sex between a husband and wife, so Mamina was matter-of-fact about preparing her daughter for it. "Your wives are your fields, so go into your fields whichever way you like," said the holy book. Mamina told Zia how to enjoy sex and to "do it this way" and "that way" in specific detail, so it would bring her pleasure as well. "It will hurt more because you are older now, but you must hide your pain. Don't let him know because it will ruin the mood." Zia giggled a little. "How it happens the first time sets the tone for the future," Mamina advised her. "You must not let him rush. Make it all go as slowly as you can. Stay relaxed."

It was a lot for Zia to digest, she knew. In Iraq, a woman's wedding was the biggest day in her life. She couldn't imagine the day without Mamina and Nunu and Aunt Sahra and Aunt Ilham, her cousin Lara, and Nunu's friend Noor. She missed Baba and longed for his approval, but no one could even tell him about the wedding. He still refused to hear about what Zia was doing in the States, or even hear Keith's name, despite the help he had offered when Zia was attacked.

A few days later, Zia sent them photos from the wedding. Keith had surprised her by asking her to get a dress, and by reserving a photographer and a chapel for the ceremony. In her spectacular white gown, with gold leaves in her hair and wearing her best jewelry, Zia was a vision to behold, but inside, Nunu understood, she felt tiny and alone.

CHAPTER THIRTY-FOUR

AS TIME WENT by and the civil war got worse, Nunu longed to confide in her sister about what was happening in Iraq.

"This will only cause her pain," Mamina said. They knew Zia felt guilty and worried for having escaped and left her family behind, and that she'd started having nightmares about Iraq. "When she hears about problems with us, she fights with Keith."

"We are fine," she told her daughter on the phone. "Don't think about us. Be a good wife to Keith and be American. Get a job and don't be a burden on your new country."

Nunu relented, not wanting to say anything that would upset her sister. She knew that Zia and Keith, while generally happy, had started bickering about little things just because of the stress and trauma of their time in Iraq, from which they hadn't yet recovered. There was no point in making her sister as unhappy as she was, she thought. That was the only light in Nunu's dark existence. But Zia felt very far away.

Until Zia's wedding, Nunu felt that she, Mamina, and Zia had been a team, experiencing the excitement of America together. After the wedding, though, the dynamic among them changed. Zia was no longer out of their lives temporarily—she was gone for good. She was an American wife now. Who knew when the three would be united again?

So when Zia would call them at the end of her day, they tried not to talk about Iraq. Zia and Keith had moved just outside Sacramento, into a community of several hundred new homes built atop what was once farmland. She had a three-car garage, a manicured front lawn, and a sidewalk running in front of her house where neighborhood children rode their bicycles. She worked part-time at Sears, and cooked and cleaned the house each day. This was the life of abundance and freedom she had dreamed of in Iraq, and yet she felt she had only one foot in her new world. At night she lay awake in the darkness worrying about her family. Zia still heard stories from the news, or from acquaintances. Someone emailed her to say that two of her friends had died in car bombings, including her childhood friend Mustafa, whom everyone called Toofy. He had been a ball of energy, a fun-loving friend who had never hurt a soul, and now a terrorist had killed him for no reason at all. Zia became preoccupied with the fear that her family would be killed. She had visions of them being blown apart by suicide bombers, kid-napped, raped, or hit by a rocket. She called constantly, just to hear their voices.

"Mama, put Nunu on," she said, one evening.

"No, Zuzu, she doesn't feel like talking now."

Zia grew agitated. "What happened?"

"No, my dear, everything's fine."

"I don't believe you!" Zia became hysterical. Maybe her sister had been killed by a bomb, or hit by a rocket—would Mamina even tell her? "Something's happened that you're not telling me."

Mamina had to put Nunu on the phone so Zia could hear her voice and reassure herself that Nunu was still alive.

"Hello?"

Zia took a deep breath. "Hi, Nunu, what's up?"

"Nothing. I did nothing today but sit inside the house and watch television," Nunu said.

They both tried, but the sisters had little to talk about anymore. Zia didn't want to tell happy stories, and Nunu was despondent and listless.

"Nunu, I can tell by your voice that something has happened."

Finally, Nunu broke down. "Noor's brother was killed," she sobbed. Nunu's one and only friend, Noor, had visited the house the prior after-noon. With a tearstained face, she told Nunu that she and her parents had returned home and found her brother shot dead on the living room floor. The militias had killed him. "Nunu, you must take care," Noor had said, trembling. "My brother knew not to open the door to anyone. So this must have been done by a friend, someone he trusted."

Zia tried in vain to comfort her. "Be strong. I'm sorry this is happen-ing for you," she said. "One day it will be over. In Jordan things were pitch black for me and I had nowhere to go. With patience, the situation got resolved and my dreams came true."

"No, things won't change in Iraq. It's too late. A generation will pass before there will be peace."

Wracked with guilt, Zia was quiet for a long time, and eventually Nunu said good night.

Months would pass before the sisters spoke again.

AFTER HER COLLEGE graduation, it became even harder for Nunu to keep her spirits strong. Without the distraction of her studies, or the goal of gaining her degree, the days felt long and pointless. Most nights, she sat alone in her bedroom listening to Radio Scheherazade. She tried to get a job, but wasn't too hopeful. None of her classmates had found jobs, and many had left Iraq. She sent in her application to ministries and universities, but never heard back. As a Shia, she couldn't work for any of the government ministries located in Sunni neighborhoods or that required her to cross through Sunni areas in her commute. She couldn't work for any foreign companies without fear of retaliation, and she couldn't work for any schools taken over by the Islamic militias, unless she was willing to wear a black cloak and headscarf, which she wasn't. Few women felt the city was safe enough to commute daily to an office. One news report said that unemployment in Iraq was at 70 percent. Uncle Khadum worked in the administration at the Ministry of Oil. He spoke to some people. "I can get you a position for six months," he said. "But they want a six-hundred-dollar bribe."

"But it will take me three months to earn back that money, and who's to say they won't fire me after that?" she said.

"They probably will," he conceded.

The months passed. Nunu barely moved more than ten yards from the kitchen to the living room to her bedroom. Sometimes, she didn't bother leaving the bedroom. Each hour was like the last. There was no difference between the days, even between night and day. Sometimes Nunu would sleep all day and stay up all night. With the curtains drawn, she didn't bother to look at the time. Each day was the same. Sometimes, in the middle of her chores, Nunu would break down and sob on the floor for minutes. But then pity made her angry at herself. She had no right to cry—at least she had her life, unlike Noor's brother, unlike so many other young people killed by the suicide attacks. She felt a responsibility to get up and live her life because she was the lucky one. She would try to continue her chores as though nothing had happened.

After a year, her skin became pale and blotchy with acne. After a while, even the crying episodes stopped, and she missed them. She felt only numbness.

Trips out of the house were few and far between. She and Mamina decided to go to the doctor, since Mamina had been bleeding and feeling pain in her abdomen, and Nunu wanted drugs for depression—a treatment that had become common in Baghdad. But they got the same response at each medical center they tried: "The doctors have left the country"; "The doctor was killed." The city they drove through looked apocalyptic: blackened, charred sites of bombings, morose passersby, date palms hacked in half and pushed across the road to create checkpoints.

Finally, they found an open clinic. The doctor diagnosed Mamina quickly: she had a dangerously large fibroid in her uterus—a serious though not uncommon problem, but one that needed to be treated with surgery. However, the hospital equipment had been looted, and the lack of electricity created a long waiting list. The surgery specialists Mamina needed had fled the country or been assassinated, the nurses told her. They gave her iron pills for anemia. She also had hypertension due to stress. She needed rest.

For Nunu's depression, they gave her small white tablets. Now she slept even more, and she couldn't even get up from the bed. Nunu turned her anger and frustration inward. She wondered if the Islamists were right: *I am a weak girl,* she thought. *I am unimportant and stupid.* Her journal entries grew darker and darker.

> I feel depressed. There are many ideas that come to me. Sometimes I think to get rid of the sadness and end it by myself, other times I say to myself that tomorrow will be better and this black cloud will die away. But I feel inside that there is no hope. I begin to lose my hope and my strength. I don't know what to do.

Almost two years had passed since Zia had left for the States, and now Nunu couldn't distinguish one month from the next.

More than anything, she wanted to reach out to her sister. Zia called twice a week but usually spoke only to Mamina or Baba. Months passed and not a word was exchanged between them. Nunu and Mamina held to their pact not to tell Zia about the violence dominating their lives. Nunu could barely summon the energy to come to the phone when Zia did call. She missed her terribly, and wanted to cry to her and tell her everything. But if Zia knew the truth, she might decide to return to Iraq to be with them. That would be her death sentence.

So everyone agreed to pretend.

WITH NO JOB, and unable to leave the house, Nunu became an unwilling spectator to the civil war. One afternoon, Baba came home pale-faced. "An explosion happened near Mustansiriya University," he said. Mustansiriya was the second-largest university in Baghdad and one of the oldest universities in the Arab world. Noor had been a student there.

Mustansiriya had an enormous walled courtyard, and only students with college ID were allowed inside. Like the ones at Baghdad University, the school guards were controlled by Muqtada al-Sadr, and they stood at the entrance harassing any girls who were dressed "improperly." Although the students felt safe inside the college walls, the buses that picked them up pulled up in front, where there was no security. Masses of cars driven by fathers and brothers were always pooled outside the gates, and 3:30 p.m. was the busiest time, when daytime classes let out and students for the evening classes were arriving. Hundreds and hundreds of students milled outside the gates, buying fruit juice, running over to the copy shop, sitting on the stone wall and gossiping. Men smoked with friends and sipped Pepsis. Groups of girls carrying books waited for the bus to arrive.

Nunu had felt the two bombs in her living room, miles away. They turned on the evening news. Nunu saw the familiar gate of the university, now blackened by smoke. That afternoon, two bombers had driven their cars to opposite ends of the college gates. The force of the blast from the first car bomb was enough to kill those standing in the immediate vicinity, decapitating many students, blowing off hands, arms, and legs. The devastation was compounded by the flying metal, the glass from the windshield, and the flaming gasoline. The sound blasted eardrums and some were blinded by the flying debris.

Nunu understood the graphic details of a suicide bombing far better than she cared to. Most victims die not from concussive force, but from pieces of steel shrapnel built into the bomb that can fly with the force of a bullet. Therefore, a bomber walking into a crowd might be less effective than a bomber standing at a short distance in a sparsely filled room, since more people would be hit by flying metal. Since the first suicide bomb at the UN building in August 2003, the attackers had refined their tactics. Since it was hard to kill large numbers of people with limited explosives strapped to the body, many bombers drove cars, or climbed onto buses, so that the gasoline could double or triple the effect. Nunu's body felt numb as she reflected on all of this.

According to the newscast, in the seconds after the blast there had been a stunned silence. Then the coughing began, followed by screams as survivors looked around them. Students could be heard in the background moaning and crying. Nunu gagged at the broadcast images of severed feet and pools of blood, of men wearing gloves to put body parts into white garbage bags.

The suicide bombers had predicted, correctly, that most students would react by rushing away to the other end of the gates, where the second car awaited them. The bomber detonated his device several minutes after the first, and there the devastation had been even greater.

The television reported sixty dead and hundreds injured. But Nunu knew the injured would probably die. The hospitals couldn't help them and the country lacked medicine, equipment, and doctors.

She was right. For several days students continued to die from injuries. Most were only eighteen or nineteen years old. For weeks, mourners came to the gates of the university to cry and lay roses for the victims whose bodies were never identified, but whose charred IDs had been uncovered amid the rubble. Almost two hundred people were killed at the gates of Iraq's oldest university.

For what? screamed a voice inside Nunu's head. She sobbed for the students. She banged her palms on the couch. Temporarily, her numbness was replaced with outrage. *Why? Why kill these beautiful young people who are just beginning their lives? Innocents who have committed no crimes!*

When Mamina spoke with Zia later on, she realized that in California her sister had not even heard about the bombings. Despite the death toll and the horrible cruelty of the attack, there was little coverage on Western channels. On the Arab channels, there was none of the outrage expressed if the troops accidentally killed even one Iraqi. Nunu could never understand why the foreign press was so much more interested in the few crimes of their own soldiers than the much worse atrocities committed by Islamic fundamentalists. Nunu and Mamina personally knew dozens of innocent Iraqis killed by the *irhabeen,* the terrorists, but no one who had been harmed by Western forces.

A far, far greater evil than even Saddam had now entered Iraq, and the thought chilled Nunu's spine. This kind of carnage was beyond what even Iraq's two largest militias, Muqtada's army or Islamic Dawa, would do. There was only one group sick enough to believe God wanted them to kill Muslim students at Mustansiriya, and that was Al Qaeda.

Indeed, days later Nunu heard that Al Qaeda had claimed responsibility. The reason given was that university officials had refused to ban female students from enrolling.

KARRADA, ONE OF the oldest settled neighborhoods in Baghdad, was in the middle of the city, the heart of the commercial downtown. It had no strong ethnic majority, and had for a long time been relatively safer than other parts of the city. Most of the ethnic cleansing had occurred in the denser religious neighborhoods on the outskirts. Shortly after the war, the Americans nicknamed Karrada the "White Rose" because citizens would emerge from their homes to offer them white roses.

By 2007, a rumor spread through the neighborhood that Al Qaeda had sworn to "turn the white rose into a red rose." Now the death squads moved closer and closer. The soldiers seemed either unwilling or unable to stop what was becoming a vicious civil war between Sunni and Shia. Mortars fired at the Americans in the Green Zone often missed their mark and fell in Karrada, killing people who were in the wrong place at the wrong time. Given the greater atrocities in the country, these kinds of deaths, by random rocket fire, rarely made the news anymore.

One day, a rocket slammed into the photographer's store at the end of their street. The family photographer, Anis, who had taken Nunu's graduation photos, the family's driver's license photos, passport photos, and even family portraits in the 1990s, was inside. He was injured, but survived. His brother was killed. The store was destroyed.

Now the neighborhoods that ringed central Baghdad had fallen under the complete control of the militias. They were being carved up by sect, and militias were going from door to door checking identity cards. Anyone from the wrong sect faced one of two fates: either they were killed on the spot and their home seized, or they were given twenty-four hours to leave—and then their home was seized. A gentle old man who had worked at IMN with both Keith and Zia had died this way: one night, Shia militias came to his door and told him and his wife, "Be out of your house by tomorrow." He was very old, and it was late, but he and his wife spent the night packing everything they had. In the morning, he went to borrow a truck from his friend, but the errand took too long. As they were packing everything into the bed of the truck, the insurgents returned. "We are leaving," the old man pleaded.

"We told you to be out by now," they said. They shot him in the head and left the body on his street. They let his wife run away, and moved into his house.

Stories like these were common. The more people killed, the more families there were that wanted revenge. In the west and north, neighborhoods such as Mansour and Adhamiya were taken over by Sunni radicals. In the east, Sadr City and and other neighborhoods were run by Shia militias. Life and death were determined by a street address. Iraqis watched in terror as their neighbors were killed or evicted; anyone who spoke up met the same fate. For those who weren't threatened, the militias offered the only security they had experienced in three years. But they were hardly a welcome form of leadership. Militia members were typically uneducated, poor, and violent; they offered no form of government or plan for the future. Nunu and Mamina knew them to be no more than cruel, power-hungry gang leaders.

One morning, fifteen minutes after Baba left to take Mamina to school, Nunu felt the house shaken by an enormous bomb that was clearly very close. She rushed outside to see giant plumes of black smoke and debris rising from the end of her street. Not stopping to think about her own safety, she pushed past the gate and joined the neighbors as they hovered around the blackened carcass of a bus, its windows blown out, its steering wheel melted, and with no passengers to be seen. Baghdad buses were used only by the poor people: day laborers, child workers, students, and widows. The entire corner had been demolished as well. As she stood there staring at the unimaginable, all of a sudden a second bomb detonated, louder than the first. Nunu was flung backward.

"Go home," a neighbor was shouting at her. She put her hands to her head and ran home.

What about Mamina and Baba? Twenty minutes later, they returned. They were sweaty and jumpy.

"There was nothing left of them. Not even body parts," Baba said about the bus passengers, sitting breathlessly on the couch.

"No, no, no!" Nunu shouted, her head in her hands. She slammed her hand against the table. "They don't want us to have a life."

She ran into her room and cried on her bed. She felt sad for those on her street who lay dying. She felt sorrow for the pieces of herself that were dying—the virtues of tolerance, forgiveness, and Iraqi pride. All she had inside these days was hatred; hatred for the terrorists and for the militias, enough hatred to make her wish she were dead.

Later, they found out that thirty-one people had died, including their neighbor's small son and Usama, the poor, gentle man who had sold trinkets at the corner for as long as Nunu could remember. Usama had not been injured by the first bomb and had rushed over to help the victims, but was wounded badly from the shrapnel of the second bomb. Baba visited him in the hospital out of respect for his baby daughter and a pregnant wife. The day after he died, people lit candles where his kiosk had stood.

For as long as Nunu could remember, this street had been her home. She had played soccer on it growing up, and ridden her bicycle there. She knew every alleyway, every family, and everyone's story. Their block was not even a quarter mile long; she could see clearly from one end to the other. It was known in Baghdad as the "street of oil paintings" because so many artists used to display their work there.

Yet now she realized she was surrounded by vacant properties, nothing but fractured families and death. At the top of the street lived a teacher whose son had been killed by the rocket that had crashed into the photographer's shop. At the other end was a small store that had been run by a man who had always been friendly to Nunu. A Sunni terrorist had kidnapped the owner's brother and held him for ransom. He tortured him and threatened to kill him, so the man sold his house and his store and turned over the money, but it turned out that the terrorist had kidnapped the brother by mistake because his name was Haider, a common Shia name. When the brother was able to prove he was Sunni they released him, but by then, too many people knew the family was Sunni, so they had had to leave for Syria.

Next to them was the home of a Ba'athist where, back in 2003, someone had scrawled "May the Ba'ath Party fall." Soon afterward the father had been gunned down. The family stayed in the house, and the son, who was Nunu's age, opened a small arcade in 2006, with billiards and other games. A religious militia threatened the store, but the son couldn't close it because he had just gotten married and had a baby girl and he needed the income. Two days after the threat, the gang arrived at his arcade and gunned him down. The mother, wife, and daughter left town.

Next door to them was an old man. His son had recently disappeared. He had driven to see a friend in Dura, a Sunni neighborhood, and he never came back. Sometimes Nunu saw the father standing alone outside, staring up and down the street.

Beyond him had been Usama.

All these neighbors made up the fabric of Nunu's small world. She knew them intimately—what time they left for work and arrived home, how they dressed, what vehicles they drove, and how they treated one another. She had grown up with them. On Nunu's street alone, four men had been murdered since the start of the war. *This is madness,* she thought. And yet her building was not an exception. When someone talked about Nunu's family, they probably said, "That is the family whose daughter was killed for working for the Americans."

NUNU AND MAMINA never told Zia about any of this. After the double bombings, few neighbors ventured outside anymore. The violence and stress took its toll within the family too. Tensions surfaced and fights began. Since they could not take their anger out on the militias, they turned on one another.

Mamina wanted Baba to line up to buy much-needed gasoline for the generator. But the lines for gasoline stretched for miles, and men began waiting before dawn. Since the gas stations were also common targets for suicide bombers, Baba refused. Mamina felt this was unfair. She left the house each morning for school, traveling on roads that were frequently violent. If she could swallow her fears, Baba could too. But he wouldn't.

Then they argued over the generator, which Baba shared with a neighbor, whom Mamina considered wasteful. "He uses the power for his fish tanks," she complained. But Baba insisted on being a good neighbor and warned Mamina not to challenge him.

Mostly, though, they fought over the television. Nunu wanted to watch talk shows and sitcoms. Baba wanted to watch only the news, which Nunu hated. Headless bodies floating down the Tigris, mass graves discovered, policemen mutilated by drills with their hands bound behind their backs. It gave her nightmares.

One evening, Baba came home while Nunu and Mamina were watching an episode of *Oprah* that featured "women who change the world." Oprah was talking to a female doctor who traveled to different countries to help sick people.

"Change this," Baba said. He wanted to watch a new show, *Terrorism in the Hands of Justice,* which aired on the American-funded station Al Iraqiya. The show broadcast "confessions" of captured insurgents, and was intended to show to average Iraqis that the insurgents were hardened criminal thugs, not glorious freedom fighters—with the interviewer often taunting the bound prisoner, the prisoners appeared more like ignorant gangsters than honorable martyrs.

The show was hugely popular among Iraqis. Baba loved it. He settled onto the couch and watched as a young man appeared with a bruised face and began answering questions.

"Why don't they execute him on the spot?" Baba demanded. "There should be no mercy."

The man said he had been tricked into working with Al Qaeda against the Americans. He was told to kidnap Shia doctors, whom Al Qaeda would hold for ransom. But Al Qaeda just murdered them outright. "Please forgive me," the man begged. "I didn't know they would be killed."

Baba shook his head. "He invited the devil into his home. How did he expect him to behave? Kill him."

Nunu sat on the couch, cross-legged and unhappy. The next detainee admitted to taking part in the gang rape of a woman whom he had kidnapped from the university.

"Didn't she beg you not to?" the interviewer's voice asked.

"Yes, but we raped her nonetheless," the man said.

"How many of you?" the interviewer asked.

"Six of us."

"Why?"

"Because she was pretty. We tricked her into coming to talk to me, and then my friends arrived with guns and we took her, and raped her."

"You raped her?"

"Yes, I was last."

Nunu's face darkened. What she heard next she would never forget.

"How could you rape this innocent girl? Didn't you hear her cries?" the interviewer asked. "Didn't you see her tears?"

The criminal answered, "By the time it was my turn, I think she was already dead."

Nunu felt all the wind collapse from her lungs. The blood rushed to her head, and she fainted.

Mamina's furious voice snapped her awake. "Turn this off! We have no escape from this violence."

Tired of arguing, Baba disappeared into his bedroom, his sanctuary, where he had air-conditioning and another, smaller television. Nunu switched the channel back to *Oprah* to try and forget what she had just heard. But in the cramped apartment, the two televisions competed with each other, and neither could be heard clearly.

Baba came back into the living room.

"This rubbish," he said, pointing to the television. "Look at that woman wearing that short skirt."

"This woman is a doctor," Nunu said. She was brimming with anger. "Maybe she doesn't pray all day. She goes out in the world and saves people."

Nunu followed Baba back to his bedroom. In the street, she could do nothing when men berated and belittled her and made her feel weak and worthless. But at home, on safer ground, she lashed out. She reached in and slammed the door closed behind him. It was a bold, unprecedented move, and before she had returned to her place on the couch, Baba threw open the door and rushed toward her.

"Don't you dare look at me in the eye," he shouted.

"I did nothing to have you treat me like this!" she screamed at him.

Baba raised his hand to beat Nunu. Mamina blocked his path.

"Stop this. You can't hit her. She is a woman now, not a little girl, and that is shameful."

"She has no manners," he shouted. Nunu felt out of control. She flung the remote control across the room and it shattered against the wall. Baba rushed to it.

"Don't worry about the remote," Mamina screamed. "Go out and get some gasoline and burn this place down. This is no way to live."

Silently, Baba returned to his bedroom and closed the door. Now the only sounds were the hum of the air-conditioning and Nunu sobbing on the couch.

"Oh, Mama," she cried. "I hate him. Why didn't you get me out of Iraq? I want to be with Zia."

Mamina cradled her sobbing daughter, her own tears falling into Nunu's hair.

"Oh, my dear daughter. I would give my life for you to have freedom from this. Please, God, protect her. Please, God, take her out of Iraq. This is no life for her."

. . .

LATER THAT WEEK, Mamina returned from school to find Nunu lying in the dark in her bedroom.

"Nunu, get up! Wake up! Don't stay in bed all day."

But Nunu had no sense of whether it was day or night. "Leave me alone, Mama," she said, her voice sluggish in the dim bedroom. "I'm making a plan. I'm going to run away to Turkey."

Mamina sat on the bed. Both women had heard stories of smuggling routes through the Kurdish mountains into Turkey or across the Shatt-al-Arab and into Kuwait. Nunu wanted to try and get out this way. Zia had escaped Iraq, as had Noor, and Nunu believed she could make it out too.

CHAPTER THIRTY-FIVE

FROM THE RELATIVE safety of Amman, Manal continued to advocate for Iraqi women through 2006 and 2007. Women for Women was still able to do some work in Iraq thanks to its twenty-four Iraqi staff members working in administration and counseling.

Even from this safe distance, the violence hit close to home. Manal and Ahmed were now happily married, but their wedding had been bittersweet. Several days before their nuptials in September 2005, Ahmed's brother-in-law had been brutally murdered by insurgents, leaving widowed Ahmed's sister Rana and three young children. Their wedding was replaced by a funeral. Manal and Ahmed had helped move Rana to Jordan into their small apartment and were caring for her and her children.

Meanwhile, Ahmed was still traveling in and out of Iraq, and he had moved their outreach efforts out of Baghdad and into the southern cities of Hilla and Karbala, where Fern had once operated. Manal had distanced herself enough that few knew the programs were U.S.-funded, which gave them a measure of protection. They offered women classes in politics, family, and nutrition. One class offered was "Equality in Raising Boys and Girls." Another class was "Stress Management," to try and help reduce the emotional impact of daily violence and chaos. Women for Women was one of the few Western nonprofits still on the ground, even though the need grew every day. *War always hurts women.* Manal had known this from the beginning, and by now its myriad effects were in full evidence: increased alcoholism among the men, depression among women, and rising reports of spousal abuse. Most Iraqi women experience war from behind locked doors in their kitchens and bedrooms, robbed of all freedoms. Although women have much smaller casualty numbers, death would, in many ways, be an escape from the lifelong grief of mourning that women face after losing their fathers, husbands, and sons to war. Some international groups counted seventy thousand Iraqi dead by 2007, but most Arab groups suggested a number double or triple that. A study published by Baghdad University and an Iraqi women's group in 2006 estimated that the combined impact of Saddam's wars and the U.S. invasion had left three million widows in Iraq. Their daughters, the report stated ominously, would make up "a generation of spinsters."

For the small number of women who attended, the group sessions held at secret Women for Women offices were the only times that victims could exchange stories and receive support. The sessions became an increasingly important part of their lives. In Hilla, many women still attended class even after a large bomb exploded in a public market. The letter-exchange program continued, and thousands of women from California, Florida, New York, and elsewhere corresponded with Iraqi women, offering sympathies and sharing a connection across the globe, no matter how different their circumstances.

Getting solid information on the status of women had become almost impossible by 2007, as all the aid agencies had been forced out of the country and journalists were unable to travel freely. Few were documenting the tragedies anymore, or counting casualties. The targeting of women's rights groups by radical Islamic groups persisted. Halima Ahmed al-Jabouri, the president of Women and Children Without Borders in Kirkuk, was gunned down in front of her children in November 2006. In another case, the director of a women's cultural center was shot five times. In Amara, a group called the Association of Widows came under threat by a religious militia. When it refused to close down, the headquarters was bombed. On April 27, 2005, Lamia Abed Khadouri, a female member of parliament, was killed in her home. The examples were endless, and horrifying.

Islamic fundamentalists, emboldened by the anarchy, were violently taking control of the country. Although the majority of Iraqis didn't want fundamentalists in charge, they were desperate for some sort of order, which the militias offered. This was how the Taliban had come to power in Afghanistan, following ten years of war with the Soviet Union and six years of civil war. It made Manal's heart ache to think Iraq was headed in the same direction.

In the south, so-called Committees for the Promotion of Virtue and Prevention of Vice roamed the cities with weapons, looking for women who were, in their opinion, violating the tenets of Islam. Such women were harshly punished. One of Manal's staffers was a Christian woman with family in Basra. She told Manal that women caught driving had their hands cut off. Women caught unveiled were whipped and in some cases beheaded. Women wearing jeans were considered prostitutes and were raped and killed. Even attending school was forbidden for girls in some places.

Women's rights groups began to see evidence of trafficking. The way young Muntaha had been, desperate Iraqi women were lured into promises of housekeeping jobs in Dubai, Kuwait, or Syria. Once they left their homes, they were forced into prostitution. In both Kirkuk and Najaf, Iraqi police units busted criminal gangs that were kidnapping young women and selling them to prostitution rings. Given the larger incidences of violence, the military paid scant attention to stopping such prostitution and trafficking. Many whispered that the soldiers themselves were involved.

Some of the crimes against women were disguised as "Islamic practices." Hanaa Adwar, a Christian woman who ran the Iraqi Women's Network, knew firsthand of incidents in which Al Qaeda fighters arriving in Iraqi villages to commit suicide bombings against U.S. soldiers or the Iraqi army would first demand to be married to a tribesman's daughter. After a night of sex, he would blow himself up. The bride, sometimes as young as thirteen, would be expected to live the rest of her life as the widow of a "martyr." In northern Iraq, the group ASUDA (Organization for Combating Violence Against Women), which ran a women's shelter, was a lone organization documenting crimes against women including honor killings, public stonings, and acid attacks. Manal had tried to send Muntaha there years earlier for protection, and she continued to fly to Sulaimaniya to run training programs. Other than Manal's help, ASUDA received no U.S. funding or attention, and was kept afloat by the efforts of local women. In May 2008, a gunman attacked the center. No one was hurt, and the women quickly returned to work.

Even those on the periphery of women's rights advocacy were not safe. Lawyers who defended women in honor-killing cases were kidnapped for their "crimes," then ransomed for thousands of dollars. One lawyer who prosecuted perpetrators of honor killing was murdered for his work. The note left by his body said: "This is the price paid by everyone who does not follow the teachings of Islam and who defends all that is dirty and evil."

AS THE VIOLENCE spread, the war spilled beyond Iraq's borders. The stream of refugees that had trickled out in 2003 and 2004 became a deluge as the civil war started in earnest. By 2006, almost two million Iraqis had fled the country. Another two million were displaced within Iraq, forced out of their neighborhoods or cities in fear of sectarian violence. Most refugees escaped to Jordan or Syria. In the building where Manal lived in Amman, ten of the twelve apartments were occupied by Iraqi refugees. Manal counted that eight of these ten families had fled after a family member was killed or kidnapped. The building collectively mourned the civil war only a few hundred miles across the border.

These were the lucky ones, however. Many poor Iraqis weren't able to find apartments in Jordan. They sneaked into the country with almost nothing, and tried to survive illegally, without access to schools, hospitals, or jobs. Many stayed inside for fear of being picked up by the Jordanian police and taken back to the border. The worst cases Manal saw were the women who traveled alone. Many were forced out of Iraq because they had been raped, widowed, or had lost their father. They had no choice but to turn to prostitution. The market was thriving, fed not only by Jordanians but also by wealthy visitors from the Gulf, lured to Amman by the bars, prostitutes, and nightclubs that were forbidden in their conservative countries. Many of those designated to help often preyed on the women instead. One woman told Manal that an Iraqi employee at the embassy in Syria was telling women his mother would help them, and to meet her at a private location. Lacking alternatives, young women would go, only to then be raped and trafficked into prostitution.

Helping these women was a challenge because many hid from the authorities in fear of being deported, arrested, or further exploited by the very people paid to help them.

Manal tried to lobby the U.S. government to accept Iraqi refugees, but it seemed hopeless. She was infuriated at the way that government abandoned those who had been most loyal to it. By 2007, a bill working its way through Congress, sponsored by Senator Edward Kennedy, would have allowed visas for seven thousand Iraqis, with precedence given to those who had worked for the Americans. That was a drop in the bucket alongside the four million refugees.

EVENTUALLY THE VIOLENCE would sputter and cease, Manal knew. Iraqis in Falluja and the rest of Anbar province were beginning to turn against Al Qaeda. Women's rights activists like Hanaa Adwar said that Iraqis had been shocked by the actions of the group's radical members. Even to religious Iraqis, sworn to expel the Americans, Al Qaeda's ideas were radical and repulsive.

A so-called Sunni Awakening, in which Sunnis had decided they were willing to stop the fighting and negotiate, had begun in 2006 and was spreading. But that was little consolation to those who'd already had their lives ruined. And what would Iraq look like for women? When Manal did imagine Iraq's future, she saw a country ruled by Islamist Shia clerics. Such a government didn't have to be repressive toward women, yet the insecurity in Iraq had opened the door to the radicals. They now had too much power, and they would set a tone of religious fervor that would condone the suppression of women. The government didn't have the authority to stop the religious militias who were patrolling the streets threatening women. In such an environment, anything could happen.

The irony was that Iraqi women themselves had voted the Shia into power in 2005. But, given the circumstances, Manal was not surprised. Iraqi women had been exposed to only three forms of governance: they could choose among a merciless dictator like Saddam, the full-blown chaos of secular American democracy, or an Islamic theocracy. They chose the latter.

Had the Americans not made so many mistakes in the beginning, perhaps they wouldn't have lost control over security, and the Iraqis could have had the time and space to try out democracy, Manal thought. But once the violence began, this was impossible. Americans had tried to do too much in one year: create a government, write a constitution, and bring about national reconciliation after thirty years of a brutal dictatorship. Few in the CPA had even considered national reconciliation an issue, preferring to work on more exciting democracy plans. But history makes clear that these things take time. It had taken South Africa ten years to get reconciliation, Manal recalled. But from the first month, Iraqis had called for the Americans to get out: there wasn't time.

Yet there were other mistakes too. Manal regretted her collusion with the military, despite her admiration for and ongoing friendship with Heather and the potential to use the money for good. The centers had been largely a wasted effort, and she had allowed her cause to be co-opted by the Bush administration. That realization was a bitter pill to swallow.

As much as she had tried to prevent it from being that way, help for women had been offered on U.S. terms, with an American vision as the goal. Bremer wanted to build women's centers, but only if he could use them to justify the occupation. Women's issues were used as political and military propaganda. Iraqis weren't going for that. They knew the Americans weren't promoting democracy for Iraqis' sake; they were promoting their own interests, wrapped up in the rhetoric of "freedom" and "liberty."

That was no way to lay the foundation for a country.

The way forward, Manal believed, was to establish rights for women within Islamic law. Was it possible? This was the contemporary debate among leading Muslim feminists. If there was any hope for Iraqi women, it was to work with progressive Muslim scholars to produce a version of feminism that was compatible with Islam. Changes were apparent everywhere in the Arab world. In 2003, the Moroccan king introduced a new family law that enshrined a woman's right to choose her husband or initiate divorce, and to limit polygamy and underage marriage. In 2005, Kuwaiti women won the right to vote. Women in Egypt were pushing for more seats in parliament. A new version of the Quran had recently been published by a female author, in which the verse that purportedly condoned spousal abuse had been reinterpreted. Although the United Nations still ranked the Arab world as the worst for women's rights, Manal did see reasons to be hopeful. But the lesson was that when change did come, it was always driven by local women.

Even in Iraq, the gains that had been made for women were many. Women had 25 percent representation in government. They had their own ministry. There were more women in cabinet posts and ministerial positions than ever before. Women had organizations. For now these gains had been swallowed up by the violence, but when the violence did cease—and it had to eventually—Iraqi women would at least have the structures in place to push for themselves. All of these gains had come from Iraqi women themselves.

Groups such as Women for Women International could help, but their role had to be as facilitators, not instigators. *Ultimately,* Manal thought, *the change must come from within.*

CHAPTER THIRTY-SIX

MAMINA TOLD BABA about Nunu's plan to run away. Surprisingly to Mamina, he was not initially against it, but the plan fell apart in the details. Baba helped arrange the visit of some Kurdish friends who knew a smuggling route out of Iraq. It would cost several thousand dollars. There were three ways to go: in a fruit container carried by a truck; by foot, walking four days across the icy border with Turkey; or by airplane, the safest but probably least successful route.

"I will take the risk," Nunu insisted.

"*Habibti,* how will you survive in Turkey?"

"I will take the train to Sweden."

Baba shook his head. "It's too dangerous." Maybe Zia could do it, but Nunu would be like a lamb separated from the flock. "She doesn't have the character to succeed in such a trip," he said, and no one disagreed.

Defeated, Nunu returned to her bedroom, rolled over, and curled up. Even she agreed with Baba. She wouldn't know how to find a train station that could take her to Sweden and didn't have the nerve to carry a gun. Their Kurdish friends had warned her that she could be raped or kidnapped and trafficked into prostitution, and that thought sickened her. But all she could think of was escape.

Zia would go.

Nunu remembered an afternoon from before Zia left, when she and Zia and Mamina had gone to the marketplace to buy Zia a new winter coat. They had greeted Usama, Nunu remembered sadly, and had passed Anis's photography store while it was still in business. A crowded marketplace was the ideal location for a suicide bomber, but avoiding the market was impractical, and those were the days when it still seemed worth the risk—the absence of electricity meant Iraqis had to shop every day because nothing could be stored.

From the crowd, a young man had suddenly moved toward Nunu. In a flash, he raised his arm and slapped her hard on her bottom. Nunu froze and went bright red.

Instantly, Zia had her gun out of her purse and in his face.

"You son of a bitch," she shouted at him. Nunu was shocked to hear her use such language. "I'll shoot you right here like a dog, and no one will care. They'll throw you in the trash."

The crowd cleared around them. His face went pale. "No, no, no," he begged. "I didn't do anything."

"You know what you did," she said.

"It happened by accident! I was trying to hit another girl."

Mamina took advantage of his fear to vent her frustrations too. She started whacking him on the head with her purse. Nunu had been terrified, and Zia had been so angry that she looked as if she almost wanted to pull the trigger, but when they saw their mother slapping him with her purse, the sisters couldn't help but laugh. Mamina always said, "The size of a woman's purse is the size of her emotions," and her purse was enormous. They all felt a rush of justice in scaring him and letting him know that he couldn't abuse women and get away with it.

By the end of the day, word had spread throughout the neighborhood about the "crazy girl with the gun." Baba's circle of friends had all heard about the incident, and Baba had been immensely proud of Zia. Many of the other young women on the street approached Nunu. "How did she get that gun? I want one."

Back in the bedroom, Zia said, "Nunu, you should get one too. You see, no one harasses me now."

But Nunu had refused. "I don't have the guts to pull the trigger."

"You don't kill him," Zia explained. "You just scare him so he thinks two thousand times before he hits another girl."

But Nunu knew in her heart that she could never pull out a gun without shaking so badly she'd be a greater danger to herself. After a lifetime of being protected by her big sister, Nunu always felt as if she wasn't made of the same ingredients as Zia. She didn't have her steeliness. "It takes guts to do what you do," she had told her sister that day.

She'd thought then that she'd always be able to stay by Zia's side. But now she knew she was going to have to start fending for herself.

THEN, AMID THE violence and bloodshed—a miracle arrived. Aunt Ilham became pregnant. She was almost forty and had been trying for years. No one could believe it.

She visited Mamina and Nunu, all done up in her lawyer's suit and briefcase, her coiffed black hair and her frosty pink lipsick. *"Congratulations!"* Nunu squealed, hugging and kissing her. Aunt Ilham beamed from ear to ear. Nunu felt so proud of her aunt; she was an intelligent, respected professional, she had a husband, and now would be a mother. It was a great blessing, at last a sign of God's presence.

Aunt Ilham hoped that the baby would bring peace to her relationship with her husband. Nothing had been easy for them in the last few years, what with the disappointment of their childless marriage. The civil war had deepened the strain, since Aunt Ilham was Shia and her husband was Sunni. Few neighborhoods were safe for both of them, and they could rarely travel together as a couple. As legal professionals in a secular justice system, they had both received death threats from religious radicals.

But the pregnancy, it seemed, only made the marriage worse. With the stress, and with her age, Aunt Ilham had a difficult time. She wanted to continue working, but her husband refused, saying it was shameful for him to have a pregnant wife on the job. She caved in to his demands and stopped working, but she told her husband she wanted to return to her job after the baby was born. He refused this as well. Aunt Ilham had always believed he was jealous of her because she had two degrees and was very well respected in judicial circles. Over the months, their fighting grew bitter and violent.

Then, one evening, there was an unexpected knock on the door. Waves of fear spread through the room, but they heard Aunt Ilham's voice. When Mamina opened the door, she saw her sister was crying and had a bruised eye.

"*Habibti!* Come in. What has happened?"

Nunu huddled close to Aunt Ilham and her swollen belly.

"We found out the baby will be a girl," she sobbed. "He is very angry. He hit me and pointed his gun at me."

Aunt Ilham stayed the night with Nunu in her bed. She fell asleep quickly, and lay there peacefully like a young girl. Next to her, Nunu lay awake, seething inside. How dare any man degrade her beautiful, brilliant, strong aunt in such a way? And only for the crime of having a daughter. *This is the reality for women,* she thought. Lying there in the dark, for the first time in her life Nunu had a thought that would have terrified her only a year earlier: *I would rather be a spinster than marry a man like Aunt Ilham's husband.*

Suddenly, this idea felt radical and empowering. It was a choice she was willing to make for herself. She felt strangely free.

As she lay there, Nunu began to wonder about her life. How had she ended up so different from her sister? Was this the character that God had given her, like her uncles said? Or had she become this way, and Zia another way, for a reason? Why could Zia stand up to her attackers on the street, while Nunu hid in the house? Why did Zia rush into life, so filled with confidence, while Nunu sat on the sidelines worrying what people thought, so concerned to be the "typical" Arab woman who always waited for a man's direction before making her move?

She hadn't always been like this, she remembered.

There was a time when she was not so shy. As a little girl, Nunu wasn't afraid of running around, pushing the boys and shouting to stick up for herself. Now that she thought back, she could remember those days vividly. She had felt so free and comfortable in her body. But what had happened? The first change, she knew, had occurred on the elementary school playground. A much-beloved teacher, Ms. Intisar, called out to her. All the little girls loved Ms. Intisar. She had black hair and was beautiful, and Nunu adored her. Excited, Nunu flew across the playground to her. But when she arrived, Ms. Intisar slapped her hard, twice, in front of all the other students. Stunned, Nunu went home crying. The next morning, Mamina stormed into the school to demand an explanation.

"Nunu was running around like a boy," Ms. Intisar said. "You should have seen her disrespectful behavior."

Mamina was furious. "She is a child," she shouted.

The headmaster intervened and apologized to Mamina.

But it was too late. After those slaps, Nunu became filled with worry that another unexpected punishment was always right around the corner. She never understood her crime, so she lost confidence in her judgment of right or wrong. She began to look to others for permission to do anything. With Zia at the helm, that was never a problem. Nunu slipped easily into the role of the follower.

In middle school, Nunu had a female math teacher, Miss Anisa, who used to belittle and humiliate the female students, especially the pretty ones, like Nunu. She was veiled and unmarried, in her late thirties. Even when Nunu gave the same answer as a boy, Miss Anisa would give the boy a higher grade. She always mocked Nunu's way of speaking, and criticized girls who dressed up their uniforms with barrettes or colored clothes. Looking back on it now, Nunu began to feel sad for Miss Anisa, as maybe she was bitter over the harsh way Iraqi society treats women who don't marry. At the time, though, Nunu felt confused and ashamed and disappeared deeper into her shell.

Nunu internalized the message of shame. Even if no one said anything, Nunu heard these voices in her head. Every now and again, though, she would receive some encouragement. She never forgot the time her aunt's husband insulted her.

He looked at her angrily in the living room. "Why do you wear your hair long and free like this? It should be covered."

Nunu froze.

But Baba was sitting nearby and overheard. "She wears her hair as she wears her hair," he said, waving his hand to dismiss the comment.

In that moment, Nunu loved her father dearly for defending her. That was the Baba she knew. Maybe he had planted a kernel of confidence in her soul that she could nurture. Zia had always blossomed under the knowledge that Baba, although he might not express his emotions very openly, took pride in her strength and intelligence. Maybe Nunu could find her own courage out of that as well.

EVENTUALLY, NUNU'S AUNT had her baby girl. The decrease in violence that had begun in the summer of 2007 allowed the women a few freedoms. The gangs still kidnapped, and robberies and carjackings were common, but the death squads and ethnic cleansing had mostly stopped. The suicide bombs reduced in number. More U.S. troops were said to be on the ground, and the militias were negotiating with the government. The Sunni tribal leaders had begun to turn against Al Qaeda. No one believed the war was over, no one felt happy or optimistic—they had seen too much—but many seemed stunned by how violent the country had become. The fury and anger left over from Saddam's years had eventually been exhausted.

When the baby was born, Mamina and Nunu decided the streets were safe enough to travel to the hospital. It was the happiest day Nunu had had in years. She tickled the baby's fat fingers and admired her long black eyelashes.

Her aunt told her that the government gave a payment to new mothers, but the amount differed depending on the sex of the baby. For a boy, a mother received 150,000 dinars, and for a girl she received 100,000.

"I suppose they think that a boy strengthens the family and girls are a burden," Aunt Ilham said. Nunu was angry, but Aunt Ilham was so happy she just laughed.

What a silly, stupid idea, Nunu thought. Surely not all people thought that way, but what a shame that anyone did. As Nunu cooed at the precious little girl, she realized the inordinate number of obstacles set up in the baby's path before she'd even left the hospital. What would Iraq look like in the next five or ten years? Nunu wondered sadly. The country Mamina had grown up in had long been crushed, and so had their hopes that the invasion would improve life for women. This baby wouldn't even grow up with the few freedoms Nunu had enjoyed under Saddam. Even with the killings diminished, Iraq was an unbearable place to live; its infrastructure was devastated, its politicians corrupt, and it was bereft of an entire class of professionals who had fled the civil war and sworn not to return. A mask of sadness became etched into Baba's face. Despite living in a region that floated on oil and was blessed with two major rivers, his country was, once again, suffering. "Iraq is like a camel," he muttered. "It carries gold and eats thorns." Mamina shook her head. She believed the country was living under a thirteen-hundred-year-old curse, going back to the days when the tribes lured the

Prophet's grandson to Karbala and beheaded him. "Iraqis are still being punished for this betrayal."

The price of peace was a country run by religious radicals, and a prison for women. Nunu hugged the baby. "No matter what happens," she swore, "I will help you be strong, even if you can only be strong in your mind." Nunu promised to encourage her to have dreams.

"You're not less than a boy," she whispered as the baby gurgled. "Don't ever feel ashamed of yourself because you're a girl."

FOR ALMOST TWO years, Nunu had lived like a prisoner in her own home. She refused to do so any longer. She began walking outside more often, to buy bread or run small errands. She didn't drive and she never went alone, but for the first time in more than a year, she went outside with Mamina, even if only for a few minutes, every day.

Then proposals came raining in.

The first suitor, the brother of Usama's widow, had seen Nunu from his window. He asked his aunt to approach the family. She stopped Mamina on the street. "My nephew wants to marry your daughter. He was born in the seventies, and is very handsome."

Mamina agreed to set up a meeting. She knew only that his name was Husam and his mother was Christian. Baba, who sat with his friends on the street for most of the day, knew him.

"Husam? But have you seen this man?" he asked his wife.

"No . . ."

"The man prefers not to look at himself in the mirror. He looks like a genie. Nunu will be scared of him."

Mamina chose to ignore him. Lately, Baba had bristled at the idea of Nunu marrying, and she worried that, as Baba aged, he was eyeing Nunu as his caretaker—a responsibility that often fell on the youngest daughter. Mamina refused to let this happen.

The day Husam was due to arrive, there was no water, gas, or electricity, and the temperature climbed to 120 degrees. With no way to prepare herself, Nunu struggled to look presentable, but as it turned out, it didn't matter. When the man arrived, they saw he was bald, with a huge chest. Baba gave Mamina a look, *I told you so,* and left the house. The next day, Mamina politely declined.

The proposals continued to arrive. An old woman spotted Nunu one afternoon and approached Mamina.

"I know this boy that is *so* handsome. He should marry your daughter. He has recently moved to the neighborhood. Come to his house tomorrow night to welcome the family and you can meet him. He looks like Redha al-Abdullah, the famous singer. Tall, dark hair, hazel eyes. He wants to travel right away."

Mamina received this news as a blessing. "You will leave Iraq immediately," she told Nunu excitedly. But the next day, Baba refused to let them go. He wouldn't say why. Normally, Mamina would never defy him, but she did this time. She quickly called her brother, and he came over to take them to the house.

The old woman greeted them at the entrance and whispered, "Oh, now you will meet Casanova!"

Nunu laughed nervously. But when she went into the house, she saw he was nothing like Redha al-Abdullah. The man was as wide as his chair, with the thickest eyebrows she had ever seen. As he stood up to greet her, his cellphone rang. He abruptly swiveled on his heel to take the call in the other room. As he waddled away, he bent back, grabbed his pants, and hiked them up over his enormous behind. Mamina and Nunu tried to suppress their laughter. When he returned, he sat next to Nunu. For a painful thirty minutes, he breathed down her neck, telling her how she would live after she married him, and how grateful she would be for what he could give her. The closer he inched his chair, the farther away Nunu inched hers. Soon, they had moved halfway across the room.

"I want an answer right away," he said.

Nunu hesitated. "I need three days to think."

"Three days is too long. Take two days. But after that, I would like to marry within the week. I have a room in my parents' house, and my mom has gotten it all ready to be moved into."

Nunu nodded noncommittally.

His mother interrupted. "We will have the wedding in Syria because it is cheaper. But don't worry, dear. His hand will be open when it comes to what you need."

Yeah, sure, Nunu thought.

Finally, Nunu and Mamina escaped. As soon as they got into the car, they burst into laughter. For the rest of the evening, Nunu did imitations of the man hiking up his pants. They called Zia and told her the whole story. It was the first time the sisters had exchanged more than a few words in months, and certainly the first time they'd laughed. As much as Mamina wanted to help her daughter escape Iraq, her pride prevented her from accepting the proposal. Her Nunu was beautiful, full figured, well mannered, and a college graduate. War or no war, she wasn't going to marry that man.

THE NEXT SUITOR to court Nunu was even stranger. One afternoon, one of her aunts called to say that the following day there would be guests coming to visit them. They had a man who wanted to make a proposal. He lived in Australia, and his parents were friends of Mamina's. This man had already proposed to Nunu when she was fifteen, and Baba had turned him down. Now, seven years later, he was back. Nunu learned that the family had been discussing this for weeks without telling her, and that the suitor was already on his way to Baghdad to propose. Maybe in the past Nunu wouldn't have minded, but now she felt bothered by the family's lack of consideration for her wishes. Besides, didn't this man know how dangerous Iraq was to visit these days?

"What man comes into this country now to take a wife?" Nunu asked Zia on the phone. "There are no girls in Australia?"

When he arrived, his entire family filled the living room. The potential bride and groom sat at opposite ends, and Nunu avoided eye contact except to sneak a glance at him when he walked in. He was not horrible, but not handsome. He looked about forty.

The first thing the man did was demand of Nunu, "Have you had a relationship with any man before?"

"If you are curious about my reputation," Nunu said boldly, waving her arm, "ask the neighborhood. Ask people at my college. Don't ask me."

As he proceeded to explain about getting her a visa to live with him, and to describe all the things he would give to Nunu once they were married, she thought about how much she disliked his authoritative tone. She didn't care for his money or his fancy country. For the man to presume she had already accepted was an insult to her. This was the male attitude she detested. *He thinks he is worth more than me because I'm a woman,* she thought. From this tone would spring a lifetime of orders, missives, and bossiness, and what could Nunu do if she was in Australia? She could tell that he presumed she was desperate to get out of Iraq, and would do anything to go to a place as *wonderful* as Sydney. Nunu wanted to tell him: I am not a naïve schoolgirl. I have traveled to Syria and Jordan.

"I would like to speak with her alone," he said, gesturing toward Nunu.

This was unusual, and Nunu shook her head.

"Okay, I understand. It is good you refuse. However, I have some questions for you and I will write them down," he said. "These are regular questions, and they are in order for me to see how you speak English and how you write."

Nunu agreed. After a minute of awkward silence as he scribbled away, Nunu accepted the piece of paper. She agreed to stand in the hallway with him and answer them verbally.

In the alcove, Nunu looked down at the paper. There were three questions:

1. Are you a virgin or not?
2. Do you want to have sex according to the Arabic style or European?
3. What do you know and what do you think of sex?

Nunu gasped. What was this? She knew nothing about sex, and even if she did, she wouldn't dream of answering these horrible questions. She was so shocked she looked him straight in the eye.

"I respect your mother, and because you are in my home, I will respect you. But you don't dare ask me this. These questions belittle me. If there are women who accept this, I am not one of those women."

"No, no. It's normal," he said. "In Australia and even in Europe people ask such questions."

"I don't care where it's normal. I am Arab and I am Muslim and I refuse such questions."

Nunu stormed back to the sitting room to see Mamina's astonished face. She explained the questions. The man trailed behind, still saying, "That's normal. It's not the first time I have asked such questions."

"Go to those women, then," Nunu said.

The suitor and his mother left.

AFTER THE SUITOR'S family was gone, Nunu's little cousin Lara skipped around the room as Nunu cleared the plates.

"Nunu, I will cut off my arm before you marry that man!"

"Don't go to the trouble," Nunu said.

Nunu longed to call Zia but there was an eleven-hour time difference. Zia had started a job with the local government and started work at 8:00 a.m., California time. Finally, Nunu reached her while she was having breakfast and relayed the story.

"Zuzu, please, you can spare me the details, but I must know if there is a difference between the Arab and European style."

The sisters laughed so hard.

"No, Nunu, I have no idea!"

At the end of the conversation, Zia told her sister, "It's good you turned him down, Nunu. He wasn't going to let you do anything, and you were wise to reject him."

"I'd rather be a spinster than marry him," Nunu said. "And I'd rather be barren than raise a daughter in this country."

Zia was speechless. "Wowww, Nunu." She whistled. "I can't believe you just said that." Zia had never heard her sister speak with such a strong opinion.

Later that evening, Nunu took out her journal.

It is not a shame if someone cleans or cooks. But men in our community now think that this is the only thing that a woman should do. Women have no rights. Even if you hear or see men talk about women's rights, deep inside they refuse to let a woman have opportunities in life. Each man in our society is an egocentric person and thinks that everything in this life should be about him, and everything should be done as he likes. That is why I refuse many proposals. Many suitors ask for my hand but I refuse them because I refuse to be treated as a slave or belittled. No, I refuse such a reality. I am a woman, yes, and I am proud of being a woman, and I don't have anything to be ashamed of.

If I get married, I need a man who will believe in me and is convinced that I am equal to him. If I get married and have children, I want my children to be proud of me, just as I am proud of my mother. I will not give up. I will not. I am not a person who accepts defeat. I will struggle till my dreams come true and make my mother and sister proud of me. May God help me.

Nunu closed her notebook. This time she didn't burn the pages.

CHAPTER THIRTY-SEVEN

IN EARLY 2006, Heather finally left Iraq. She had spent three years on the ground, longer than almost any other American in that period. She left behind a devastated country. It was worse than it had been under Saddam, she felt, and she hated the idea that she hadn't been able to do more.

She moved to Washington, D.C., into a bright, two-bedroom apartment in the eclectic neighborhood of Adams Morgan. She had a small porch, hanging plants, shiny wooden floors, stacked bookshelves, and windows that let in lots of sunlight. She kept her bike downstairs, and could come and go as she pleased. On her hallway walls, she hung photos of what she considered her only three happy days in Iraq: the transfer of control of the warehouses to the Ministry of Trade, the Hindiya Club elections, and the opening of the Mansour Women's Center. By her couch, a collection of recently released books about Iraq grew taller and taller: *The Politics of Insurgent Violence* and a number of other Iraq-related "lessons learned" books.

Each morning, she rode her bicycle to her job at the U.S. Institute of Peace, where she became a senior program officer in the Center for Mediation and Conflict Resolution. Heather felt signs of posttraumatic stress disorder—she was short-tempered, nervous, anxious, frustrated—but she never sought counseling. Why should she, when so many soldiers and Iraqis had been through so much worse? She was lucky to have come home at all, when women such as Fern Holland, Margaret Hassan, Marla Ruzicka, and countless other Westerners and Iraqis had lost their lives. There were nights when she couldn't sleep very well. For a while, she had such vivid nightmares that she woke up exhausted. In one, she dreamed she was supposed to be guarding Saddam Hussein, and she got into such an intense discussion with him that she didn't notice he'd slipped out of the room and escaped. The theme was always the same: letting Iraqis down.

She worked to bring some of her Iraqi staff to the USA or to other safe havens, but the State Department was still refusing Iraqi applications. For a while she had held out hope for Iraq, writing an op-ed for the *Christian Science Monitor* arguing: "Those who wait for the headline 'Iraq completes constitution' or 'Iraq misses constitution deadline' will have missed all the intervening steps that really mattered." The violence would have to taper off eventually, she argued, and if the process and policies could just be put in place to guarantee democracy and protections for the minority, then as soon as there was a window of calm, women's and other civic groups could reemerge. Perhaps this would take ten years, but it could be possible if everyone laid the right groundwork.

But Heather feared she was watching the same failures and mistakes from afar as she had seen from the conference rooms inside the Green Zone. As for the U.S. efforts to export women's rights, Heather felt the end effect was the opposite. Any involvement the Americans had with women's issues only provoked accusations of Western influence and tainted the Iraqi women involved. Better, she thought, to have a light touch and let Iraqi women run the show.

After the bombing of the Askari mosque in Samarra in spring 2006, Heather finally gave up hope. The newspaper reports of the start of the civil war were grisly: beheaded bodies floating down the Tigris; mass executions and ethnic cleansings of entire neighborhoods. This was the nightmare scenario Heather had feared for so long. Wherever she went—to work, on the Metro, in a bar with friends—she tried to concentrate on the friendly chatter around her, but found herself drifting off, staring silently, miserably into the distance. Washingtonians debated a troop surge, but Heather felt it was too late to save Iraq. All the fatal decisions had been made early on. The Americans' credibility had been shattered. The window of opportunity for nation-building in Iraq had slammed shut on American fingers. "We sold the Iraqis out," she sighed to friends. "The same way Saddam sold them out."

Sometimes she ran into old colleagues from the CPA. Most of them felt as she did: disappointed, ashamed, and angry. But occasionally, Heather ran into those "bright idea fairies"; to her amazement, they still insisted on depicting the Iraq situation sunnily. Once, at a party, Heather ran into a woman who had worked at the CPA's program review board, which had given Heather final approval for the $1.4 million for the women's centers.

Heather tried to make a dark joke. "Oh, how could you have approved that money?" she said. "Why didn't you stop me from destroying the country?"

She smiled wryly, expecting the woman to agree. Instead, the woman gave her an icy look and walked away.

We destroyed the country, Heather thought bitterly. *Why are you still playing this game?*

In 2007, a number of books and movies came out assailing America's role in the war. Heather agreed with almost all the criticism. The purging of all the Ba'ath Party members from government had left the ministries with no experienced leaders; disbanding the Iraqi army had created too much unemployment; and the bureaucrats working in the CPA were underqualified, unprepared, and had been chosen more for their loyalty to the Republican Party than for their expertise. Troop levels were too low, she agreed, although she felt the number of troops was not nearly as important as the kind of people on the ground. While Bush tried to push the blame onto the Iraqis for not "stepping up," his approval ratings had sunk to the lowest in the history of the presidency. Not far from Heather's apartment, antiwar marches closed down streets as protesters demanded the USA get out of Iraq.

Then Paul Bremer's memoir, *My Year in Iraq: The Struggle to Build a Future of Hope,* was released. Heather blamed Bremer for many of the early mistakes, and the book proffered the same head-in-the-sand analysis of the situation as had existed in the early days. Had we learned nothing at all? she wondered. The book included a few paragraphs about women's issues and described his dawn visit to her and Manal's women's center:

"Monday, March 8, was International Women's Day," he wrote. "I opened the first of nine Women's Centers we planned for Baghdad, a chance to emphasize the importance we attached to helping Iraq's women. As we sat on the floor and ate sweets and dates, I told the women at the center that the TAL required Iraq's electoral law to guarantee that 25 percent of Iraq's parliament be women, one of the highest percentages in the world."

That was the last straw. The idea that Bremer had the nerve to now try to take credit for the 25 percent quota of women infuriated Heather.

After that, she began lecturing on the issue, and was more honest and self-critical than most others. By then there were nascent signs that Iraq's civil war was exhausted. The Bush administration had increased troops on the ground, and some of the Sunni Awakening councils had turned against Al Qaeda and teamed up with the U.S. military. However, nothing could erase the painful damage already done. In late 2007, she published a piece in *The American Interest* entitled "Amateur Hour: Nation-Building in Iraq." She argued that the USA went into Iraq relying largely on the military to deal with everything from humanitarian crisis intervention to large-scale reconstruction efforts to democracy building—none of which it was trained or prepared to do. Such tasks required professional planning, specialized expertise, and a large resource base—if it could be done at all, she wrote. Even if the troops had sealed the borders, stopped the looting, and never disbanded the Iraqi army, they still wouldn't have had any idea what to do next.

"You wouldn't ask an expert engine mechanic to remove your inflamed appendix. So why ask combat arms experts to deal with electricity grids, sanitation, and banking problems when they not only do not understand the language, but can't even read the script."

She openly used her own experiences as an example of mistakes made. The military should never have been in the role of promoting women's rights and building women's centers. Expectations were inflated, and then, in the rush to meet them, "the perfect became the enemy of the good." Reconstruction missions require time for people to adjust and learn the democratic process, as well as to build relationships and trust, she wrote. She knew that a lot of what she understood now, in retrospect, Manal had tried to tell her all along.

If anything *could* still be done, Heather believed it should be to create quick employment programs tied to building up the legitimacy of local institutions and grants to local NGOs and other organizations. The idea was not to simply give things to Iraqis, but to let Iraqis choose what they needed from the Americans. She had never felt strongly about whether Iraqi women lived under Islamic or secular law. Heather wanted to establish a governmental structure in which a diversity of opinions could flourish, and the rights of minorities were protected. After that, the Iraqis could, and should, decide for themselves.

These were all valuable lessons, except they had come too late.

Despite her grave disappointment, there was still a spark of idealism in her argument, a deep-seated belief that the USA could—and should—right the world's wrongs. Had they just done a few things differently, she insisted, it could have worked.

"My three years in Iraq were largely frustrated ones," her article concluded. "I went to Iraq with high hopes of what we could achieve there. I had not understood how completely unprepared we were to do what we had promised. Many argue that failure was inevitable; that the task itself was impossible. Perhaps," she surmised. "But I don't think so."

EPILOGUE

ZIA WAS UP at six o'clock each morning, ready to commute to her new job as an accountant in the Sacramento County government offices. Everyone was really friendly. When they learned she was Iraqi, they all looked at her with curiosity and surprise. But after a few initial questions, no one wanted to know more. She understood—who wanted to spend their lunch hour hearing about suicide bombings and assassinations? As 2008 approached, people changed the channel when Iraq news came on—they were tired of it. Once, when the staff was changing offices, she tried to make a joke. The entire office had been packed up and everything was in boxes. The image reminded Zia of preparations her family had taken before evacuating their neighborhood when Saddam invaded Kuwait. "All we need is some bags of flour and rice and it will be just like the first Gulf War," she laughed.

The entire office stopped and stared at her in confusion. *Oh well,* Zia thought.

In recent months, Zia had begun to see a therapist. She had been feeling so depressed, she had stopped eating. She was shriveling away to nothing—at five feet six inches, Zia weighed barely one hundred pounds. She and Keith bickered often, and she had begun talking about leaving him and returning to Iraq as a U.S. soldier. In her darker moments, she felt that she would rather die fighting for peace and democracy in her country than stay on the sidelines any longer.

The therapist helped her a lot. Zia learned that she had posttraumatic stress disorder and survivor's guilt. Although this didn't ease the pain of missing her family or her fear for them, she began to see things more clearly. Some of her anger eased, and she began to talk about the war with Keith. Seeing things more clearly, however, made her realize what a dangerous situation her family was still in. Zia began to go online and read the news accounts of the beheadings, and she learned about the suicide bombings at Mustansiriya University and the rocket attacks on their street, all the news her family had shielded her from. She learned that at least 85,000 Iraqis had been killed since the start of the war.

Zia felt snapped out of a deep sleep. She knew she had to somehow help them to leave.

Then, one day she couldn't reach them. At first, she didn't worry too much, since the Iraqi phone network shut down so frequently. But after several days, she became increasingly concerned. Each time she called she received the same "out of network" message. She felt like stomping on her shiny silver phone, yet for the past two years that little machine was all she had had of her family. Zia tried not to imagine the worst.

By the fifth day, she was in an absolute panic, and there was nothing Keith could do to calm her. At night, she woke up crying. During the day, she called constantly. Now she did imagine the worst and begged God to spare her family. The landline was working, but no one picked up. Her emails went unanswered.

THEN, LATE ONE evening, she received a call from a long foreign number that started with 968. She answered. It was Nunu.

"We left Iraq!" she shouted. "We're in Oman."

Zia was crying so hard she couldn't even see in front of her. "Why didn't you tell me?" she cried.

Mamina had taken the phone. "We were afraid to worry you. And then it happened so quickly."

They were with Nunu and Zia's friends Suad and Bedria, two Omani sisters who had studied at Baghdad University; they had returned to Oman in 2004 out of fear they'd be kidnapped. For almost a year, Bedria had been trying to help Nunu get a work visa for Oman, but every avenue seemed closed. Then, finally, in late summer of 2007, Bedria suggested they apply for tourist visas to attend the country's annual Khareef Festival, in Salalah. Mamina and Nunu were granted permission, but Baba was denied. He refused to allow the women to go until Mamina's older sister, Aunt Huda, had agreed to cook for Baba and look after him.

Zia could hear the airport commotion in the background.

"Do you have residency?" Zia asked.

"We only have temporary visas," Mamina said, but she thought they had a good chance of receiving work permits.

Getting this far had been difficult. Their plan was only short-term, yet it was the best one on offer. They had decided that they had to take a risk, or life would never change. Zia could hear angry voices.

"Where are you?" she asked.

"We're still at the airport. They've lost our bags."

Behind Mamina, Zia could hear Nunu's voice grow louder. She was telling off the baggage-claim man.

"You'd better find our bags," she was saying. "Those bags are important." Zia had never in her life heard her sister sound so demanding.

When Nunu came back on the phone, Zia was laughing. "Nunu, what's gotten into you?"

"Oh, Zia, it's really hot here and every woman wears an abaya, but at least there are no curfews and no rockets." *Exactly,* Zia thought. They were safe, for the moment. Zia took a deep breath. It felt like the first one she'd taken in years.

"Hey, Nunu," she said. "I'm really proud of you. It really takes guts to do what you did."

FOR AS LONG as they could, Nunu and Mamina had enjoyed their relative freedom in Oman, a small country on the eastern edge of the Arabian Peninsula, at the entrance to the Persian Gulf. They moved into a hotel apartment in a newly developed section of the city, extended their tourist visa to three months, and applied for permanent work visas. Nunu was employed as a secretary at a medical center, and Mamina in a school teaching English.

The first three months in Oman were wonderful and relaxing, but after that their applications for work visas were rejected and they were forced to quit their jobs. They could stay in Oman illegally for only so long before the police would track them down and they would be sent back to Baghdad. For months they went into hiding in their apartment. Returning to Baghdad seemed the only option.

Zia was determined not to give up and let her sister and mother return to Iraq—to likely death. So she started furiously working the phones. She called her state senators, her congressman, and Senator Barbara Boxer's office. She considered going on a hunger strike outside Governor Schwarzenegger's office. Day and night she drafted letters to her representatives and called lawyers and friends in Washington, D.C., asking for advice on asylum, visas, or refugee claims. Zia could barely believe her own persistence and determination. In Iraq, people just didn't do things like this. If you wanted a favor from the government, you had to have a connection or pay a bribe. You couldn't just *ask*.

But Zia had been learning a lot about the United States, and from an unlikely source: Marla Ruzicka. Zia had been reading her biography, *Sweet Relief*. Marla was the twenty-seven-year-old aid worker from California who had died in the suicide bomb attack on the Baghdad airport road. Zia felt a special connection with Marla. They were close in age, and she had been on the same road where Marla was killed, moments after the bomb had detonated. Had things been different, she could have died, not Marla. And it was Marla's connection with Senator Patrick Leahy that had helped convince the embassy officials to approve Zia's visa. Since she'd gotten to the States, Zia had written to Marla's parents, who lived only a few hours from Sacramento, telling them how much Marla had meant to Iraqis.

If there was one thing Zia was learning in America, it was that persistence could pay off. Unlike in Iraq, where individuality was crushed, one person *could* make a difference here. She had cried through most of Marla's book, as she learned about Marla's Rollerblading down the halls of the Capitol building, teaming up with aides who would, eventually, earmark $50 million to help innocent victims of war. *Why would this beautiful, spirited young American leave her home and travel across the world just to help Iraqis?* she wondered. Why was it that even in the most violent, inhumane periods of war, when everything felt dark, there were so many examples of good, kind human beings? Each time Zia felt like giving up, she thought of Marla.

Zia found that Marla was only one of many Americans who cared about Iraqis. As she continued her campaign to help her mother and sister, she was stunned to see Americans from all walks of life put down what they were doing and help her. Zia's email campaign eventually made its way to the desk of Jody Lautenschlager, the former sergeant in Iraq who was now working for the State Department. After returning from Iraq, in her free time and with her own money, she had formed a group to help Iraqi refugees. She agreed to take on Zia's case. Whereas before, Zia couldn't get past a voice recording, suddenly she had a contact inside the State Department.

Former army lieutenant Lorne Segerstrom offered to write a letter of support for Zia. He had served as Central Region program manager for IMN while Zia was site manager.

"I remember very well during the fourteen months while in Iraq, the situation was particularly dangerous for IMN employees . . ." he wrote. "I have no doubt that Zia's family has a well-founded fear of serious harm, persecution, and/or death if they were to return to Iraq."

Another young woman who responded to Zia's emails was twenty-six-year-old Erica Gaston, a Harvard Law graduate working on refugee issues in Kabul, Afghanistan. She explained the refugee process to Zia and shared her contacts inside the United Nations High Commission for Refugees (UNHCR) for the Gulf region. When Zia had called the UN in Oman, she had been hung up on. Now, just like that, thanks to Erica, Zia was exchanging emails with officials at the UNHCR in Geneva.

But the biggest help of all would come from Senator Boxer's office in San Francisco. Zia knew that Senator Boxer had tens of millions of constituents, and for months she didn't bother trying. But after she read Marla's book, Zia felt inspired to beat back her feelings of fear and insecurity and began writing letters.

Dear US Sen. Barbara Boxer:

I currently live in California and work for the Sacramento County government, however I am born and raised in Iraq. From 2003 to 2005, I worked for the US government in Baghdad, first as a translator for Iraqi Media Network and later as a facility manager for the US embassy. In 2005, several attempts were made on my life by insurgents, and I was granted a visa to come to the US, where I am now married to an American man.

I contact you on behalf of my sister and mother, who have just left Baghdad and who I have not seen in more than two years. I kindly ask you to write a letter of support on my behalf, which we can present to the US embassy in Oman.

My sister, Nariman, 23, graduated with honors from Baghdad University, and speaks fluent English. My mother, Madiha, 50, is a school teacher for 20 years.

During my two years in the United States, I have established a productive life for myself. My husband and I are fully employed, and I am proud to have a green card, and being on track to becoming an American.

Zia's passionate plea and doggedness caught the senator's attention, and after several months Senator Boxer agreed to write a letter of support. No one thought it possible that the U.S. embassy in Oman would issue American visas to two Iraqis, but Zia called Mamina and Nunu anyway. "Go to the U.S. embassy and apply for visas," she said. "I think we have a shot."

FOUR MONTHS LATER, in the summer of 2008, Nunu's plane touched down at Sacramento International Airport. Keith had flown to London to meet her and ensure safe passage through U.S. immigration in San Francisco. Bedraggled and exhausted, they struggled off the plane and into the terminal, where Zia waited with arms filled with flowers and balloons.

After three years apart, during which Zia felt certain she would never see her little sister again, they both let the tears flow unchecked. "Nunu, you've gotten so fat!" Zia exclaimed through her sobs. Nunu laughed.

But Mamina was still in Oman. Her visa had been delayed for unspecified reasons. It would be two months before the good news arrived, before she followed the path Nunu had pioneered, meeting Keith in London and flying with him to America.

ON A BRIGHT summer day, Zia and Nunu stood anxiously together in the San Francisco airport. Americans in T-shirts and shorts walked past, pulling wheeled suitcases and hurrying to and from different destinations. The day was sunny, and a light breeze swayed the trees outside the glass doors.

Suddenly, the monitor changed and digitized letters read: LANDED. As Mamina emerged through the sliding doors, Zia saw her own beloved husband smiling broadly by her mother's side, carrying her luggage. When Mamina caught sight of her daughters standing together, she broke down in tears. They hugged one another fiercely, never wanting to let go. "I have my children gathered around me, at last," Mamina said.

THEY HAD LEFT behind a country in pieces, and still the war was not over. Iraq was a nation of desperate women, with millions of war widows, childless mothers, and young girls forced into prostitution. Iraq's suffering would not soon be healed by a peace treaty or a constitution. Mamina and Nunu were not sure it would ever heal.

But for Zia, the war was over. For the first time in as long as she could remember, she would not go to bed at night wondering if her sister was still alive. She would not fear that her mother would die before they saw each other again. They would share their lives together and live in peace. Maybe one day Baba would join them, but he was at least safer in Iraq than they ever could have been. A way had been parted for them; a second chance at a new life. And they were finally together.

Zia hugged her mother as tightly as she could. "We'll never part again."

BY 2009, HEATHER and Manal were both still involved in Iraq, and things were looking up. They teamed up to help a young woman who'd been shot by a militia, and they managed, together, to resettle her and her family in the States. Heather is still working at USIP, focusing on conflict resolution. Manal also joined USIP as a program officer, and she has recently become head of the board of directors of ASUDA-USA and is raising money for it. In Iraq, the security situation has improved since 2007. Elections for local councils were held in January 2009 and hundreds of women ran—even campaigning publicly. The risks continue: one woman candidate was assassinated in Baghdad, but hundreds of others won seats.

With Zia's attorney's help, Nunu and Mamina both applied for asylum. By 2009, as their cases were being processed, Nunu received another offer of marriage. This one was welcomed. One of Zia's Iraqi friends who lived in the United States had a brother, Nawar. He saw Nunu on Zia's Facebook page. After courting her for a month through Facebook, he contacted her male relatives in the UK and informed them of his intentions. They approved, as did Baba, over the phone. In his mid-twenties, Nawar was born in the United States to Iraqi parents and had been raised in both countries. He flew to California, and they spent four days getting to know each other, under Mamina's supervision. Nunu found her suitor to be gentle, easygoing, and respectful of women. She fell in love. In February 2009, with Zia, Mamina, and Keith by Nunu's side, they were married.

ACKNOWLEDGMENTS

I'm grateful to many people for their help in the reporting and writing of this book and for risking their lives to share their stories about this long and confusing war. For their company and conversation in Iraq, I thank the following colleagues: Maya Alleruzzo, Tara Sutton, Matt McAllester, Willis Witter, Adam Davidson, Jen Banbury, Jon Lee Anderson, Ilana Ozernoy, Victoria Whitford, Jeremy Kahn, Ray LeMoine, Jeff Neumann, Jens Munch, Patrick Graham, and Marla Ruzicka. Special thanks to Rajiv Chandrasekaran, whose thoughtfulness opened the door for this book and whose groundbreaking reporting paved the way for many of the ideas in it.

I'm grateful to *The New York Times* for giving me the initial assignment in Iraq, to the BBC crew for taking me from Kuwait into Baghdad at the start of the war, and to editors Jimmy Kilpatrick and Xan Smiley for supporting me while I was there. Reporting from Iraq would not have been possible without a staff of dedicated Iraqi journalists and translators who worked under threat of death. I appreciate the work of Abu Hassan, Ali, Sarmaad and his mother, Abu Salah, Quais, Haider, and Ahmed "Triple A."

Following the lives of Zia, Nunu, and Mamina as they were trapped in Baghdad during the height of the civil war was an emotionally challenging assignment. Many Iraqi women lost their lives or their loved ones during the course of my reporting. Yet despite their losses, these women demonstrated kindness and bravery. Many asked not to be named, but I recognize here those who I can for their work: Hanna Adwar, Khanum Rahim Latif, Maysoon al Damluji, Rend al Rahim, Nariman Othman, and Zainab al Suwaijj.

In the United States, I'd like to thank the following people for their empathy and actions on behalf of Zia and her family: Tim Reiser and U.S. senator Patrick Leahy; Nicole Boxer and her mom, U.S. Senator Barbara Boxer; Nikki Asquith-Dubois, Jody Lautenschlager, Nancy and Cliff Ruzicka, and Marla Bertagnolli-Keenan; and Sarah Holewinski and Erica Gaston at CIVIC.

The Woodrow Wilson International Center provided me with an intellectual home for my project, and I'm very grateful to the people there who made the Center such a friendly and productive environment. Thanks to Lucy Jilka for steering me to the Center; to my spirited and insightful adviser Haleh Esfandiari, for devoting time to talk with me about women's rights, the Quran, and the Shia of Iraq; to Sarah Courteau for graciously volunteering her keen eye to several early chapters; and to my intern, Rega "Ahmed" Jabar, for going way beyond intern duties in traveling to Jordan to meet with Mamina and Nunu and to harangue government bureaucrats, bouncers, and taxicab drivers.

The work of a number of Muslim scholars and journalists helped me understand the more nuanced aspects of Sharia law, the Quran, and Islam; these include Albert Hourani, Isobel Coleman, Fatima Mernissi, Nadji al Ali, Leila Ahmed, Amina Wadud, and M.A.S. Abdel Haleem.

For taking the time to explain their work to me, I'd like to thank Jonathan Morrow, Idong Essiet, Gordon Adams, Camille Elhassani, Peter Bergen, Keith Flossman, Ahmed Gutan, and the staff at Women for Women in Baghdad and Jordan. For their history lesson on the U.S. women's rights movement in the 1960s, I thank Heather Coyne's parents, Leila and Don Coyne. I also thank Manal's parents, Dr. Mohammed Omar and Lamah Omar, for talking to me about Palestinian women's rights, and Zia and Nunu's father, Baba, for educating me on Iraqi history.

Thank you to Michelle Peluso, Nikki Asquith-Dubois, Sophie Fairweather, Maya Alleruzzo, and Catherine Philp for reading early drafts and giving constructive, honest feedback. I'm grateful to Sebastian Junger for always taking time out of his busy life to talk me through a rough writing patch. By pure serendipity, I met Nichole Bernier at the Bethesda Writer's Center and would never have gotten the proposal off the ground if not for her excellent edit. I appreciate Ron Roach for introducing me to the Center and for our long conversations about neoconservatism. Thanks to fellow scribe Rufus Fairweather for coining the book's title, and to Cherry Fairweather for providing home-cooked meals and warm fires throughout the long writing process (and thanks to both for hosting the best wedding a bride could ask for in the middle of it all). My mentor, Mark Bowden, has been the most thoughtful and inspiring role model a journalist could ever wish to know—I'm grateful for all his advice and friendship over the years.

At William Morris, thanks to my agent, Mel Berger, and to his assistants Evan Goldfried and Graham Jaenicke.

At Random House, I'm very lucky to have worked with editor Tim Bartlett, whose strong sense of detail, narrative, and history pushed me to write and rewrite and kept the project alive during difficult times. Millicent Bennett was a master at moving the story along quickly, and I'm grateful for the consideration she put into the final edit. Thank you also to production editor Janet Wygal.

I would especially like to thank my parents, Lynn and Phil Asquith. It must not be easy for parents to watch their daughter go off alone to Iraq at the start of a war, nor to hear gunfire at the other end of a distant phone line. Yet they gave me a lot of support and wisdom, and I hope this book makes them proud.

A foreign correspondent's life can be a lonely one, and writing a book is usually a painfully solitary process. But I'm incredibly fortunate to have had a companion. Jack Fairweather, who I met my second day in Baghdad, has been by my side, across the world, for every stage of this book, and I could not have written it without him. I thank him for being an adventurous reporter, a dogged editor, a war historian, a creative thinker, and a supportive and loving best friend and husband.

Lastly, I would like to thank the five women whom I have come to know intimately in writing this book: Heather Coyne, Manal Omar, Zia, Nunu, and Mamina. They trusted me in sharing their stories honestly. A long war that is distant to most was profoundly personal for them. Observing their struggles, tears, and victories over the last five years has been an honor, and has demonstrated to me women's capacity not only to endure the toughest of circumstances, but to do so with humility, empathy, dedication, self-sacrifice, and love.

ABOUT THE AUTHOR

After graduating from Boston University, CHRISTINA ASQUITH worked as a staff reporter for *The Philadelphia Inquirer* before leaving the newsroom to teach for a year in an inner-city school. Shortly after the Iraq war began, she took an assignment in Baghdad for *The New York Times* and spent the next two years covering the war for the *Times, The Economist,* and *The Christian Science Monitor.* A journalist for more than fifteen years, she has also written about women's rights in Afghanistan, Oman, and Jordan. Asquith is currently teaching about women in Islam at the University of Vermont. She lives in Burlington with her husband and their daughter.

ABOUT THE TYPE

This book was set in Fairfield, the first typeface from the hand of the distinguished American artist and engraver Rudolph Ruzicka (1883–1978). In its structure, Fairfield displays the sober and sane qualities of the master craftsman, whose talent has long been dedicated to clarity. It is this trait that accounts for the trim grace and vigor, the spirited design, and the sensitive balance of this original typeface.

Rudolph Ruzicka was born in Bohemia and came to America in 1894. He set up his own shop, devoted to wood engraving and printing, in New York in 1913, after a varied career working as a wood engraver, in photo-engraving and banknote-printing plants, and as an art director and freelance artist. He designed and illustrated many books and was the creator of a considerable list of individual prints—wood engravings, line engravings on copper, and aquatints.